Communications
in Computer and Information Science

733

Commenced Publication in 2007
Founding and Former Series Editors:
Alfredo Cuzzocrea, Xiaoyong Du, Orhun Kara, Ting Liu, Dominik Ślęzak,
and Xiaokang Yang

More information about this series at http://www.springer.com/series/7899

Costantino Grana · Lorenzo Baraldi (Eds.)

Digital Libraries and Archives

13th Italian Research Conference on Digital Libraries, IRCDL 2017
Modena, Italy, January 26–27, 2017
Revised Selected Papers

 Springer

Editors
Costantino Grana (iD)
University of Modena and Reggio Emilia
Modena
Italy

Lorenzo Baraldi (iD)
University of Modena and Reggio Emilia
Modena
Italy

ISSN 1865-0929   ISSN 1865-0937   (electronic)
Communications in Computer and Information Science
ISBN 978-3-319-68129-0   ISBN 978-3-319-68130-6   (eBook)
DOI 10.1007/978-3-319-68130-6

Library of Congress Control Number: 2017955784

Printed on acid-free paper

This Springer imprint is published by Springer Nature
The registered company is Springer International Publishing AG
The registered company address is: Gewerbestrasse 11, 6330 Cham, Switzerland

Preface

The Italian Research Conference on Digital Libraries (IRCDL) is an annual event for the Italian research community, both on the computer science and on the humanities side, interested in digital libraries, digital cultural heritage, and related topics. The IRCDL conferences were launched in 2005 by Maristella Agosti and Costantino Thanos and initially sponsored by DELOS, an EU FP6 Network of Excellence on digital libraries together with the Department of Information Engineering of the University of Padua. Over the years, IRCDL has become a self-sustainable event supported by the Italian Digital Library Research Community.

This edition followed the road designed by the previous editions, with a focus on the multidisciplinary nature of research on digital libraries, which not only ranges from humanities to computer science but also crosses over areas in the same field ranging, for example, from archival to librarian sciences or from information systems to human–computer interaction.

This volume contains the revised accepted papers from among those presented at the 13th Italian Research Conference on Digital Libraries (IRCDL 2017), which was held at the Department of Engineering Enzo Ferrari of the University of Modena and Reggio Emilia, during January 26–27, 2017.

The recognized scope of IRCDL is to bring together the Italian research community interested in the diversified methods and techniques that allow the building and operation of digital libraries. A national Program Committee was set up composed of 28 members, with representatives of the most active Italian research groups on digital libraries.

Of the original 25 submissions, after receiving three reviews per paper, 20 papers were presented to the conference and 15 were accepted for extension after a further rebuttal stage. The covered topics are related to the different aspects that need to support information access and interoperability, including:

- Multimedia digital libraries
- Algorithms and techniques for automatic content analysis
- System interoperability and data integration
- Data integration between galleries, libraries, archives, and museums (GLAM)
- Ontologies and linked data for digital libraries
- Metadata creation, management, and curation
- Information access, usability, and personalization
- Social networking and networked information
- Education and learning
- Evaluation of research quality and impact (including novel metrics)
- Exploitation of digital cultural heritage collections

In addition to the presentations of the accepted papers, the program of IRCDL 2017 featured two keynote talks. The first keynote talk was given by Simona Caraceni of the

Visit-Lab of the Department of Supercomputing, Applications and Innovation of Cineca; it was entitled "Virtual Heritage: An Open Pipeline" and focused on the powerful combination of supercomputing resources and virtual reality applied to improve the creation and presentation of cultural heritage collections. The second invited speaker was instead Marcello Pellacani, director of Expert System UK, who provided examples of the real-world application of the power that semantic relations may give to the data analysts. His talk "Semantics for Digital Libraries" presented strategies for text mining, topic extraction, semantic search, content recommendation, and linked data connections.

IRCDL 2018, the 14th edition of IRCDL, will be held at Palazzo di Toppo Wassermann in Udine during January 25–26, 2018.

We would like to thank those institutions and individuals who made the conference and this volume possible. In particular, we would like to thank the Program Committee members, the Steering Committee members, the authors, and the Department of Engineering Enzo Ferrari of the University of Modena and Reggio Emilia.

August 2017   Costantino Grana
                                                              Lorenzo Baraldi

Organization

Program Chairs

Costantino Grana   University of Modena and Reggio Emilia, Italy
Lorenzo Baraldi   University of Modena and Reggio Emilia, Italy

IRCDL Steering Committee

Maristella Agosti   University of Padua, Italy
Tiziana Catarci   University of Rome La Sapienza, Italy
Alberto Del Bimbo   University of Florence, Italy
Floriana Esposito   University of Bari, Italy
Carlo Tasso   University of Udine, Italy
Costantino Thanos   ISTI CNR, Pisa, Italy

Program Committee

Maristella Agosti   University of Padua, Italy
Andrew David Bagdanov   University of Florence, Italy
Valentina Bartalesi Lenzi   ISTI-CNR, Italy
Stefano Berretti   University of Florence, Italy
Marco Bertini   University of Florence, Italy
Maria Teresa Biagetti   University of Rome La Sapienza, Italy
Simone Calderara   University of Modena and Reggio Emilia, Italy
Diego Calvanese   Free University of Bozen-Bolzano, Italy
Vittore Casarosa   ISTI-CNR, Italy
Michelangelo Ceci   University of Bari, Italy
Rita Cucchiara   University of Modena and Reggio Emilia, Italy
Alberto Del Bimbo   University of Florence, Italy
Stefano Ferilli   University of Bari, Italy
Nicola Ferro   University of Padua, Italy
Maria Guercio   University of Rome La Sapienza, Italy
Donato Malerba   University of Bari, Italy
Federica Mandreoli   University of Modena and Reggio Emilia, Italy
Paolo Manghi   ISTI-CNR, Italy
Simone Marinai   University of Florence, Italy
Nicola Orio   University of Padova, Italy
Antonella Poggi   University of Rome La Sapienza, Italy
Marco Schaerf   University of Rome La Sapienza, Italy
Giuseppe Serra   University of Modena and Reggio Emilia, Italy

Gianmaria Silvello	University of Padua, Italy
Carlo Tasso	University of Udine, Italy
Francesca Tomasi	University of Bologna, Italy
Roberto Vezzani	University of Modena and Reggio Emilia, Italy
Paul Gabriele Weston	University of Pavia, Italy

Contents

Cultural Heritage

Applications

Bibliometrics and Education

Analysing and Discovering Semantic Relations in Scholarly Data

Angelo Di Iorio[1], Andrea Giovanni Nuzzolese[2], Silvio Peroni[1],
Francesco Poggi[1(✉)], Fabio Vitali[1], and Paolo Ciancarini[1]

[1] DASPLab, Department of Computer Science and Engineering,
University of Bologna, Bologna, Italy
{angelo.diiorio,silvio.peroni,francesco.poggi,
fabio.vitali,paolo.ciancarini}@unibo.it
[2] STLab, Institute of Cognitive Science and Technologies,
National Research Council, Rome, Italy
andrea.nuzzolese@istc.cnr.it

Abstract. Scholarly publishing has seen an ever increasing interest in Linked Open Data (LOD). However, most of the existing datasets are designed as flat translation of legacy data sources into RDF. Although that is a crucial step to address, a lot of useful information is not expressed in RDF, and humans are still required to infer relevant knowledge by reading and making sense of texts. Examples are the reasons why authors cite other papers, the rhetorical structure of scientific discourse, bibliometric measures, provenance information, and so on. In this paper we introduce the *Semantic Lancet Project*, whose goal is to make available a LOD which includes the formalisation of some useful knowledge hidden within the textual content of papers. We have developed a toolchain for reengineering and enhancing data extracted from some publisher's legacy repositories. Finally, we show how these data are immediately useful to help humans to address relevant tasks, such as data browsing, expert finding, related works finding, and identification of data inconsistencies.

1 Introduction

Scholarly papers are key tools for disseminating, developing and evaluating research results. There is an ever increasing interest in making scholarly data available as Linked Open Data (LOD), on top of which building sophisticated services for the users. The current landscape is variegated, and a lot of information is available through SPARQL end-points and user-friendly interfaces: bibliographic data on journal papers as in BioTea [2], scientific events as in Semantic Web Dog Food [8], citations as in the OpenCitation [18], and so on.

However, existing RDF datasets are built as *conversion of existing data sources into RDF*. A lot of valuable information is still hidden in the text of the papers. Consider for instance the citations: though the bibliographic references to a paper being cited are available, there is no information about the possible reasons why that paper is cited – or at least the context where it was cited.

© Springer International Publishing AG 2017
C. Grana and L. Baraldi (Eds.): IRCDL 2017, CCIS 733, pp. 3–19, 2017.
DOI: 10.1007/978-3-319-68130-6_1

The presence of the abstracts is another example: abstracts are made available as plain text but there is no explicit connection with the entities they refer to, nor a formal representation of their content. Having these data would instead help users to access, understand and compare papers and research results.

We claim that the next generation of LOD of scholarly papers should make such information available, in order to support users (researchers, reviewers, publishers, data curators, etc.) in their daily work and to improve the access to relevant research products. It will be more and more important to provide a broad view of the relations among research papers and to make their content and worth *explicitly formalised* as much as possible.

This paper introduces the *Semantic Lancet Triplestore (SLT)*, a freely available LOD dataset designed with the aforementioned goal in mind. SLT includes rich data about scholarly papers, that range from a large network of citations (that also includes citation contexts and functions) to semantically-enriched abstracts, from provenance data to time-aware descriptions of the scientific production. The paper also shows how these data can be exploited to complete common tasks in a faster and more effective way. In particular, we show how:

- the presentation of such data can be provided in an intuitive way (supporting users at browsing data about authors and their scientific publications);
- the assessment of the impact of a researcher can benefit from the citation functions (that allow users to have a more precise understanding of the nature citation);
- the search of related works can benefit from semantic abstracts (that allow users to find papers not only with a plain text-based analysis but also taking into account entities, events and roles referred by the abstract);
- the maintenance of such data can benefit from provenance information (that allows users to spot and fix errors and inconsistencies).

SLT has been built with a chain of tools that produces data from legacy sources (i.e., Elsevier's repositories), accessed by REST APIs. The overall workflow – that guarantees a very high level of maintainability and extensibility – is presented in this work as well.

This paper is structured as follows. Section 2 describes some desiderata for a LOD dataset of scholarly papers. Section 3 presents the ontological models used within SLT, and Sect. 4 describes the reengineering process used to populate the SLT dataset. Section 5 shows how SLT can be exploited to support common research tasks. Section 6 compares the SLT and the current LOD landscape, and Sect. 7 draws conclusions and future works.

2 Enhancing Scholarly Papers for Analysis and Discovery

The idea of creating LOD for scholarly publications is not new. Several repositories of scientific publications have been published as RDF datasets that can be queried through SPARQL and provide information about research results, articles, etc. In this section we discuss some data that LOD triplestores should contain in order to be exploited in sophisticated services for the final users.

The basic building pieces must obviously be the general **(meta)data** about each paper, such as title, venue, volume, issue, citations, and so on. The information about the authors, editors and any other **actor** involved in the publication of each work is also needed, together with data about the **affiliations**. The **abstract** in textual form and the classification of a paper provided by the authors is a further information that we expect. These data are already available in scholarly repositories – for instance, the **subjects** from a taxonomy (as in the case of ACM classification) and the **keywords** – and should be available in RDF datasets as well.

The network of citations is a first area in which a lot of improvement is possible. The minimum requirement is obviously to connect citing and cited papers in a complete network of citations and express it in RDF. Nonetheless, citations are very different in use and scope, because they can have very different functions. It is then important to store them and be able to analyse the original **citation context** [15], i.e., the sentence (or a larger part) of the original paper where a particular work was cited.

The step forward is to make explicit the reason why a paper was cited. As described by Teufel *et al.* [20], the "function of a citation" is the reason why an author cite another paper. This kind of data could be very helpful to understand the nature of each citation and to give it more or less relevance. The automatic identification of the **function of a citation** is not simple – as shown in [1], it is very difficult for humans too and there is a very low agreement in completing such a task – but it can be helpful to better exploit citations.

Many other valuable information can be extracted from the textual content of each paper and made available in RDF datasets. A straightforward application is the extraction of the main **research topics** in a paper, which could be used for automatic reasoning and searching. The issue here is to build a representation that is as faithful as possible to the actual meaning the author had in mind. That is extremely difficult but in some cases it can be encoded through a simple model, e.g., by linking entities to DBpedia in order to represent some semantic aspects of a certain text. In general, the representation as LOD of the content of a paper, from natural language to a graph of entities, enables the development of a new generation of services that can leverage the whole LOD ecosystem for sophisticated access, searching and reasoning.

There are many other scholarly-related data that could be published as LOD. For instance, information about funding agencies or grants associated to each paper. The list of requirements discussed in this section, in fact, is not meant to be exhaustive. However, it allowed us to build both a dataset and a set of applications on top of it that make easier and faster to address some tasks that are specific to the research community, as described in Sect. 5.

3   Ontologically Modelling Scholarly Knowledge

In this section we briefly introduce the ontologies we used within our framework, providing a bird's-eye view of their main components. Several works have proposed RDFS vocabularies and OWL ontologies for describing particular aspects of the publishing domain, even if they have mainly focused on the description of the metadata concerning bibliographic resources – e.g., DCTerms (http://purl.org/dc/terms) and BIBO (http://purl.org/ontology/bibo) – rather than their content or contextual information. This is one of the reasons why we built our system around the *Semantic Publishing and Referencing (SPAR)* ontologies (http://www.sparontologies.net) [12]. SPAR is a suite of orthogonal and complementary OWL 2 ontologies that enable multiple aspects of the publishing process to be described as machine-readable metadata statements, encoded using the Resource Description Framework (RDF).

Particularly interesting for our discussion is the SPAR's ability to enable the characterisation of the nature (or type) of citations, to describe the structure of the paper content and to fully describe agent's roles. The SPAR ontologies in fact allowed us to capture and represent all the aspects that have been introduced in Sect. 2 – excluding the organisation of the scientific discourse that has been modelled according to the output of one of the tools we have used, i.e. FRED [14] (described in the next section). In particular:

- FaBiO (http://purl.org/spar/fabio) and PSO (http://purl.org/spar/pso) has allowed us to describe the basic metadata of a publication, as well as its current status (e.g. open-access, subscription-access, in-print);
- PRO (http://purl.org/spar/pro) has been used for describing the roles of the contributors of a publication (e.g. author, publisher, etc.);
- BiRO (http://purl.org/spar/biro), CiTO (http://purl.org/spar/cito) and C4O (http://purl.org/spar/c4o) have been used to describe bibliographic reference lists, as well as the citation acts with their related contexts and functions;
- DoCO (http://purl.org/spar/doco) has been used to describe the components of a publication (abstracts, sentences, etc.).

4   Building the Semantic Lancet Triplestore

The *Semantic Lancet project*[1] (SLT) is our contribution towards the creation of LOD datasets of scholarly resources, semantically described and enriched as discussed in the previous sections. The aim of the Semantic Lancet Project is twofold. On the one hand, we want to implement a workflow to automatise the production of proper RDF data compliant with the chosen semantic models (i.e. the SPAR Ontologies). On the other hand, we want to make an RDF triplestore of scholarly data publicly-available, starting from the published by Elsevier's

---

[1] http://www.semanticlancet.eu.

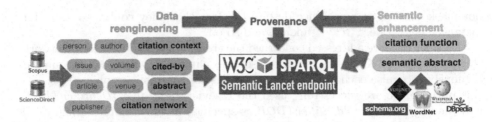

Fig. 1. The semantic lancet framework.

Science Direct and Scopus APIs. This is a first step towards the management of heterogeneous data coming from different publishers and repositories.

The three main components of the Semantic Lancet framework are summarised in Fig. 1. First we have the *data reengineering* component that is responsible for the conversion of raw data coming from existing repositories into OWL according to SPAR. Then, the *semantic enhancement* component enriches SLT data semantically according to the information from different sources, such as Wikipedia, DBPedia [6], VerbNet [17], WordNet [7], and Schema.org. Finally, the *provenance* component is responsible for adding provenance information about the data added/modified by the aforementioned two components. In the next subsections we describe these three components in more detail.

4.1 Data Reengineering

The data reengineering component (shown in Fig. 1, on the left) takes care of the translation of the raw data coming from Scopus and Science Direct into RDF. Basically, two kinds of data are retrieved using the API made available by Elsevier[2]: the metadata and the full text of the articles. Metadata are retrieved for all papers of a given journal (identified by a ISSN) by querying both Scopus and Science Direct indexes. The full text in XML format is obtained querying Elsevier's repositories by using their Text and Data Mining (TDM) API[3].

These data are used by all the other scripts of our data reengineering process – one script for each blue block of the data reengineering section shown in Fig. 1 – and are converted into proper SPAR-based RDF statements. Finally, all these RDF statements are published on the Semantic Lancet triplestore and, thus, are made available to Web users for free browsing and download.

Achieved results and open issues: during this phase, we had to deal with several issues that emerged from the intrinsic complexity of the data. First of all, the recognition of the sentences was a crucial activity in order to extract citation contexts. Of course, the tokenisation of the sentences has been addressed by means of existing natural language processing tools for sentence recognition. However the main issue we faced was the identification of stop-words that did

---

[2] http://www.developers.elsevier.com/devcms/content-apis.

[3] http://www.elsevier.com/about/policies/content-mining-policies.

not mark the end of a sentence despite the fact that they contained "." – for instance "e.g.", "i.e.", "cf.", "a.k.a.", and so on.

Another issue we addressed concerned the creation of the full citation network starting from the XML-based full text of the papers. It was crucial to unambiguously recognise each cited paper, regardless of the bibliographic styles. For this purpose, we are successfully used the Elsevier *Electronic IDentifier* (*EID*) and the *Digital Object Identifier* (*DOI*) as specified in the various bibliographic references of the full text of the downloaded articles, that have to be identified and mined from the actual natural language text fulltext of the papers.

Finally, a side note on a particular issue that is addressed in the next stage of our process, i.e., the disambiguation of people. The approach we currently adopt during this phase is quite basic: we create a new entity in the SLT for each person by normalising the concatenation of the given and family names available in the Elsevier repository. This method allowed us to identify most of the authors but could not handle correctly composite, incomplete and homonymous names, that are managed in the semantic enhancement stage, as described in Sect. 4.2.

4.2 Semantic Enhancement

The *semantic enhancement* component enriches the triplestore with more semantic data, resulting from a further refinement of those produced during the data reengineering phase, such as abstracts and citation contexts.

Currently, we have implemented a module for generating *semantic abstracts*, i.e., the formal representations of paper abstracts as RDF graphs, defined starting from the original abstracts written in natural language text. To this end, we rely on FRED[4] [14], which is a tool that implements deep machine reading methods based on Discourse Representation Theory, Linguistic Frames and Ontology Design Patterns for deriving a logical representation (expressed in OWL) of natural language sentences. By using FRED, we can also perform named entity recognition and linking to existing entities in the Web and Linked Data (e.g., Wikipedia, DBPedia, VerbNet, WordNet, Schema.org), thus enabling a rich enhancement of textual abstracts. Moreover, other complex tasks on the processed text such as relation finding, taxonomy induction, semantic role labelling, event recognition and word-sense disambiguation are performed. A run of this module queries the triplestore and extracts their related semantic abstracts that will be then linked to the original natural language ones through LMM [13] (i.e., an ontology for expressing semiotical relations) by using the property *semiotics:expresses*.

For example the sentence below extracted from the abstract of [10] *"The Web Ontology Language (OWL) is a new formal language for representing ontologies in the Semantic Web..."* returns the RDF/OWL representation depicted in Fig. 2 when parsed with FRED.

---

[4] FRED: http://wit.istc.cnr.it/stlab-tools/fred.

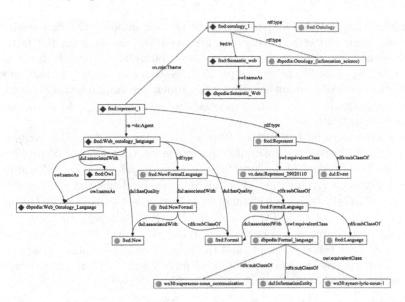

Fig. 2. Semantic enhancement obtained with FRED from the sentence *"The Web Ontology Language (OWL) is a new formal language for representing ontologies..."*.

The semantic features extracted from the previous example (cf. Fig. 2) are:

- events, i.e., *fred:Represent*, disambiguated with respect to VerbNet [17];
- semantic roles, i.e., *vn.role:Theme* and *vn.role:Agent*[5];
- named entities, i.e., *fred:Semantic_Web*, *fred:Web_ontology_language*, *fred:Owl* and *fred:ontology_1*, that are also linked when possible to entities in the linked data, i.e., DBpedia;
- entity types derived from the natural language text, i.e., *fred:NewFormal-Language*, with relative taxonomies, i.e., *rdfs:subClassOf* axioms, and detected alignments to WordNet (by means of word-sense disambiguation), D0 and DBpedia, i.e., *owl:equivalentClass* and *rdfs:subClass* axioms.

Besides the extraction of semantic abstracts our approach also performs additional and complementary activities, such as the disambiguation of authors. Being able to uniquely recognise an author (aka *author disambiguation*) is a basic building block for the realisation of our vision but, even if FRED typically produces valuable results, it is not an easy task yet. For example, one of the authors of this paper, Andrea Giovanni Nuzzolese, has two entries in the ScholarlyData dataset[6], namely *sd-person:andrea-nuzzolese* and *sd-person:andrea-giovanni-nuzzolese*. Each entry reports the same facts (affiliation, papers, roles

---

[5] vn.role:Theme and vn.role:Agent identify the theme and the agent of an event, respectively.

[6] The Scholarlydata dataset is the reference linked dataset of the Semantic Web community about papers, people, organisations and events. It is available at http://www.scholarlydata.org/.

in program committees, etc.) for each entity, but none of the two related to the other by an *owl:sameAs* axiom. This situation results from the fact that NER systems generally take into account only plain literals in which the name of an author appears. To solve this problem we consider other information such as affiliations, emails, co-authorships, etc., which are fundamental to correctly interpret cases such as the aforementioned and successfully perform the author disambiguation task.

The citation typing is a further step we are taking. In fact, the frequency a work is cited is a partial indicator of its relevance for a community. More effective results can be obtained by looking for the *citation function*, i.e. "the author's reasons for citing a given paper". For this task, we implemented another module based on *CiTalO* [1], which is a chain of tools to automatically identify the nature of citations according to CiTO (one of the SPAR ontologies), in a way that is comparable with humans. For each paper in the SLT, a run of this module filters all the in-text reference pointers[7] and the related citation sentences introduced during the data reengineering phase, and links them to their related citation functions through OA annotations [16].

Achieved results and open issues: we had to handle several issues for producing data related to semantic abstracts and citation functions, mainly derived from the reliability of the external tools we used.

For the production of the semantic abstracts, one of the problems we addressed was due to the size of the natural language abstracts we used as input. In particular, running FRED with long sentences resulted either in crashes of the service or in quite long computations, which are unacceptable for processing huge quantities of data as in our case. In order to bypass these issues, we split the abstracts into separate sentences (by using a strategy similar to that one introduced in Sect. 4.1 for citation contexts), ran FRED on each sentence, and merged the results. Even if this process prevented us from using the FRED capabilities for anaphora resolution on multiple and subsequent sentences, it drastically reduced crashes and computational time without a drop in quality.

Another issue was the identification of a citation function in case of CiTalO crashes. Instead of not associating any function to such citation acts, we decided to assign the most generic property in CiTO, i.e., *cito:citesForInformation*, which is the most frequent and neutral citation function (even according to humans, as described in [1]). The main open issue to be addressed still remains how to handle the cases in which these services do not work as expected.

4.3   Data and Their Provenance Information

Since data changes, it is crucial to trace who added and updated each piece of information in the dataset. There is also another tricky issue: data come from different sources. The integration of different data sources with different degrees of correctness, quality, precision and completeness, and the intervention

---

[7] An *in-text reference pointer* is the entity in the body of a citing work that denotes a bibliographic reference in the reference list, e.g. "[3]" and "(Handler et al. 2012)".

of different agents in the process at different times, means that each piece of information may have been originated by different actors, may have been the result of a number of different actions, or may have been added in different moments in time. Thus it is important to record everything about the origin and the transformation that each data item has undergone. Cumulatively, this meta-information about the metadata itself is called *provenance*.

Thus, the SLT actually contains two datasets, one with those data called *Scholarly Data Dataset* (SDD) and one for provenance data called *Provenance Data Dataset* (PDD)[8]. Provenance data are generated by an additional module and stored in the PDD according to the Provenance Ontology (PROV-O) [4], i.e., the W3C Recommendation for tracking provenance information. In particular, we track:

- all the *new RDF statements* created and published in the previous steps (including, for example, their creation date, the agent responsible for such data, the source graph where these data are actually stored in the SDD, and the description of the related creation activities, etc.);
- all the *new provenance data* generated by this step (including temporal information, the description of the creation activities, etc.).

These provenance data are helpful to maintain the SDD (as we will discuss in the next section), and are stored separately so as to not interfere with the currently-available scholarly data used by external applications.

5   Exploiting the Triplestore

Though SLT can be queried via SPARQL and data are freely available for a smooth integration in the LOD, we want also to show the value of this information for supporting users (e.g., researchers, editors, data curators) in their daily tasks. For this purpose, we have developed a set of tools that provide an interface to the data and enhancement modules developed within the Semantic Lancet project. In particular, in this section we focus on four specific activities: the exploration and analysis of citation networks, the assessment of researchers' relevance in the context of a particular community, the discovery of existing works related to a certain research, and the identification of issues and mistakes in the data published in the triplestore.

5.1   Exploring Bibliographies and Citation Networks

The *Bibliography EXplorer* (BEX)[9] [9] is an interactive web-based tool that leverages the rich information about citation networks (i.e. citations functions, citation contexts, etc.) in the SLT to support the analysis, exploration and

---

[8] Available at http://two.eelst.cs.unibo.it/data and http://two.eelst.cs.unibo.it/prov, respectively.
[9] http://eelst.cs.unibo.it:8089/.

sensemaking process of scientific works. The navigation starts with three search functionalities: besides searching a title or author, the user can also search relevant papers according to their content. This search is performed by calling the Abstract Finder service described in more detail in Sect. 5.3. Thus, through BEX a user can write in the search box a tentative abstract for her/his paper to retrieve meaningful works that match with it from a pure textual but also semantic point of view. Figure 3 shows the main interface of BEX and the output of a search.

Search results are organized as a list of papers, ordered by default from the most recent to the oldest one. Through the sorting box at the top of the interface, the user can easily define custom criterion to order the results (i.e. year, number of citations) and the order type (i.e. ascending or descending). For each returned paper, BEX shows a summary of basic information (e.g. title, publication year, author list, etc.) and a link to the official page of the paper on Elsevier's ScienceDirect.

In order to gather more information about a paper in the list, the user can open a sliding box showing the full abstract and data about citations, organized in two separate sections: *outgoing* and *incoming*.

By clicking on the "Show Items" button, the user can get access to the data about the *outgoing citations*, as shown in the central part of Fig. 3. BEX organizes the cited papers in a vertical list. For each cited paper it shows the following information: the number of times in which the paper is referenced by the paper under examination, some general information about the paper, and a piechart summarising the number and type of citations received from the focus paper. Moreover, abstracts and citation contexts are shown in popups windows.

In the *incoming citation* section, two counters show the number of *global* and *internal* citations received by the paper under examination. The term 'global' here indicates citations for a paper as counted by external services (Scopus); the term 'internal' indicates the citations given by papers described in our dataset (published in the Journal of Web Semantics).

Further details about the citation functions of incoming internal citations are available. This information is presented in a popup window organized in three parts: a pie chart gives an overview of the number and type of incoming citations (top left), a column chart shows the distribution of the citation functions on a time axis (top right), and details about the citation contexts are presented in the bottom. In the two charts at the top of the page, different colors are used to encode the function of each single citation, and citations with the same function are grouped together. Finally, the last component shows, for each paper citing the paper under focus, the list of the citation contexts.

Finally, BEX provides a rich list of filtering capabilities and ordering criteria that can used to focus on different aspects of the internal citation network. In addition to traditional functionalities, BEX provides additional features, such as filter papers by citation function, and include/exclude the self-citations.

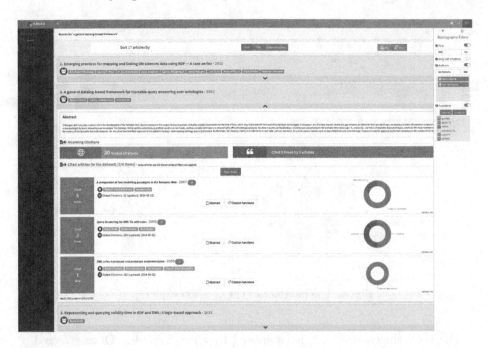

Fig. 3. The main interface of BEX and the list of papers returned by a search. Abstracts and data on citations can be collapsed/expanded on the user's demand.

5.2   Evaluating the Relevance of a Researcher

The investigation functionalities provided by BEX, though rich, can be refined by other tools to support other specific tasks that are relevant for scholars' activities and tasks. For example, it is often useful to evaluate the impact and relevance of researchers for a community. Let us consider the following scenario: the editors-in-chief of a journal have decided to give a prize to the most representative and influential author in the history of the journal. The objective of the selection process is evaluating the impact on the community life in terms of both influence and active participation in the debate on the research topics of the journal.

The network of citations can provide valuable information for this task. In particular, a network that also includes some bibliometric indicators and the citation functions provides the editors with a more precise and exhaustive view on the history of each researcher. SLT gives us all the data useful for this analysis, as discussed in Sect. 2. To help users read and exploit these data, we implemented the *Citation Explorer* [10], an interactive web based tool for analysing and making sense of the citations.

---

[10] http://www.semanticlancet.eu/citationexplorer.

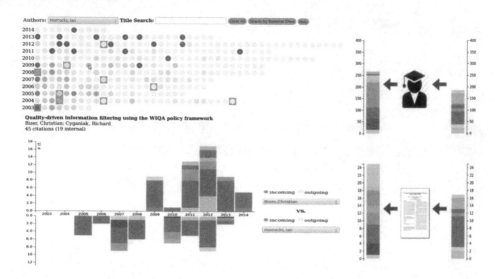

Fig. 4. The interface of the citation explorer.

The tool, shown in Fig. 4, is composed by three modules. Once selected a particular journal (i.e., *Web Semantics* in our example), the top-left area shows the overview of all the papers (i.e., the circles) published in the journal and their citation network. This view is based on the attribute-based layout described in [19].

The second module, shown in the right part, summarises the functions (depicted by using different colours) of the incoming and outgoing citations related to each paper (shown in the bottom) and each author (top). This tool provides new elements to evaluate citations: for example, users can grasp the different impact of an article referenced several times *as an authority* from another cited more times but for a generic reason (e.g., *for information* or *as a related work*).

The last module, shown on the left-bottom, allows users to compare the activity of two authors by showing the distribution of their citations (and the related functions) on a time axis. This time-aware perspective highlights the role played by an author within the particular journal under consideration.

5.3 Searching Related Works

A third very common task for scholars is searching related works. What a researcher usually does is using a search engine combined with some citation services to make sense of possible interesting articles that talk about a particular topic. However, this is a time-consuming and stressing task to address, since it relies on the ability of the researcher in making connections among papers – that usually must be read totally or in part (e.g., their abstract) to really understand if they are of interest or not. The natural language text of the abstracts (graph *abstract*) and its related formal characterisation (graph *semantic abstract*) available in the Semantic Lancet SDD can be exploited to simplify and, at least, reduce the cognitive effort the researcher uses for addressing such task.

In fact, we have developed a prototypical service called *Abstract Finder*[11]. It is a service for searching relevant papers according to their textual and semantic abstracts, by exploiting the semantic information about concepts, events, roles and named entities produced by the *semantic abstract* module of the semantic enhancement component described in Sect. 4.2. This tool works in two phases. First, it creates a semiotic index of the semantic abstracts with respect to the related taxonomy of types defined within them – that are aligned to WordNet synsets and DBpedia resources. In this way we can index the papers according to the textual content of their abstracts as well as to the concepts represented in that content. Finally, a simple interface allows users to query for papers having abstracts similar to the input text, and ranks the results according to a similarity measure that takes into account both the textual content of the input text and its formal translation.

Thus, through the Abstract Finder a researcher can, for instance, write in the search box a tentative abstract for her/his paper to retrieve meaningful papers that match with it from a pure textual but also semantic points of view.

5.4 Spotting and Fixing Data Errors

As discussed in Sect. 4.3 the datasets on scholarly papers need to be maintained and updated. One of the worst nightmares of data curators is to deal with duplicate, incomplete, and inconsistent data. In order to prevent or, at least, to monitor such scenarios, it is valuable to have some mechanisms for debugging datasets and looking for imperfections and errors.

That applies to the SLT as well. In fact, each of the modules in the Semantic Lancet Project pertains the creation of particular kinds of data. What we would like to have, thus, is a dynamic report that spots all the issues of interest, by showing provenance data about them – such as where (i.e., the graph) the problematic RDF statements are stored and what were the modules responsible for their creation. In this way, we can infer whether and when some mistakes have been made, and what we have to fix for addressing such issues.

In order to reach this goal, we have developed the *Web Data Reporter*[12] (WDR), a Web application that queries both SDD and PDD and presents such kinds of situations as a Web page. The current implementation allows us to spot:

- potential *mistakes* in the datasets, e.g., papers that have multiple DOIs;
- data *incompleteness*, e.g., resources associated to no label, type or author;
- data *duplication*, e.g., RDF statements that are defined twice in different graphs.

Finally, since WDR's modular architecture is based on SPARQL queries, new checks and analyses can be easily developed and integrated at any time.

---

[11] http://www.semanticlancet.eu/abstractfinder.
[12] http://www.semanticlancet.eu/reporter.

6 Related Work

Several RDF datasets on scientific publications are available today. In this section we summarise the most relevant ones, highlighting their main strengths and weaknesses. The most relevant and complete ones have been created for the biomedical domain. One of the first was the Nature Linked Data platform[13]. It includes data about papers published by Nature from 1845 and counts about 400 millions of triples, structured according to Dublin Core, FOAF, PRISM and BIBO vocabularies. **Pros:** the platform relies on an automatic workflow for converting data into RDF, facilitating its maintainability. It is also connected to external services, for instance CrossRef to handle citations. Data are very high-quality and cover several aspects (e.g. bibliographic metadata, unambiguous authorship information, basic network of citations, content-based article types - such as survey papers, in-use papers, system papers, etc.). **Cons:** however, some information is not present for all papers. For instance, some abstracts are missing, and some papers are classified by subjects, some others by keyword, others are not classified at all. The citation network also is partially covered by the dataset. The citation network is quite basic, with no information about contexts and functions. Moreover, data about authors' affiliations and how they changed over time are missing.

Citations are indeed the key part of the JISC OpenCitation corpus [18], which makes freely available data about papers published in PubMed Central[14]. **Pros:** particularly interesting is the adoption of the PRO ontology to describe roles and to model authorship information, that takes into account time-awareness issues. The dataset also contains several abstracts, data about affiliations ad some classification data, though these are not available for all papers. The website makes available a tool for extracting OpenCitation data from XML sources with an automatic workflow. **Cons:** although the dataset is very well-structured and of high-quality, one of the main problem is that it is not currently active. Moreover, no provenance data are included, and advanced features about citations (e.g. citation contexts and functions) and article types are missing.

A very similar research is carried on in BioTea [2]. The goal of the project is to make the biomedical literature from PubMed Central available as RDF, taking papers again from PubMed Central. The BioTea dataset describes about 270000 papers, published in 2400 journals, according to different ontological models (BiBO, Dublin Core, FOAF, etc.). **Pros:** this is a very complete dataset: for example, it contains bibliographic, authorship and affiliation data for all papers. It contains information about the document structure (e.g. sections, subsections, paragraphs, etc.), content fragments are annotated to identify meaningful entities, such as proteins, genes, etc., and the abstracts are fully available. **Cons:** one of the main issue with this dataset is the absence of bibliometric information. Moreover, also some advanced features like data about the rhetorical structure of the papers and citation contexts and functions are missing.

---

[13] http://data.nature.com.
[14] http://www.ncbi.nlm.nih.gov/pmc/tools/openftlist/.

Publishers of computer science papers have also made several datasets available. One of them is DBLP++[15] that makes available RDF data corresponding to those collected in DBLP, and coming from multiple publishers and publications. The dataset uses the SWRC ontology[16]. **Pros:** the dataset contains metadata about papers. Particular attention is given to the keywords and the topics of the papers, on top of which the system provides a facet-based search engine. There are also some abstracts in textual form taken from existing scholarly repositories on the Web. **Cons:** the goal of the original project (i.e. tracking the bibliography of each researcher) does heavily impact the type of information in the dataset. For instance, it does not contain any data about affiliations nor about the citations. The quality of the data is also quite heterogeneous.

The situation is much easier to control in smaller datasets, associated to single journals. For example, the Semantic Web Journal SPARQL end-point[17] publishes bibliographic records and rich data for the homonymous journal. It contains about 21000 triples, structured according to a specific Semantic Web Journal ontology, FOAF, Dublin Core and BIBO. **Pros:** the peculiarity of this dataset, that is actually derived from the peculiar open reviewing process of the journal, is that each paper is also supplied with time-aware information about the reviewing process (e.g. reviews, reviewers information, etc.). It contains rich bibliographic data, contributions and all the abstracts. **Cons:** only few data about citations are provided, and information about citation contexts and functions are completely missing. Moreover, no data about affiliations and how they change over the time are provided.

To summarise, the situation today is very fragmented. In particular, the semantic annotation of the content and the exploitation of that enhanced content is still under-explored. SLT plays well in this arena, though it still misses some information that others datasets already make available, even in a larger scale, for instance on affiliations and classifications.

7   Discussion and Conclusions

This paper presents a LOD on scholarly papers, a toolchain for producing and updating the dataset, and a set of tools for browsing, investigating and leveraging the information included in the dataset. The triplestore implements our vision of semantic scholarly dataset, that combines basic bibliographic and authorship data with semantically-enriched data extracted from the text of the papers.

Currently SLT contains data about all the papers published in the Elsevier's Web Semantics journal, but we plan to extend it incrementally: the dataset, in fact, is populated and updated by an automatic workflow that generates content from XML sources. Moreover, we are also enriching the set of information included in the dataset. For instance, the next release will include data about authors' affiliations and documents' internal components, just to name a few.

---

[15] http://dblp.l3s.de/dblp++.php.

[16] http://ontoware.org/swrc/.

[17] http://semantic-web-journal.com:3030/.

The integration of multiple sources, cross-checked and merged together, is a further step: we are also investigating these aspects, experimenting novel interfaces to access SLT and adding support for new tasks. Nonetheless, going back to the ideal characteristics of a semantic publishing dataset, we think that the richness of our dataset is acceptable.

Another key aspect of the project is the overall quality of both the data, applications and services built to support their use. These aspects have been separately evaluated in other previous works, focusing on the different modules composing the SLT project. For what concerns the data reengineering process, all the models used to represent the data in the SLT and discussed in Sect. 3 have been presented and discussed in our previous work [12]. Also the two main modules that perform the semantic enhancement described in Sect. 4.1, extracting information from the analysis of natural language texts, have been introduced and evaluated: CiTalO, which computes the citation functions [1], and FRED, the tool used to generate the semantic abstracts [5]. Finally the Bibliography EXplorer (BEX), the main tool presented in Sect. 5 that provides an interface to the data and the enhancement modules developed for the SLT, has been discussed and evaluated in [9]. As future work, we plan to perform thorough tests on the whole SLT ecosystem for measuring the overall quality of both the dataset and the developed tools.

Acknowledgements. This paper was supported by MIUR PRIN 2016 GAUSS Project. We would like to thank Elsevier for granting access to Scopus and ScienceDirect APIs.

References

1. Ciancarini, P., Iorio, A., Nuzzolese, A.G., Peroni, S., Vitali, F.: Evaluating citation functions in CiTO: cognitive issues. In: Presutti, V., d'Amato, C., Gandon, F., d'Aquin, M., Staab, S., Tordai, A. (eds.) ESWC 2014. LNCS, vol. 8465, pp. 580–594. Springer, Cham (2014). doi:10.1007/978-3-319-07443-6_39
2. García-Castro, L., McLaughlin, C., García Castro, A.: Biotea: RDFizing PubMed central in support for the paper as an interface to the web of data. J. Biomed. Semant. **5**(Suppl1), S5 (2013)
3. IFLA Study Group on the FRBR (2009). Functional Requirements for Bibliographic Records. http://www.ifla.org/publications/functional-requirements-for-bibliographic-records. Accessed 7 Nov 2016
4. Lebo, T., Sahoo, S., McGuinness, D.: The PROV Ontology. W3C Recommendation, 30. World Wide Web Consortium. http://www.w3.org/TR/prov-o/. Accessed 7 Nov 2016
5. Gangemi, A., Presutti, V., Reforgiato Recupero, D., Nuzzolese, A.G., Draicchio, F., Mongiovì, M.: Semantic web machine reading with FRED. Semantic Web, Under review (2016). http://www.semantic-web-journal.net/system/files/swj1297.pdf
6. Lehmann, J., et al.: DBpedia - a large-scale, multilingual knowledge base extracted from wikipedia. Semantic Web. **6**(2), 167–195 (2015)
7. Miller, G.A.: WordNet: a lexical database for English. Commun. ACM **38**(11), 39–41 (1995)

8. Möller, K., Heath, T., Handschuh, S., Domingue, J.: Recipes for semantic web dog food: the ESWC and ISWC metadata projects. In: Aberer, K., et al. (eds.) ASWC/ISWC -2007. LNCS, vol. 4825, pp. 802–815. Springer, Heidelberg (2007). doi:10.1007/978-3-540-76298-0_58
9. Di Iorio, A., Giannella, R., Poggi, F., Peroni, S., Vitali, F.: Exploring scholarly papers through citations. In: Proceedings of the 2015 ACM Symposium on Document Engineering, pp. 107–116. ACM (2015)
10. Horrocks, I., Patel-Schneider, P.F., van Harmelen, F.: From SHIQ and RDF to OWL: the making of a web ontology language. Web Semant. Sci. Serv. Agents World Wide Web **1**(1), 7–26 (2003). doi:10.1016/j.websem.2003.07.001
11. Ogbuji, C.: SPARQL 1.1 Graph Store HTTP Protocol. W3C Recommendation, 2013. World Wide Web Consortium (2013). http://www.w3.org/TR/sparql11-http-rdf-update/. Accessed 7 Dec 2016
12. Peroni, S.: The semantic publishing and referencing ontologies. Semantic Web Technologies and Legal Scholarly Publishing. LGTS, vol. 15, pp. 121–193. Springer, Cham (2014). doi:10.1007/978-3-319-04777-5_5
13. Picca, D., Gliozzo, A.M., Gangemi, A.: LMM: an OWL-DL MetaModel to represent heterogeneous lexical knowledge. In: Proceedings of the Sixth International Conference on Language Resources and Evaluation (LREC 2008) (2008)
14. Presutti, V., Draicchio, F., Gangemi, A.: Knowledge extraction based on discourse representation theory and linguistic frames. In: Teije, A., Völker, J., Handschuh, S., Stuckenschmidt, H., d'Acquin, M., Nikolov, A., Aussenac-Gilles, N., Hernandez, N. (eds.) EKAW 2012. LNCS (LNAI), vol. 7603, pp. 114–129. Springer, Heidelberg (2012). doi:10.1007/978-3-642-33876-2_12
15. Qazvinian, V., Radev, D.: Identifying non-explicit citing sentences for citation-based summarization. In Proceedings of the 48th Annual Meeting of the Association for Computational Linguistics, pp. 555–564. Pennsylvania, USA (2010)
16. Sanderson, R., Ciccarese, P., Van de Sompel, H.: Designing the W3C open annotation data model. In: Proceedings of the 5th Annual ACM Web Science Conference (WebSci13), pp. 366–375. ACM Press, New York (2013)
17. Schuler, K.: A broad-coverage, comprehensive verb lexicon (2005). http://repository.upenn.edu/dissertations/AAI3179808. Accessed 1 Apr 2016
18. Shotton, D.: Publishing: open citations. Nature **502**(7471), 295–297 (2013)
19. Stasko, J.: Value-driven evaluation of visualizations. In: Proceedings of the Fifth Workshop on Beyond Time and Errors: Novel Evaluation Methods for Visualization, pp. 46–53. ACM (2014)
20. Teufel, S., Siddharthan, A., Tidhar, D.: Automatic classification of citation function. In: Proceedings of the 2006 Conference on Empirical Methods in Natural Language Processing (EMNLP 2006), pp. 103–110 (2006)

The Road Towards Reproducibility in Science: The Case of Data Citation

Nicola Ferro and Gianmaria Silvello[(⊠)]

Department of Information Engineering, University of Padua, Padua, Italy
{ferro,silvello}@dei.unipd.it

Abstract. Data citation has a profound impact on the reproducibility of science, a hot topic in many disciplines such as as astronomy, biology, physics, computer science and more. Lately, several authoritative journals have been requesting the sharing of data and the provision of validation methodologies for experiments (e.g., Nature Scientific Data and Nature Physics); these publications and the publishing industry in general see data citation as the means to provide new, reliable and usable means for sharing and referring to scientific data. In this paper, we present the state of the art of data citation and we discuss open issues and research directions with a specific focus on reproducibility. Furthermore, we investigate reproducibility issues by using experimental evaluation in *Information Retrieval (IR)* as a test case. (This paper is a revised and extended version of [33,35,57]).

1 Motivations

Data citation plays a central role for providing better transparency and reproducibility in science [16], a challenge taken up by several fields such as Biomedical Research [2], Public Health Research [27] and Biology [18]. Computer Science is also particularly active in reproducibility, as witnessed by the recent *Association for Computing Machinery (ACM)* policy on result and artifact review and badging[1]. For instance, the Database community started an effort called "SIGMOD reproducibility" [38] "to assist in building a culture where sharing results, code, and scripts of database research"[2]. Since 2015, the *European Conference in IR (ECIR)* [34,41], allocated a whole paper track on reproducibility and in 2015 the RIGOR workshop at SIGIR was dedicated to this topic [12]. Moreover, in 2016 the "Reproducibility of Data-Oriented Experiments in e-Science" seminar was held in Dagstuhl (Germany) [3] bringing together researchers from different fields of computer science with the goal "to come to a common ground across disciplines, leverage best-of-breed approaches, and provide a unifying vision on reproducibility" [33,35].

In recent years, the nature of research and scientific publishing has been rapidly evolving and progressively relying on data to sustain claims and provide

---

[1] https://www.acm.org/publications/policies/artifact-review-badging.
[2] http://db-reproducibility.seas.harvard.edu/.

© Springer International Publishing AG 2017
C. Grana and L. Baraldi (Eds.): IRCDL 2017, CCIS 733, pp. 20–31, 2017.
DOI: 10.1007/978-3-319-68130-6_2

experimental evidence for scientific breakthroughs [44]. The preservation, management, access, discovery and retrieval of research data are topics of utmost importance as witnessed by the great deal of attention they are receiving from the scientific and publishing communities [21]. Along with the pervasiveness and availability of research data, we are witnessing the growing importance of citing these data. Indeed, data citation is required to make results of research fully available to others, provide suitable means to connect publications with the data they rely upon [59], give credit to data creators, curators and publishers [20], and enabling others to better build on previous results and to ask new questions about data [19].

In the traditional context of printed material, the practice of citation has been evolving and adapting across the centuries [21] reaching a stable and reliable state; nevertheless, traditional citation methods and practices cannot be easily applied for citing data. Indeed, citing data poses new significant challenges, such as:

1. the use of heterogeneous data models and formats – e.g., flat data, relational databases, *Comma Separated Value (CSV)*, *eXtensible Markup Language (XML)*, *Resource Description Framework (RDF)* – requiring different methods to manage, retrieve and access the data;
2. the transience of data calling for versioning and archiving methods and systems;
3. the necessity to cite data at different levels of coarseness – e.g., if we consider a relational database, then we may need to cite a specific attribute, a tuple, a tuple sets, a table or the database as a whole – requiring methods to individuate, select and reference specific subsets of data;
4. the necessity to automatically generate citations to data because a citation snippet is required to allow the data to be understood and correctly interpreted and it must be composed of the essential information for identifying the cited data as well as contextual information. Such contextual information must be extracted from the given dataset and/or from external sources automatically, because we cannot assume one knows how to access and select additional relevant data and to structure them appropriately.

As a consequence, traditional practices need to evolve and adapt in order to provide effective and usable methods for citing data.

IR represents a challenging field for data citation as well as for reproducibility. In particular, experimental evaluation in IR represents an effective testbed for new ideas and methods for reproducing experiments and citing data. Indeed, reproducing IR experiments is extremely challenging and there are three main different areas that are of major concern for reproducibility: experiments (or system runs), experimental collections, and meta-evaluation studies. Experiments can be seen as the output of a retrieval system – e.g., a ranking list of documents – given a corpus of documents and an information need; to reproduce an experiment we need to get access to the corpus or sub-corpus and to the information needs used in the experiments as well as the software and the methods employed.

Meta-evaluation studies are even more complex since they often involve manipulation of the data used in the actual analysis; this, among other things, requires to keep track of the provenance of the data and to include provenance information also in the citations to data.

This paper is organized as follows: Sect. 2 briefly presents the state of the art of research in data citation and some open issues and research lines focusing also on provenance which is particularly important for reproducibility in IR. Section 3 describes the main issues concerning reproducibility in IR evaluation with a specific focus on the role of data citation in this context. Finally, Sect. 4 draws some final remarks.

2   Data Citation: Open Issues and Research Directions

Data citation is a complex problem that can be tackled from many perspectives and involves different areas of information and computer science. Overall, data citation has been studied from two main angles: the scholar publishing viewpoint and the infrastructural and computational one.

The former has been investigating the core principles for data citation and the conditions that any data citation solution should meet [1,37]; the need to connect scientific publications and the underlying data [17]; the role of data journals [26]; the definition of metrics based on data citations [45]; and the measurement of datasets impact [11,53].

The latter has been focusing on the infrastructures and systems required to handle the evolution of data such as archiving systems for XML [23], RDF [49] and databases [51]; the use of persistent identifiers [47,58]; the definition frameworks and ontologies to publish data [40]; and, the creation of repositories to store and provide access to data [4,25].

As described in [22], from the computational perspective the problem of data citation can be formulated as follows: "Given a dataset D and a query Q, generate an appropriate citation C". Several of the existing approaches to address this problem allow us to reference datasets as a single unit having textual data serving as metadata source, but as pointed out by [51] most data citations "can often not be generated automatically and they are often not machine interpretable". Furthermore, most data citation approaches do not provide ways to cite datasets with variable granularity.

Until now, the problem of how to cite a dataset at different levels of coarseness, to automatically generate citations and to create human- and machine-readable citations has been tackled only by a few working systems. In [51] an approach relying on persistent and timestamped queries to cite relational databases has been proposed; this method has been implemented to work with CSV files [52]. On the other hand, this system does not provide a suitable means to automatically generate human- and machine-readable citations. In [24] a rule-based citation system that creates machine- and human-readable citations by using only the information present in the data has been proposed for citing XML. This system has been extended into a methodology that works with database views provided that the data to be cited can be represented as a hierarchy [22]; this work has been further extended for general queries over relational databases in [28–30]. [55] proposed a methodology for citing XML data based on machine learning techniques, which allows us to create citations with variable granularity learning from examples and reducing the human effort to a minimum. In [54] a methodology based on named meta-graphs to cite RDF sub-graphs has been proposed; this solution for RDF graphs targets the variable granularity problem and proposes an approach to create human-readable and machine-actionable data citations even though the actual elements composing a citation are not automatically selected. In the context of RDF citation, [40] proposed the nano-publication model where a single statement RDF triple is made citable in its own right; the idea is to enrich a statement via annotations adding context information such as time, authority and provenance. The statement becomes a publication itself carrying all the information to be understood, validated and re-used. This solution is centered around a single statement and the possibility of enriching it.

A great deal of attention has been dedicated to the use of persistent identifiers [9,47,58] such as Digital Object Identifiers (DOI), Persistent Uniform Resource Locator (PURL) and the Archival Resource Key (ARK). Normally, these solutions propose to associate a persistent identifier with a citable dataset and to create a related set of metadata (e.g., author, version, URL) to be used to cite the dataset. Persistent identifiers are foundational for data citation, but they represent just one part of the solution since they do not allow us to create citations with variable granularity, unless we create a unique identifier for each single datum in a dataset, which in most of the cases may be unfeasible. As a consequence, the use of persistent identifiers as well as their study and evaluation is mainly related to the publication of research data in order to provide a handle for subsequent citation purposes rather than a data citation solution itself.

Data citation is a compound and complex problem and a "one size fits all" system to address it does not exist, yet. Indeed, as we have discussed above, flat data, relational databases, XML and RDF datasets are intrinsically different one from the other, present heterogeneous structures and functions and, as a consequence, require specific solutions for addressing data citation problems. Furthermore, different communities present specific peculiarities, practices and policies that must be considered when a citation to data has to be provided.

As a consequence, within the context of data citation, there are several open issues and research directions we can take into account:

Automatic Generation of Citations. Most of the solutions addressing this problem work for XML data because they exploit its hierarchical structure to gather the relevant (meta)data to be used in a citation. On the other hand, there is no ready to use solution for non-hierarchical datasets as it may be a relational database or a RDF dataset. A further problem is to automatically create citations for data with no structure at all.

Citation Identity. This problem refers to the necessity of uniquely identifying a citation to data and of being able to discriminate between two citations referring to different data or different versions of the same data and between two different citations referring to the same data.

Citation Containment. We need to define some methods to check if a citation refers to a superset or a subset of the data cited by another citation; somehow, we may need to define hierarchies of citations in order to identify the relationships they have one with the other.

Citation identity and containment have a direct impact on the definition of data citation indexes that can be used to assess the overall impact of a dataset and to quantify the impact and the contribution of a data creator/curator as we now do with bibliometrical indicators based on traditional citations.

Versioning. One of the main differences between traditional citations and data citations is that data may not be fixed, but it may evolve through time; indeed, new data may be added to a dataset, some changes may occur, some mistakes may be fixed or new information may be added. All these changes in a dataset reflect on the citations to data that have been produced. Indeed, a citation needs to ensure that the data a citation uses is identical to that cited [8]. Several archiving and versioning systems have been proposed especially for relational databases and XML data, but they have not been incorporated with data citation solutions, yet.

Provenance. Provenance information plays a central role because we may need to reconstruct the chain of ownership of a data object or the chain of modifications that occurred to it in order to produce a reliable citation. New solutions have to be provided to integrate data citation with currently employed systems controlling and managing the data workflow.

A further challenge is represented by streaming data which may not been always available or which keep constantly changing through time.

Groups of Citations and the Empty Set. Most of the solutions we discussed above are oriented to the citation of a single datum such as a single node, a set of connected nodes in a hierarchy or a set of connected statements in a RDF dataset. On the other hand, we may need to provide a suitable citation for hundreds or thousands of independent data; let us imagine a query to a relational database returning a hundred of possibly unrelated tuples, how do we provide a single citation for this result set?

Vice versa, a related problem is how to define a suitable citation for the empty set. In other terms, how do we create a citation for a query that returns no results?

Supporting Scientific Claims. Scientific claims are often based on evidence gathered from data. They could be related to a single datum or to multiple data coming from the same source or from different sources. Data citation can be used to support such claims and to provide a means to verify their reliability. Actionable papers aim at connecting the presented results with the data from which they have been derived; in this case, we are foreseeing an evolution of such papers, where every single component of a scientific statement can be related to a piece of evidence (data) supporting it and some sort of automatic inference can be carried out.

3 Reproducibility Open Issues: The Example of IR Evaluation

Performances of IR systems are determined not only by their efficiency but also and most importantly by their *effectiveness*, i.e. their ability to retrieve and better rank relevant information resources while at the same time suppressing the retrieval of not relevant ones. Due to the many sources of uncertainty, as for example vague user information needs, unstructured information sources, or subjective notion of relevance, *experimental evaluation* is the only mean to assess the performances of IR systems from the effectiveness point of view. Experimental evaluation relies on the Cranfield paradigm which makes use of *experimental collections*, consisting of documents, sampled from a real domain of interest; topics, representing real user information needs in that domain; and, relevance judgements, determining which documents are relevant to which topics [43].

Reproducing IR experiments is extremely challenging, even when they are very well-documented [14,15,36]. There are three main different areas that are of major concern for reproducibility: system runs, experimental collections, and meta-evaluation studies.

The most common concern for reproducibility are *system runs*, i.e. the outputs of the execution of an IR system, since they are what typically researchers and developers want to compare their new ideas against. Even if you use the same datasets and even if you rely on shared open source software, there are often many hidden parameters and tunings which hamper the reproducibility of algorithms and techniques. The situation is even more challenging when you also rely on user-interaction data. Approaches like Evaluation-as-a-Service [42], based on open interfaces and virtual machines as in *The Incredible Research Assistant (TIRA)*[3] [50], or Open Runs [61], i.e. system runs backed by a software repository that captures the code to recreate the run, are now starting to explore how to face these issues.

Experimental collections are the core of evaluation and they are used for many years, often for purposes different from those that led to their creation. Nevertheless, they are not yet a primary focus for reproducibility, even if they should be, given their central role in experimentation. Indeed, it is important to understand their limitations and their generalizability as well as to reproduce the process that led to their creation. This is not always trivial since, for example, documents may be ephemeral data such as tweets [10], topics may be

---

[3] http://www.tira.io/.

sampled from real system logs, relevance judgments are made by (disagreeing) humans [60] and, more and more often, using crowdsourcing [7].

Even if IR has a long tradition in ensuring that the due scientific rigor is guaranteed in producing experimental data, it has not a similar tradition in managing and taking care of such valuable data [5,32]. This represents a serious obstacle to facing the above mentioned challenges. For example, there is a lack of commonly agreed formats for modeling and describing the experimental data as well as almost no metadata (descriptive, administrative, copyright, etc.) for annotating and enriching them. The semantics of the data themselves is often not explicit and it is demanded to the scripts typically used for processing them, which are often not well documented, rely on rigid assumptions on the data format or even on side effects in processing the data. Finally, IR lacks a commonly agreed mechanism for citing and linking data to the papers describing them [57].

As there are many different terms relating to various kinds of reproducibility [31], the *Platform, Research goal, Implementation, Method, Actor, and Data (PRIMAD)* (pronounce "primed") model, proposed by [3,35], can act as a framework to distinguish the major components describing an experiment in computer science (and related fields):

Research Goal characterizes the purpose of a study;
Method is the specific approach proposed or considered by the researcher;
Implementation refers to the actual implementation of the method, usually in some programming language;
Platform describes the underlying hard- and software like the operating system and the computer used;
Data consists of two parts, namely the input data and the specific parameters chosen to carry out the method;
Actor refers to the experimenter.

As an example, consider a student performing a retrieval experiment. The research goal is to achieve a high retrieval quality, and as method chosen is the BM25 formula. Experiments use the LEMUR system as implementation, under the operating system Ubuntu 15.10 on a Dell xyz server. The GOV2 collection serves as input data, and a specific setting of the BM25 parameters is chosen. The actor is the student performing the runs.

When another researcher now tries to reproduce the experiment described above, she will change one or more of the components. In case she tries to rerun the experiment without changing anything else[4], then we have another actor, that is, A is changed to A', the actor is "primed". If successful, this experiment would demonstrate that the original researcher has supplied enough information to ensure reproducibility. In case the results of the experiment are the same, then the original findings have been successfully reproduced and thus confirmed.

Now let us look at changes of the other components:

R → R' : When the research goal is changed, then we *re-purpose* some of the components of the experiment for another research question (for example,

---

[4] Actually, this would be difficult to achieve.

performing interactive retrieval experiments). So method and implementation usually are also changed, and other components as well.

M → M' : Most of the research in the field of IR deals with the investigation of alternative methods (retrieval models, formulas). This implies also a new implementation I', which often runs on a different platform. However, for performing comparisons, the (input) data should be the same.

I → I' : Here a researcher uses a different implementation, say Terrier instead of Lemur, or does their own reimplementation.

P → P' : In most cases, independent researchers do not have access to the platform used in the original experiment. Even different versions of system libraries, or external resources such as dictionaries, might have subtle effects on the outcome of experiments.

D → D' : Rerunning an experiment with different parameters might be useful for testing the robustness of a method. Applying the implementation to different input data (for example, test collections) aims at investigating the generality of the method.

For ensuring reproducibility, there is the need to be able to share as many PRIMAD components as possible. Research goal and method are what we currently share via publications in conference proceedings or journals (although details of the method are often missing). Sharing implementations are possible via making it open source and uploading it on Web sites focusing on this task (for example, Github). Platforms can be shared by means of virtual machines or dockers, or by "evaluation as a service". For the input data, there are a number of standard test collections which are generally available. When researchers use their own test collection, however, reproducibility can only be ensured in case this collection is shared with the community, ideally via a trustworthy repository.

However, also in this case, we note a lack of attention to data citation. Indeed, the PRIMAD model allows us to have a common framework to describe what has changed from one experiment to another and to clearly define the kind of reproduciblity we are achieving (or not). Nevertheless, all these changes modeled by the framework should be backed by a proper data citation mechanism that allows us to track them and to reference back to them.

There have been early examples of systems to manage IR experimental data, such as EvaluatIR [13] and *Distributed Information Retrieval Evaluation Campaign Tool (DIRECT)*[5] [4,6], but they have not been designed with reproducibility and/or data citation as goals. More recently, steps forward more fine grained models and systems have been proposed, as for example LOD-DIRECT[6] [56] which uses semantic Web and *Linked Open Data (LOD)* technologies to model IR evaluation data and make them linkable, or nanopublications for IR evaluation [48].

All these examples provide bit and pieces which may exploited or further developed to support reproducibility and data citation in IR evaluation but a more comprehensive and holistic approach would be needed. Indeed, a full

---

[5] http://direct.dei.unipd.it/.

[6] http://lod-direct.dei.unipd.it/.

fledged abstract conceptual framework for describing IR experiments with reproducibility and data citation in mind, e.g. an evolution of PRIMAD, should be paired with semantic models clearly formalizing it, e.g. a further development of LOD-DIRECT, and proper systems should be developed to implement and operationalize it, e.g. starting from DIRECT and TIRA.

4   Final Remarks

In this paper we discussed reproducibility in science by highlighting why it is important and the main issues that need to be addressed. Data citation plays a central role for enabling reproducibility, but despite its importance and the attention dedicated by the information and computer science communities, there still are several open issues that need to be tackled in order to have a general and usable data citation system. Hence, we outlined the main open issues and research direction in data citation. Moreover, we presented the concrete use case of IR experimental evaluation highlighting the state of the art, the open problems and where data citation can play a central role for enabling effective reproducibility in IR.

References

1. Out of Cite, Out of Mind: The Current State of Practice, Policy, and Technology for the Citation of Data, vol. 12. CODATA-ICSTI Task Group on Data Citation Standards and Practices, September 2013
2. Reproducibility and reliability of biomedical research: improving research practice. Technical report, The Academy of Medical Science (2015)
3. Freire, J., Fuhr, N., Rauber, A. (eds.): Report from Dagstuhl Seminar 16041: Reproducibility of Data-Oriented Experiments in e-Science. Dagstuhl Reports, vol. 6, no. 1. Schloss Dagstuhl-Leibniz-Zentrum fuer Informatik, Germany (2016)
4. Agosti, M., Di Buccio, E., Ferro, N., Masiero, I., Peruzzo, S., Silvello, G.: DIREC-Tions: design and specification of an IR evaluation infrastructure. In: Catarci, T., Forner, P., Hiemstra, D., Peñas, A., Santucci, G. (eds.) CLEF 2012. LNCS, vol. 7488, pp. 88–99. Springer, Heidelberg (2012). doi:10.1007/978-3-642-33247-0_11
5. Agosti, M., Di Nunzio, G.M., Ferro, N.: The importance of scientific data curation for evaluation campaigns. In: Thanos, C., Borri, F., Candela, L. (eds.) DELOS 2007. LNCS, vol. 4877, pp. 157–166. Springer, Heidelberg (2007). doi:10.1007/978-3-540-77088-6_15
6. Agosti, M., Ferro, N.: Towards an evaluation infrastructure for DL performance evaluation. In: Tsakonas, G., Papatheodorou, C. (eds.) Evaluation of Digital Libraries: An Insight into Useful Applications and Methods, pp. 93–120. Chandos Publishing, Oxford (2009)
7. Alonso, O., Mizzaro, S.: Using crowdsourcing for TREC relevance assessment. Inf. Process. Manage. 48(6), 1053–1066 (2012)
8. Altman, M., Crosas, M.: The evolution of data citation: from principles to implementation. IAssist Q. 37(1–4), 62–70 (2013)
9. Altman, M., King, G.: A proposed standard for the scholarly citation of quantitative data. IASSIST (2006). http://www.iassistdata.org/conferences/archive/2006

10. Amigó, E., Corujo, A., Gonzalo, J., Meij, E., de Rijke, M.: Overview of RepLab 2012: evaluating online reputation management systems. In: Forner, P., Karlgren, J., Womser-Hacker, C., Ferro, N. (eds.) CLEF 2012 Working Notes. CEUR Workshop Proceedings (CEUR-WS.org), ISSN 1613–0073 (2012). http://ceur-ws.org/Vol-1178/

11. Angelini, M., Ferro, N., Larsen, B., Müller, H., Santucci, G., Silvello, G., Tsikrika, T.: Measuring and analyzing the scholarly impact of experimental evaluation initiatives. Procedia Comput. Sci. **38**, 133–137 (2014)

12. Arguello, J., Crane, M., Diaz, F., Lin, J., Trotman, A.: Report on the SIGIR 2015 workshop on reproducibility, inexplicability, and generalizability of results (RIGOR). SIGIR Forum **49**(2), 107–116 (2015)

13. Armstrong, T.G., Moffat, A., Webber, W., Zobel, J.: EvaluatIR: an online tool for evaluating and comparing IR systems. In: Allan, J., Aslam, J.A., Sanderson, M., Zhai, C., Zobel, J. (eds.) Proceedings of 32nd Annual International ACM SIGIR Conference on Research and Development in Information Retrieval (SIGIR 2009), USA, p. 833. ACM, New York (2009)

14. Badan, A., Benvegnù, L., Biasetton, M., Bonato, G., Brighente, A., Cenzato, A., Ceron, P., Cogato, G., Marchesin, S., Minetto, A., Pellegrina, L., Purpura, A., Simionato, R., Soleti, N., Tessarotto, M., Tonon, A., Vendramin, F., Ferro, N.: Towards open-source shared implementations of keyword-based access systems to relational data. In: Ferro, N., Guerra, F., Ives, Z., Silvello, G., Theobald, M. (eds.) Proceedings of 1st International Workshop on Keyword-Based Access and Ranking at Scale (KARS 2017) - Proceedings of the Workshops of the EDBT/ICDT 2017 Joint Conference (EDBT/ICDT 2017). CEUR Workshop Proceedings (CEUR-WS.org), ISSN 1613–0073 (2017). http://ceur-ws.org/Vol-1810/

15. Badan, A., Benvegnù, L., Biasetton, M., Bonato, G., Brighente, A., Marchesin, S., Minetto, A., Pellegrina, L., Purpura, A., Simionato, R., Soleti, N., Tessarotto, M., Tonon, A., Ferro, N.: Keyword-based access to relational data: to reproduce, or to not reproduce? In: Greco et al. [39]

16. Baggerly, K.: Disclose all data in publications. Nature **467**, 401 (2010)

17. Bardi, A., Manghi, P.: A framework supporting the shift from traditional digital publications to enhanced publications. D-Lib Magaz. **21**(1/2) (2015). http://dx.doi.org/10.1045/january2015-bardi

18. Bloom, T., Ganly, E., Winker, M.: Data access for the open access literature: PLOS's data policy. PLoS Biol. **12**(2), e1001797 (2014)

19. Borgman, C.L.: The conundrum of sharing research data. JASIST **63**(6), 1059–1078 (2012). http://dx.doi.org/10.1002/asi.22634

20. Borgman, C.L.: Why are the attribution and citation of scientific data important? In: Board on Research Data and Information, Policy and Global Affairs Division, National Academy of Sciences (eds.) Report from Developing Data Attribution and Citation Practices and Standards: An International Symposium and Workshop, pp. 1–8. National Academies Press, Washington DC (2012)

21. Borgman, C.L.: Big Data, Little Data, No Data. MIT Press, Cambridge (2015)

22. Buneman, P., Davidson, S.B., Frew, J.: Why data citation is a computational problem. Commun. ACM (CACM) **59**(9), 50–57 (2016)

23. Buneman, P., Khanna, S., Tajima, K., Tan, W.C.: Archiving scientific data. ACM Trans. Database Syst. (TODS) **29**(1), 2–42 (2004)

24. Buneman, P., Silvello, G.: A rule-based citation system for structured and evolving datasets. IEEE Data Eng. Bull. **33**(3), 33–41 (2010). http://sites.computer.org/debull/A10sept/buneman.pdf

25. Burton, A., Koers, H., Manghi, P., La Bruzzo, S., Aryani, A., Diepenbroek, M., Schindler, U.: On bridging data centers and publishers: the data-literature interlinking service. In: Garoufallou, E., Hartley, R.J., Gaitanou, P. (eds.) MTSR 2015. CCIS, vol. 544, pp. 324–335. Springer, Cham (2015). doi:10.1007/978-3-319-24129-6_28
26. Candela, L., Castelli, D., Manghi, P., Tani, A.: Data journals: a survey. J. Assoc. Inf. Sci. Technol. **66**(9), 1747–1762 (2015). http://dx.doi.org/10.1002/asi.23358
27. Carr, D., Littler, K.: Sharing research data to improve public health: a funder perspective. J. Empir. Res. Hum. Res. Ethics **10**(3), 314–316 (2015)
28. Davidson, S.B., Deutsch, D., Milo, T., Silvello, G.: A model for fine-grained data citation. In: Greco et al. [39]
29. Davidson, S.B., Deutsch, D., Tova, M., Silvello, G.: A model for fine-grained data citation. In: 8th Biennial Conference on Innovative Data Systems Research (CIDR 2017) (2017)
30. Davidson, S.B., Buneman, P., Deutch, D., Milo, T., Silvello, G.: Data citation: a computational challenge. In: Proceedings of the 36th ACM SIGMOD-SIGACT-SIGAI Symposium on Principles of Database Systems (PODS 2017), USA, pp. 1–4 (2017). http://doi.acm.org/10.1145/3034786.3056123
31. De Roure, D.: The future of scholarly communications. Insights **27**(3), 233–238 (2014)
32. Dussin, M., Ferro, N.: Managing the knowledge creation process of large-scale evaluation campaigns. In: Agosti, M., Borbinha, J., Kapidakis, S., Papatheodorou, C., Tsakonas, G. (eds.) ECDL 2009. LNCS, vol. 5714, pp. 63–74. Springer, Heidelberg (2009). doi:10.1007/978-3-642-04346-8_8
33. Ferro, N.: Reproducibility challenges in information retrieval evaluation. ACM J. Data Inf. Qual. (JDIQ) **8**(2), 8:1–8:4 (2017)
34. Ferro, N., et al. (eds.): ECIR 2016. LNCS, vol. 9626. Springer, Cham (2016)
35. Ferro, N., Fuhr, N., Järvelin, K., Kando, N., Lippold, M., Zobel, J.: Increasing reproducibility in IR: findings from the dagstuhl seminar on "reproducibility of data-oriented experiments in e-science". SIGIR Forum **50**(1), 68–82 (2016)
36. Ferro, N., Silvello, G.: Rank-biased precision reloaded: reproducibility and generalization. In: Hanbury et al. [41], pp. 768–780
37. FORCE-11: Data Citation Synthesis Group: Joint Declaration of Data Citation Principles. FORCE11, San Diego, CA, USA (2014)
38. Freire, J., Bonnet, P., Shasha, D.: Computational reproducibility: state-of-the-art, challenges, and database research opportunities. In: Proceedings of the ACM SIGMOD International Conference on Management of Data, SIGMOD 2012, pp. 593–596 (2012). http://doi.acm.org/10.1145/2213836.2213908
39. Greco, S., Saccà, D., Flesca, S., Masciari, E. (eds.): Proceedings of 25th Italian Symposium on Advanced Database Systems (SEBD 2017) (2017)
40. Groth, P., Gibson, A., Velterop, J.: The anatomy of a nanopublication. Inf. Serv. Use **30**(1–2), 51–56 (2010)
41. Hanbury, A., Kazai, G., Rauber, A., Fuhr, N. (eds.): ECIR 2015. LNCS, vol. 9022. Springer, Cham (2015). doi:10.1007/978-3-319-16354-3
42. Hanbury, A., Müller, H., Balog, K., Brodt, T., Cormack, G.V., Eggel, I., Gollub, T., Hopfgartner, F., Kalpathy-Cramer, J., Kando, N., Krithara, A., Lin, J., Mercer, S., Potthast, M.: Evaluation-as-a-service: overview and outlook. CoRR abs/1512.07454, December 2015
43. Harman, D.K.: Information Retrieval Evaluation. Morgan & Claypool Publishers, San Rafael (2011)

44. Hey, T., Tansley, S., Tolle, K. (eds.): The Fourth Paradigm: Data-Intensive Scientific Discovery. Microsoft Research, Redmond (2009)
45. Huang, Y.H., Rose, P.W., Hsu, C.N.: Citing a data repository: a case study of the protein data bank. PLoS ONE **10**(8), e0136631 (2015)
46. Kanoulas, E., Lupu, M., Clough, P., Sanderson, M., Hall, M., Hanbury, A., Toms, E. (eds.): CLEF 2014. LNCS, vol. 8685. Springer, Cham (2014). doi:10.1007/978-3-319-11382-1
47. Klump, J., Huber, R., Diepenbroek, M.: DOI for geoscience data - how early practices shape present perceptions. Earth Sci. Inform. 1–14 (2015). http://dx.doi.org/10.1007/s12145-015-0231-5
48. Lipani, A., Piroi, F., Andersson, L., Hanbury, A.: An Information Retrieval Ontology for Information Retrieval Nanopublications. In: Kanoulas et al. [46], pp. 44–49
49. Papavasileiou, V., Flouris, G., Fundulaki, I., Kotzinos, D., Christophides, V.: High-level change detection in RDF(S) KBs. ACM Trans. Database Syst. **38**(1), 1 (2013)
50. Potthast, M., Gollub, T., Rangel Pardo, F., Rosso, P., Stamatatos, E., Stein, B.: Improving the reproducibility of PAN's shared tasks: plagiarism detection, author identification, and author profiling. In: Kanoulas et al. [46], pp. 268–299
51. Pröll, S., Rauber, A.: Scalable data citation in dynamic, large databases: model and reference implementation. In: Hu, X., Young, T.L., Raghavan, V., Wah, B.W., Baeza-Yates, R., Fox, G., Shahabi, C., Smith, M., Yang, Q., Ghani, R., Fan, W., Lempel, R., Nambiar, R. (eds.) Proceedings of the 2013 IEEE International Conference on Big Data, pp. 307–312. IEEE (2013)
52. Pröll, S., Rauber, A.: Asking the right questions - query-based data citation to precisely identify subsets of data. ERCIM News **100** (2015)
53. Robinson-Garcia, N., Jiménez-Contreras, E., Torres-Salinas, D.: Analyzing data citation practices according to the data citation index. J. Am. Soc. Inf. Sci. Technol. (JASIST) **67**, 2964–2975 (2015)
54. Silvello, G.: A methodology for citing linked open data subsets. D-Lib Magaz. **21**(1/2) (2015). http://dx.doi.org/10.1045/january2015-silvello
55. Silvello, G.: Learning to cite framework: how to automatically construct citations for hierarchical data. J. Am. Soc. Inf. Sci. Technol. (JASIST), 1–28 (2017)
56. Silvello, G., Bordea, G., Ferro, N., Buitelaar, P., Bogers, T.: Semantic representation and enrichment of information retrieval experimental data. Int. J. Digit. Libr. (IJDL) **18**(2), 145–172 (2017)
57. Silvello, G., Ferro, N.: Data citation is coming. Introduction to the special issue on data citation. Bullet. IEEE Tech. Committee Digit. Libr. (IEEE-TCDL) **12**(1), 1–5 (2016)
58. Simons, N.: Implementing DOIs for research data. D-Lib Magaz. **18**(5/6) (2012). http://dx.doi.org/10.1045/may2012-simons
59. Vernooy-Gerritsen, M.: Enhanced Publications: Linking Publications and Research Data in Digital Repositories. Amsterdam University Press, Amsterdam (2009)
60. Voorhees, E.M.: Variations in relevance judgments and the measurement of retrieval effectiveness. Inf. Process. Manage. **36**(5), 697–716 (2000)
61. Voorhees, E.M., Rajput, S., Soboroff, I.: Promoting repeatability through open runs. In: Yilmaz, E., Clarke, C.L.A. (eds.) Proceedings of 7th International Workshop on Evaluating Information Access (EVIA 2016), pp. 17–20. National Institute of Informatics, Tokyo, Japan (2016)

Digital Libraries in Open Education: The Italy Case

Anna Maria Tammaro[1](✉) [iD], Laura Ciancio[2] [iD],
Rosanna De Rosa[3] [iD], Eleonora Pantò[4] [iD], and Fabio Nascimbeni[5] [iD]

[1] University of Parma, Parma, Italy
annamaria.tammaro@unipr.it
[2] ICCU Ministero Beni Culturali, Rome, Italy
laura.ciancio@beniculturali.it
[3] Università di Napoli Federico II, Naples, Italy
rderosa@unina.it
[4] CSP Innovazione nelle ICT, Turin, Italy
eleonora.panto@csp.it
[5] Universidad Internacional de La Rioja, La Rioja, Spain
fabio.nascimbeni@unir.net

Abstract. Open Education strategies, and specifically MOOC (Massive Open Online Courses) and OER (Open Educational Resources), play an important role in supporting policies for educational innovation, lifelong learning, and, more generally, the enlargement of educational opportunities for all. While there is an increasing interest in Open Education, there is little awareness about the role of Digital Library as learning incubators for learning enhancement. The paper presents briefly the state of art of Digital libraries in the light of the most recent initiatives of Open Education in Italy, towards an integrated model of Digital libraries as "knowledge and learning open hubs".

Keywords: MOOCs · OER · Open education · ICCU · EMMA · Digital libraries · Internet culturale

1 Introduction: Key Drivers

In Europe, in the context of the Higher Education modernisation process [1], the European Commission has highlighted how digital technologies represent an opportunity to improve quality of education and to increase access and equality for all. In particular, Open Education promotes the objectives of the Bologna Process for higher education and that of lifelong learning, enhancing internationalization, democratization of education, active and collaborative learning, as well as the co-creation of content by teachers and students. In 2013, the European Commission launched the "Open Education Europa" [2] portal to collect and promote existing national initiatives, aiming to exploit the potential of OER by including digital technologies into current practices of university and continuing professional development initiatives. A stimulus in this direction came in 2013 with the Communication Opening Up Education [3], promoting those approaches removing barriers to participation in education at all levels through

C. Grana and L. Baraldi (Eds.): IRCDL 2017, CCIS 733, pp. 32–41, 2017.
DOI: 10.1007/978-3-319-68130-6_3

use of ICT. The approaches "Open" serve as an example for Open Education policies at the level of EU member states.

Open Education represents a key strategy to meet the growing need for connections between the worlds of formal, non-formal and informal learning towards lifelong learning, and can contribute to learning modernisation towards educational systems that are:

- Centered on the learner,
- Based on collaborative learning;
- Combined with constructivist pedagogy;
- Personalized in various training programs;
- Focused on continuous training on competencies (such as information literacy).

In order to achieve the ambitious goal of continuous learning, the availability of OER and MOOC is not enough, however, and a favorable context that can facilitate learning, such as digital libraries, is needed. Digital libraries can become incubators and instructional hubs, where learning can be enhanced.

1.1   Digital Libraries in Open Education

The Report "Digital Libraries in Education: analytical survey" published by UNESCO in 2003 [4] emphasizes the need to coordinate the development of Open Education initiatives with the growth of Digital libraries. In the definition given by UNESCO Digital libraries are distinguished from "hybrid" libraries and even from traditional libraries. According to UNESCO, the benefits that digital libraries can bring to Open Education developments are very ambitious: "as a way of restructuring the current higher-education enterprise into a global" knowledge and learning "industry" [4, p. 7]. Instead of being tied to the traditional metaphor of libraries, UNESCO explains that Digital libraries are intended as advanced tools for collaborative construction of: "knowledge and learning". The definition of the Digital library which is adopted is the following: "… an environment bringing together collections, services, and people to support the full cycle of creation, dissemination, discussion, collaboration, use, new authoring, and preservation of data, information, and knowledge" [4, p. 7].

Digital libraries as suggested in the UNESCO report, can offer essential features:

- They are made for specific users' learning needs;
- They offer re-use of a large amount of educational resources;
- They allow open access to anyone, anytime and anywhere.

How do Digital libraries have achieved this ambitious goal of enhancing learning? Best results can be evidenced for the technological infrastructure. Digital libraries are, however, quite behind when it comes to the objectives of applying a constructivist pedagogy and facilitating collaboration.

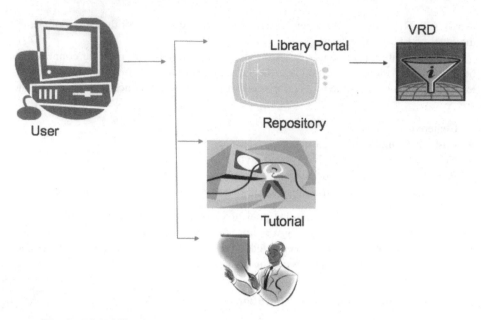

Fig. 1. Digital libraries and Open Education: Model 1 (source: Tammaro, 2005).

2 Digital Libraries as Infrastructure

From a technological point of view, the experiences of European Digital libraries in relationship with Open Education have experimented two possible ways of collaboration. First, Digital libraries as collections of educational resources (learning object) integrated into the OER management platforms and MOOC (LMS-Learning Management System); second, Digital libraries as learning platforms themselves (VLS - Virtual Learning System). Both approaches are based on Web technology (standards and protocols) that are transversal to Digital libraries and Open Education.

In the UNESCO view, Digital libraries should indeed become essential components of the basic infrastructure for research, learning and teaching: learning incubators, pillars of "knowledge and learning". What has been achieved since the publication of the UNESCO report?

ELAG (European Library Automation Group) in 2005 and in 2006 established a working group to understand the technological and organizational issues of the possible cooperation between the libraries community (not just Digital) and education (not just Open). The research question which was investigated was:"..a student is working in the e-learning environment and is recommended to read a given article, which is within a licensed database or a library repository; how can this be enabled with minimum effort and minimum confusion on the part of the user?" [5, p. 1].

Three models were identified:

1. Content and support: this model is essentially that of the integration of the additional resources indicated by UNESCO, in which the digital content is static and is delivered through link to the resource;

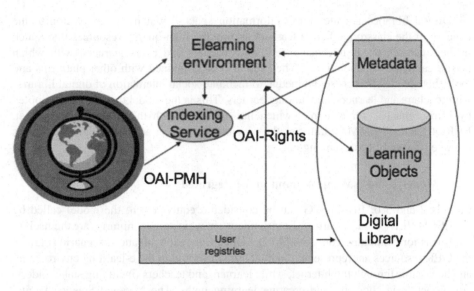

Fig. 2. Digital libraries and Open Education: Model 2&3 (source: Tammaro, 2005).

2. <u>Wrap around</u>: this model provides a dynamic resources pool, with which students can interact, becoming themselves content creators;
3. <u>Integrated</u>: this model indicates a learning community facilitated by a platform that can be the digital library itself, where there is an explicit reference to the OER, with the student's ability to interact with resources and with a learning community with the same interests [6].

2.1 Model 1: Content and Support

The quality of educational content is definitely the strong point of Digital libraries, since these provide a set of resources that are selected, organized, preserved and maintained, along with a set of metadata that describe the content of educational resources and general support (Fig. 1).

Access to resources of Digital libraries is accompanied (within copyright limits) by the capability of re-using and combining resources, stimulating creativity and innovation. This opportunity is made possible by specific metadata that describe the educational value of the resource within a specific learning context. This value is usually assigned by the teachers, who select the resources in a Resource Based Learning (RBL) educational approach (abandoning the obsolete textbook), but it can also be left to the selection of the learners, in order to make them more responsible and constructive in their learning process. Even in the case where there is not a default path orienting the user, the Digital library value stands in its selection of high quality resources, as well as in the curation of the digital collection, which distinguishes the digital library from the Web in general.

Digital libraries are therefore "information spaces" which can revolutionize the concept of the classroom: here a learner can find the high-quality resources that match his/her research needs but also meets with teachers and peers learners, with which he/she can learn collaboratively. They can also be combined with other platforms and tools that are classified as social media, to facilitate social interaction of digital libraries with teachers and learners, and among learners. This is the model that has been adopted by Europeana [7], for example, which has launched with the European Schoolnet, EUROCLIO and EMMA platforms the possibility of direct access to digital resources retrieved through its search engine.

2.2   Model 2 and 3 Wrap Around and Integrated

Models 2 and 3 of ELAG WG can be considered equivalent to the model called by UNESCO VLE (Virtual Learning Environment), in which digital libraries are themselves platforms for continuing education. In this Open Education advanced scenario (Fig. 2), the OER resources are represented in the Digital Library, in the e-learning environment and accessible through the Internet, while learners and teachers (including stakeholders) are proactive in choosing and creating learning paths. The National Science Digital Library (NSDL) is an example of a Digital Library as an integrated platform where OERs are organized for educational purposes and where users are stimulated to be creators of content. Some private companies such as Questia have also tried to realize this typology of digital library with an advanced role in learning support [8].

However, despite the attention that the research on Digital library has given to VLS (Virtual Learning Systems), Digital libraries as platform for learning "compete" with many other services and platforms. The integration of Digital libraries within the contexts of e-learning platform and the relationship with Open Education has been and still is difficult. The lack of educational metadata in organizing the collection is an obvious example of the difficulty of Digital libraries to take on an educational role.

The reason for this is to point to the weakness of the digital libraries for pedagogy. Following the distinction made by Lynch [9], it is evident that digital libraries do not play an educational role because they are not able to educate, but only to support lifelong learning.

3   Digital Libraries and Pedagogy

The difficulty for Digital libraries is to integrate new educational theories, according to the vision of the constructive approach of Open Education indicated above. Lynch [9] distinguishes between learning needs for training and for education, indicating that digital libraries are not for education. While Thomas Carlyle in the last century could say "true university today is a collection of books" Lynch affirms that today it would not be possible to state that the Digital library would be the university, given the amount of educational resources freely available on the Internet in the forms of MOOCs and OERs. In other words, access to information should not be confused with access to education!

To become themselves platforms for education and training, Digital libraries should become able of promoting meaningful educational approaches, stimulating some form of social interaction among teachers and learners and administering the assignments on which then give feedback. The interaction with the learners should also seek to involve the participants and motivate them to be engaged in learning, interacting with resources and with other learners.

The negative opinion of Lynch is only partly contradicted by the advanced experiences of Digital libraries in education nominated before, such as within the collaboration between European Schoolnet and Europeana, or the US National Science Digital Library (NSDL) project, which is working with communities of teachers and learners in the science area. These advanced experiences depict a digital library environment which is human-teacher intensive, in which digital libraries not only facilitate the interaction of teachers and learners, but are meaningfully supporting teaching, for example by adding metadata on learning outcomes, providing tutorials, preparing bibliographical guides. And above all Digital libraries should be giving the opportunity to the learning community to be participatory, offering the capability to create content and to foster the re-use of digital assets, in an Open Education philosophy. The collaboration with teachers is fundamental. Europeana [7] has produced in 2015 the Policy Recommendations for Education and Learning, focusing on the need to improve dialogue between teachers and Digital libraries.

One aspect to which Digital libraries cannot provide support is the assessment and validation of learning achievements, since a feedback to the learners on their learning results, as well as the support and guide towards learning outcomes, cannot be achieved with the simple administration of self-assessment tests and other certification devices such as badges. The collaboration with teacher and their assessment role is in this way crucial for Digital libraries.

In conclusion, an educational role of digital libraries seems to be the weakest part of the Digital libraries in Open education, they cannot replace the university education and advanced training. Digital libraries are well positioned instead for lifelong learning and adult education, to provide support for developing professional skills.

4 Digital Libraries and Open Education: State of the Art in Italy

A number of recent developments related to Open Education in Italy must be mentioned.

Given the exponential growth of the MOOC phenomenon, at the beginning of 2016 the Conference of Italian University Rectors (CRUI) has launched a set of shared guidelines for the preparation of high quality MOOC by Italian universities. Also, CRUI has developed an institutional framework for the mutual recognition of credits by universities and finally has established a system of benchmarking for the evaluation of MOOCs quality. This ambitious project on the one hand has the merit of turning the spotlight on the little known OER phenomenon in Italian universities, while on the other tends to pursue an overly regulatory approach for a start-up phase that would require greater freedom to experiment. EDUOPEN and RUIAP are university networks which have been created to offer MOOCs both for university students and for professional and have reached a higher degree of consolidation. Other Italian institutions are active in a number of European projects dealing with Open Education, such as EMMA [10] and OER-Up [11].

In the Italian scenario, there are also private players that offer free online courses, such as the ILO project, which started in 2009 as a platform specifically dedicated to high school students and funded by private investors. ILO Website gives an explicit reference to the Creative Commons license BY-NC-ND 2.5, applicable unless otherwise specified: for example, the 3000 lessons offered by Umberto Eco Encyclomedia project have copyrights reserved to the publisher EM Publishers Srl.

Finally, in a context in which the audiovisual format is becoming more and more dominant, it becomes crucial the role of RAI, the national television broadcasting services. RAI Education offers thematic channels on history, philosophy, art and a service to create collections of videos on the portal RAI School which, however, are not exportable or downloadable.

Parallel to these Open Education development, starting from the late '90 s Digital libraries have become important in Italy,

The Italian Digital Library was officially born in 2001, during the National Conference of Libraries in Padua. The development of digital libraries in Italy has been slow but steady, connected from its inception to EUROPEANA and European projects (many with an Italian coordination) but characterized by fragmentation of initiatives as it can be evidenced in the professional literature.

Collaboration between Digital libraries and Open Education is still in its initial state in Italy, and to describe it, we can list some initiatives of digital libraries in the Open Education field and some Open Education initiatives that are run in collaboration with libraries.

4.1 Initiatives Connecting Digital Libraries and Open Education

Starting in 2010, the portal Internet Culturale has been developed as a search engine giving integrated access to catalogues and to digital content of the collections of Italian libraries. Internet Culturale is working across the various collections of Italian libraries, linking various digital assets and for any discipline. Internet Culturale aims to promote Italian culture and was the first Digital library initiative to put clearly the goal of being a support to learning. In the new version (released in 2017), Internet Culturale gives more and more value to a participatory approach in digital content, opening to the collaboration of accredited users, such as teachers, "students" or other content provider partners, in order to create content for the digital library. These "special" users may agree with the Internet Culturale portal management, to contribute particular collections. Students can give their editorial contributions, experiencing a participatory experience and achieving knowledge of digital tools.

In particular, teachers have the possibility of finding digital resources for their research, students can take special paths, those selected by the teachers, and those selected by the Internet Culturale portal. The features that are provided for inexperienced students are: "similar documents" and "suggested documents" which are "search" features that guide to bibliographical lists, exhibitions, texts and other resources. Media resources are also available, such as 3D objects, classified according to thematic areas and classes of indexing.

Also the 2016 Piano Nazionale Scuola Digitale (PNSD) has included innovative school libraries which promotes the use of digital collection. These are defined as: "biblioteche scolastiche capaci di assumere (…) la funzione di centri di documentazione e alfabetizzazione informativa, (…) aperti al territorio circostante, nei quali moltiplicare le occasioni per favorire esperienze di scrittura e di lettura, anche con l'ausilio delle tecnologie e del web. Le reti saranno anche centri di formazione per i docenti sulle tematiche della gestione di risorse informative cartacee e digitali (…)" [12, p. 100].

The access to digital resources is seen by school libraries primarily as a "digital lending" service for reading, especially entrusted to MLOL (Media Library OnLine) platform as a service aggregator for school libraries.

In the Librare Project [13] another approach was adopted, working on the "book", imagining that the books will have a leading role in the digital world, overcoming the paper-digital dichotomy through the interaction between people, objects, tools and knowledge. The underlying idea of the Librare research project (2015–2016) was to "transform" books from paper volumes in virtual objects, following the model of the Internet of Things, becoming traceable objects, collecting more and more information entered by users, according to the pattern of the Internet of Persons. At the same time, in Librare the interaction between paper books and online digital content was facilitated, allowing a better integration of activities that take place on the Web and out of the school, with educational activities that take place in the flipped classroom. These activities have been realized following the Living Labs approach where students, teachers, citizens were involved in the innovation processes. In Librare, students and teachers from all the degrees of schools (Primary and Secondary) were involved in Torino, and in other parts of Italy; a core group of about five classes carried out all the activities proposed by the project. What have been developed, concretely? First of all a Web platform (server side) was set up to manage data flows and interactions that take place in "informal libraries" (i.e. school libraries or book crossing places). Second, reading activities were stimulated, individually or collaboratively, with paper books or online editions. On the client side, two mobile applications (Librare and Librando) were provided to the users, a geographic mapping system (FirstLife), and a Web app for online collaborative reading (the Cbook).

Barriers and obstacles to the use of digital libraries must be highlighted. In Librare many challenges were encountered: schools (mostly primary, but also some secondary professional schools) were not totally equipped with wi-fi connection in the classroom and with tablets; some secondary schools have important library but others have no library at all, or very poor and not managed library; students and family were very concerned about their privacy and the possibility of being tracked, and the project managed very carefully the data, and also many corrective actions (creation of closed group) were put in place. Cbook was very appreciated by teachers and students, but the scarcity of digital resources titles (mostly Italian classics like Divina Commedia, Promessi Sposi) limited the adoption but increased the awareness of intellectual property rights [14].

4.2   Initiatives Connecting Open Education and Digital Libraries

EMMA is the first experience of Open Education which tried to work with Digital libraries. The EMMA technological approach was to enter the digital resources of Europeana into the platform, in order to allow the interaction of learners with the resource (Wrap around Model). The approach wants to be a bridge between EMMA and EUROPEANA and to strengthen the definition of a European Area of Higher Education (European Higher Education Area). One of the MOOC proposed by EMMA (Digital Library in Principle and Practice, MOOC in Italian, English and Spanish) has been specifically addressed to K12 teachers in schools of all types and levels for giving the capability to build and use Digital libraries in flipped classrooms. EMMA has organized a Webinar with EUROPEANA to analyze the opportunities and challenges of collaboration of the MOOC with EUROPEANA.

The Italian landscape of Open Education [15] is trying, also if not in a systematic way, to offer tools and open resources in Italian language, available to be re-mixed and re-used for educational purposes. Even if the National Plan for Digital School (PNSD) indicates a specific action on the OER, it provides no funding and have had to be concluded in March 2016. It will be interesting to see the result of the recent Call for Digital Curricula, for the creation of resources released in open format to facilitate their reuse.

5   Conclusions and Next Steps

The opportunities offered by OER and MOOCs and other Open Education approaches are especially relevant from the point of view of lifelong learning and innovative teaching, because more easily adaptable to the time constraints of adult learners as well as the ability to connect open learning resources to effective pedagogical approaches methods. The use then of systems that allow the students to control their own learning and their performance contribute to strengthen the autonomy and willingness to learn, with the resulting enhancement of OER in institutional policy.

The integration of Digital libraries within Open Education approaches remain at an early stage in Italy, with limited exchange of metadata and with a traditional vision of the library as a repository of resources. With the experience gained from the Internet Culturale and the pioneer experiences of Digital library as advanced systems for the construction of knowledge we have described, we must now be able to do more.

The vision is that of Digital libraries as "knowledge and learning" open hubs. What is missing? First of all, we would need a real partnership between teachers, students and Digital libraries, so to close the gap - not just digital - that is preventing the full exploitation of the current possibilities offered by digital libraries in Italy and the real experience of teachers and students who use them. In parallel, with the definition of technological infrastructure, we need to concentrate on the real possibilities of collaboration between the Digital library and the teachers, following the most advanced model of integration indicated by UNESCO "knowledge and learning". This implies the need to analyze the pedagogical and organizational problems of the realization of the integrated model, starting from the design of the course and its learning objectives, to include a participatory approach of the learning community.

References

1. European Commission. Supporting growth and jobs – an agenda for the modernisation of Europe's higher education systems (2011). http://eur-lex.europa.eu/legal-content/EN/ALL/?uri=CELEX:52011DC0567
2. Open Education Europa. https://www.openeducationeuropa.eu
3. European Commission. Opening up Education: Innovative teaching and learning for all through new Technologies and Open Educational Resources (2013). http://eur-lex.europa.eu/legal-content/EN/TXT/?uri=CELEX%3A52013DC0654
4. UNESCO: Digital Libraries in Education: Analytical Survey. IITE, Moscow (2003)
5. Tammaro, A.M.: Libraries and e-learning. ELAG 2005 Workgroup (2005)
6. Akeroyd, J.: Information management and e-learning: some perspectives. Aslib Proc. **57**, 157–167 (2005)
7. Europeana Foundation: Europeana for Education and Learning. Policy Reccomendations (2015). http://pro.europeana.eu/files/Europeana_Professional/Publications/Europeana%20for%20Education%20and%20Learning%20Policy%20Recommendations.pdf
8. Tammaro, A.M.: Biblioteche per la didattica. Biblioteche oggi, pp. 62–64, Aprile 2003. http://www.bibliotecheoggi.it/2003/20030306201.pdf
9. Lynch, C.: Digital libraries, learning communities, and open education. In: Opening up education the collective advancement of education through open technology open content and open knowledge, pp. 105–118 (2008). http://mitpress.mit.edu/books/chapters/ 0262033712 chap7.pdf
10. EMMA. https://platform.europeanmoocs.eu
11. OERUp. http://www.oerup.eu
12. Piano Nazionale Scuola Digitale (PNSD). www.istruzione.it/scuola_digitale/allegati/Materiali/pnsd-layout-30.10-WEB.pdf
13. Librare was co-funded under the ERDF 2007/2013 of the Piemonte Region with the support of European, National and Regional resources of the ERDF. http://www.librare.org/
14. Pantò, E., Comass-Quinn, A.: The challenge of open education. J. e-Learning Knowl. Soc. **9**, 1 (2013). http://www.je-lks.org/ojs/index.php/Je-LKS_EN/article/view/798
15. Tammaro, A.M.: Oer nelle Università italiane: risultati di un'indagine conoscitiva. In: MOOC Risorse educative aperte, a cura di M. Cinque, Universitas Quaderni, issue 30, pp. 53–66 (2015). http://www.rivistauniersitas.it/files/fileusers/Mooc%20QU30.pdf

Multimedia

Indexing of Historical Document Images: Ad Hoc Dewarping Technique for Handwritten Text

Federico Bolelli[✉]

Dipartimento di Ingegneria "Enzo Ferrari", Università degli Studi di Modena e Reggio Emilia,
Via Vivarelli 10, 41125 Modena, MO, Italy
federico.bolelli@unimore.it

Abstract. This work presents a research project, named XDOCS, aimed at extending to a much wider audience the possibility to access a variety of historical documents published on the web. The paper presents an overview of the indexing process that will be used to achieve the goal, focusing on the adopted dewarping technique. The proposed dewarping approach performs its task with the help of a transformation model which maps the projection of a curved surface to a 2D rectangular area. The novelty introduced with this work regards the possibility of applying dewarping to document images which contain both handwritten and typewritten text.

Keywords: Document indexing · Page rectification · Dewarping

1 Introduction

XDOCS is designed with the intention of extending to a much wider audience of scholars, or even simply curious people, the possibility to access a variety of historical documents published on the web[1].

To that purpose, the project is developing an innovative data capturing technique able to extract document indexes in quasi-automatic mode from their handwritten contents. The devised solution intervenes after the dematerialisation action of scanning the historic documents and obtaining one image per couple of adjacent pages, and it is intended to be especially applied to a long series of documents such as the large number of civil registries that are available since the constitution of the Italian state.

Since warping affects, as well as documents readability, most of the high level text processing such as OCR, word spotting, and handwritten recognition, dewarping digital text is one of the fundamental requirements to perform a correct extraction of indexes. This process starts from a curled page, usually captured by a flatbed scanner or by a digital camera, and aims to obtain an output image constituted only of horizontal straight text lines, without suffering from any distortion due to perspective or page warping.

---

[1] http://www.antenati.san.beniculturali.it/.

© Springer International Publishing AG 2017
C. Grana and L. Baraldi (Eds.): IRCDL 2017, CCIS 733, pp. 45–55, 2017.
DOI: 10.1007/978-3-319-68130-6_4

Over the last two decades many methods for document dewarping have been proposed. These approaches are usually classified in two categories according to the surface model adopted: restoration approaches based on 2D document image processing [8,13] and restoration approaches based on 3D document shape reconstruction [5,7]. Most of the dewarping techniques proposed in the past, of both categories, are specifically designed for typewritten text. These methodologies produce bad results when applied to handwritten text or, worse, to documents containing a mix of handwritten and typewritten text. In order to improve the XDOCS indexes extraction, the coarse dewarping technique originally proposed by Stamatopoulos *et al.* [12] was adjusted to address also handwritten documents.

The remainder of the paper is organized as follows. Section 2 presents an overall description of the indexing process. In Sect. 3, the dewarping adopted technique is detailed. Section 4 reports some visual experimental results. Finally, in Sect. 5, are drawn the conclusions.

2   Indexing Process

The XDOCS indexing process is split into two main phases, namely "image rectification" and "indexing & publication". The former is depicted in Fig. 1(a), showing the steps that move from a scanned image up to its final squaring. More specifically:

(a) Image rectification.

(b) Indexing & publication.

Fig. 1. Phases of the XDOCS indexing process.

- *Repository* is the place where the original scanned images are found.
- *Preprocessing* is the document image processing step, filtering out noise due to the intrinsic features of the original image and to the digitization process.
- The *Extraction* step aims to find the projection of the curved surface represented by two almost vertical straight lines and by two third degree polynomial curves surrounding the document page (see Sect. 3.2 for details). This is required by the proposed dewarping method.
- *Adjust* is the manual operation required whenever the *Extraction* operation fails.
- *Dewarping* is the core step of the "image rectification" phase; its purpose is to compute the dewarping, which transforms the original image into a rectified and normalized one.
- *Save* is the final step associating the rectified image to the original one in the *Repository* for further processing.

The latter phase of the indexing process is depicted in turn in Fig. 1(b), showing the steps that cut individual registrations from the rectified image and lead to indexing each of those registrations. More specifically:

- *Portal* is the place where the registrations and their indexes are made available for consultation.
- *Cut* is the image processing step separating and normalizing the three registrations that are present in every rectified image.
- *Save* is the step storing the normalized registrations into the Portal.
- *Extract* is the image processing function which extracts and compares parts of images, corresponding to names, places and numbers (mainly dates of birth) [4].
- *Publish* is the final step associating the extracted indexes to the corresponding registration in the Portal.

Of course, the degree of completeness and confidence of the extracted indexes are strongly affected by the quality of the handwritten text and the state of preservation of the original registry. Those factors can however be increased by driving the *Extraction* action by templates representing the limited areas to be examined for the purpose of finding out each of the desired indexes. The templates are manually defined on the normalized registrations and in principle can depend on the single registry (year, municipality, handwriting style of the registrar).

Figure 2 reports two examples of birth registry, the first one dated June 1888 and the second one September 1900. Each image shows two pages containing three birth registrations: one on the left-upper side, one on the right-bottom side and one split between the two pages. The three registrations share the same structure and present the intended indexes in equivalent and well identified positions. Moreover, the most critical indexes, namely family name and given name, appear twice in each registration and this redundancy can increase the level of confidence in the indexing.

The metadata identifying the double page image are: registry type, year and volume, place of registration (typically, a municipality). The intended indexes are in turn: birth month and day, name and family name, sex, father's name, mother's name and family name, possibly grandparents names.

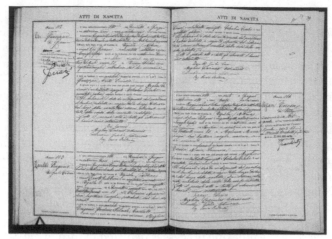

(a) Historical birth act dated June 1888.

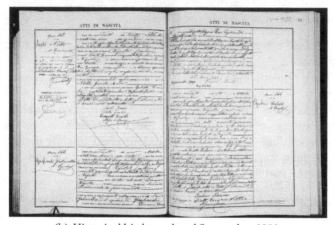

(b) Historical birth act dated September 1900.

Fig. 2. Examples of warped digital document images.

3   The Proposed Dewarping Approach

This section describes in detail "Image Rectification" phase focusing on *Preprocesing*, *Extraction* and *Dewarping* steps.

3.1   Preprocessing

Before proceeding with the dewarping step, which is detailed in the following, the gray level images are mapped into black-white ones using the adaptive threshold described in [11] (see Fig. 3(a) as example). Then, noise is filtered out principally using information related to statistics of connected components calculated using [9]. An example of preprocessing output is reported in Fig. 3(b).

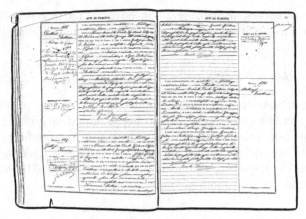

(a) Output binary image.

(b) Output of preprocessing step.

Fig. 3. Example of preprocessing results.

3.2   Extraction

The extraction step aims at identifying the 2D projection of the curved surface defined by the four polynomial curves which surround the document text on every single page (see Fig. 5).

According to the warping model characterizing historical documents, the right and left polynomial curves are supposed to be lines and generically defined as:

$$y = ax + b \tag{1}$$

To identify these lines the approach combines the information obtained by the Hough transform [6] and the position of A, B, C and D vertexes of the curved surface projection retrieved using the Harris algorithm and starting from a thinned image [10].

Top and bottom curves, instead, are supposed to be third degree polynomial lines and their coefficients are fitted with the Least Square Estimation algorithm and have the following general expression:

$$y = ax^3 + bx^2 + cx + d \tag{2}$$

More accurate results could be achieved modeling these curves as higher polynomial functions. This change increases dewarping computation time slightly improving accuracy, so it is not recommended. Boundary extraction significantly influences the quality of the dewarping process, and then the indexes extraction: if it fails the *Adjust* step leaves the user the possibility to correct curves via a GUI: examples of the automatic extracted 2D projections are reported in Fig. 4.

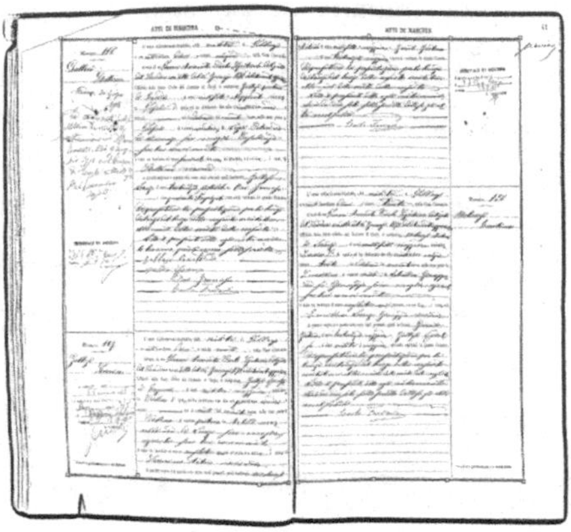

(a) 2D projection correctly extracted.

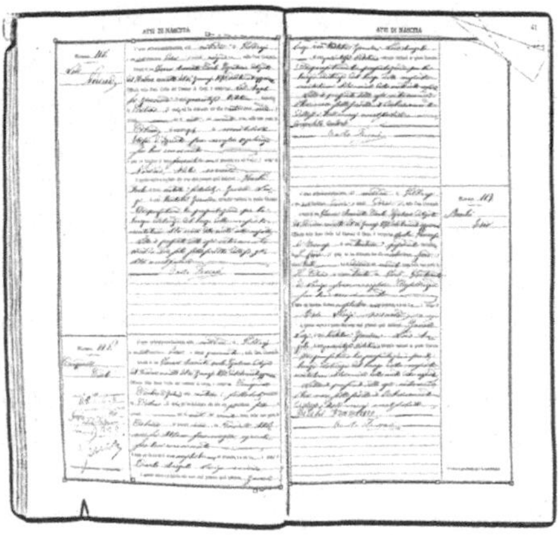

(b) 2D projection badly extracted.

Fig. 4. Example of curved 2D projection extraction during the *Adjust* phase. Best viewed in color. (Color figure online)

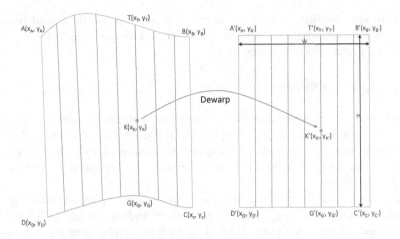

Fig. 5. Dewarping transformation model: projection of the curved surface on the left side, 2D rectangular destination area on the right side.

3.3 Dewarping

This is the core step of the dewarping approach which aim to map the projection of the curved surface to a 2D rectangular area with fixed dimensions H and W (see Fig. 5 for details). Stages of the mapping process are detailed in this section using the following notation: $A(x_A, y_A)$, $B(x_B, y_B)$, $C(x_C, y_C)$, and $D(x_D, y_D)$ are the vertexes of the projection surface whereas $A'(x'_A, y'_A)$, $B'(x'_B, y'_B)$, $C'(x'_C, y'_C)$, and $D'(x'_D, y'_D)$ are the ones of the rectangular destination area. Moreover, the euclidean distances between points A and D, B and C are respectively called $|AD|$ and $|BC|$, and the lengths of the polynomial curves $|\widehat{AB}|$ and $|\widehat{CD}|$ are defined as:

$$|\widehat{AB}| = \int_{x_A}^{x_B} \sqrt{1 + [f'(x)]^2} \, dx \tag{3}$$

$$|\widehat{DC}| = \int_{x_D}^{x_C} \sqrt{1 + [g'(x)]^2} \, dx \tag{4}$$

where f(x) and g(x) are the functions describing the polynomial lines.

Therefore, given a generic point $K(x_K, y_K)$ on the warped image, the corresponding one on the 2D rectangular area $K'(x'_K, y'_K)$ can be found preserving proportions between dimensions of projected curves and 2D destination area. First of all it is necessary to find the two points $T(x_T, y_T) \in |\widehat{AB}|$ and $G(x_G, y_G) \in |\widehat{DC}|$ such that $K \in TG$ and $|\widehat{AT}| : |\widehat{AB}| = |\widehat{DG}| : |\widehat{DC}|$. The transformation equations are then defined as follows:

$$x'_K = x'_A + W * \frac{|\widehat{AT}|}{|\widehat{AB}|} \tag{5}$$

$$y'_K = y'_A + H * \frac{|TK|}{|TG|} \tag{6}$$

To compute the final page dewarping every pixel in the dewarped image is mapped to a floating-point coordinate in the warped image, therefore the process is concluded using a simple interpolation.

4   Experimental Results

Common practices in the evaluation of dewarping techniques consist of comparing the error rate of OCR software applied on the original and dewarped images or are simply based on visual pleasing impressions. Unfortunately, the first strategy is unfeasible for documents which contain handwritten text, so the second one is adopted in this paper.

Figure 6 reports an example result of the proposed dewarping technique applied to a regular modern form image, which contains a bounding box and both handwritten and typewritten text. It is possible to see that the horizontal lines in the dewarped image are perfectly aligned with the horizontal boundaries of the box.

Figure 7 instead, shows another result applied on the typical historical documents treated in this work. Also here both handwritten and printed text is present and the detection phase is complicated by the presence of many distracting elements.

The method has been tested on more than 4.000 birth acts and on almost 200 generic digital documents similar to the one reported in Fig. 6. Experimental results reveal that more than 85% of curved 2D projections are correctly extracted and do not require the manual *Adjust* step before performing the dewarping procedure.

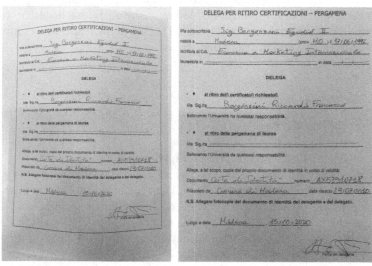

(a) Original warped document.   (b) Dewarping Result.

Fig. 6. Example of dewarping applied on generic digital document image.

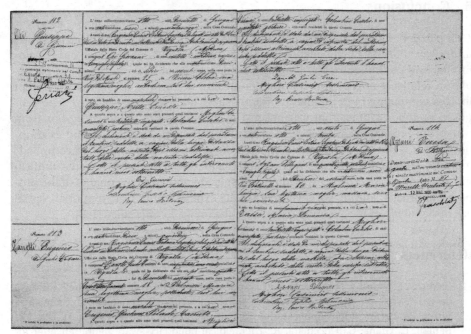

(a) Historical birth act dated June 1888: original image is depicted in Figure 2(a).

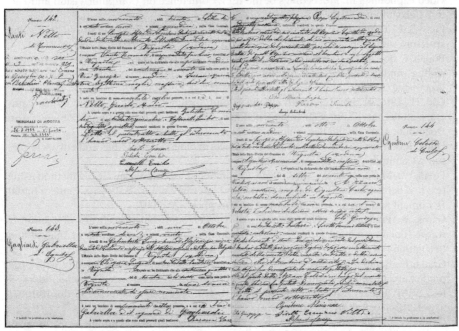

(b) Historical birth act dated September 1900: original image is depicted in Figure 2(b).

Fig. 7. Examples of dewarping applied on historical digital document images.

5 Conclusions

This paper describes the rationale and objectives of a research project presently underway at SATA s.r.l. in collaboration with the University of Modena and Reggio-Emilia, and co-funded by the Emilia-Romagna regional administration. In particular, a relatively novel approach for performing dewarping on digital document images containing both handwritten and typewritten text was detailed. The proposed method assumes that original text is surrounded by a bounding box from which the projection of the curved surface is extracted. This is a strong assumption, but it is not uncommon to find such documents: most of the "precompiled" modules present this kind of structure and the historical documents tested confirm the assumption. Moreover, experimental results demonstrate the quality of the proposed approach. Future work will require the exploration of Convolutional Neural Networks architectures, in order to improve the image *Extract* stage [1–3].

References

1. Balducci, F., Grana, C., Cucchiara, R.: Classification of affective data to evaluate the level design in a role-playing videogame. In: 2015 7th International Conference on Games and Virtual Worlds for Serious Applications (VS-Games), pp. 1–8. IEEE (2015)
2. Baraldi, L., Grana, C., Cucchiara, R.: Hierarchical boundary-aware neural encoder for video captioning. In: Proceedings of the IEEE Conference on Computer Vision and Pattern Recognition (2016)
3. Baraldi, L., Grana, C., Cucchiara, R.: Recognizing and presenting the storytelling video structure with deep multimodal networks. IEEE Trans. Multimed. **19**(5), 955–968 (2017)
4. Bolelli, F., Borghi, G., Grana, C.: Historical handwritten text images word spotting through sliding window hog features. In: 19th International Conference on Image Analysis and Processing (2017)
5. Cao, H., Ding, X., Liu, C.: Rectifying the bound document image captured by the camera: a model based approach. In: Proceedings of the Seventh International Conference on Document Analysis and Recognition, pp. 71–75. IEEE (2003)
6. Duda, R.O., Hart, P.E.: Use of the hough transformation to detect lines and curves in pictures. Commun. ACM **15**(1), 11–15 (1972)
7. Fu, B., Wu, M., Li, R., Li, W., Xu, Z., Yang, C.: A model-based book dewarping method using text line detection. In: Proceedings of the 2nd International Workshop on Camera Based Document Analysis and Recognition, Curitiba, pp. 63–70 (2007)
8. Gatos, B., Pratikakis, I., Ntirogiannis, K.: Segmentation based recovery of arbitrarily warped document images. In: Ninth International Conference on Document Analysis and Recognition (ICDAR 2007), vol. 2, pp. 989–993. IEEE (2007)
9. Grana, C., Baraldi, L., Bolelli, F.: Optimized connected components labeling with pixel prediction. In: Blanc-Talon, J., Distante, C., Philips, W., Popescu, D., Scheunders, P. (eds.) ACIVS 2016. LNCS, vol. 10016, pp. 431–440. Springer, Cham (2016). doi:10.1007/978-3-319-48680-2_38
10. Grana, C., Borghesani, D., Cucchiara, R.: Decision trees for fast thinning algorithms. In: 2010 20th International Conference on Pattern Recognition (ICPR), pp. 2836–2839. IEEE (2010)
11. Sauvola, J., Pietikäinen, M.: Adaptive document image binarization. Pattern Recognit. **33**(2), 225–236 (2000)

12. Stamatopoulos, N., Gatos, B., Pratikakis, I., Perantonis, S.J.: A two-step dewarping of camera document images. In: The Eighth IAPR International Workshop on Document Analysis Systems (DAS 2008), pp. 209–216. IEEE (2008)
13. Ulges, A., Lampert, C.H., Breuel, T.M.: Document image dewarping using robust estimation of curled text lines. In: Eighth International Conference on Document Analysis and Recognition (ICDAR 2005), pp. 1001–1005. IEEE (2005)

A Video Library System Using Scene Detection and Automatic Tagging

Lorenzo Baraldi$^{(\boxtimes)}$, Costantino Grana, and Rita Cucchiara

Dipartimento di Ingegneria "Enzo Ferrari", Università degli Studi di Modena
e Reggio Emilia, Via Vivarelli 10, 41125 Modena, MO, Italy
{lorenzo.baraldi,costantino.grana,rita.cucchiara}@unimore.it

Abstract. We present a novel video browsing and retrieval system for edited videos, based on scene detection and automatic tagging. In the proposed system, database videos are automatically decomposed into meaningful and storytelling parts (i.e. *scenes*) and tagged in an automatic way by leveraging their transcript. We rely on computer vision and machine learning techniques to learn the optimal scene boundaries: a Triplet Deep Neural Network is trained to distinguish video sequences belonging to the same scene and sequences from different scenes, by exploiting multimodal features from images, audio and captions. The system also features a user interface build as a set of extensions to the eXo Platform Enterprise Content Management System (ECMS) (https://www.exoplatform.com/). This set of extensions enable the interactive visualization of a video, its automatic and semi-automatic annotation, as well as a keyword-based search inside the video collection. The platform also allows a natural integration with third-party add-ons, so that automatic annotations can be exploited outside the proposed platform.

Keywords: Scene detection · Tagging · Video browsing · Interfaces

1 Introduction

Video is currently the largest source of internet traffic: after having been used mainly for fun and entertainment in the last decades, it is now employed into novel contexts, like social networks, online advertisement, and education.

Unfortunately, the vast majority of video content available on the web is not provided with annotations, and is therefore cumbersome to retrieve. Furthermore, video browsing platforms like Youtube, Facebook and Dailymotion treat the video as an indivisible entity, so that the user receives no help in finding the portion of the video that really interests him. The user must either watch the entire video or move from one portion of the video to another through seek operations. In the case of educational video clips, which are usually longer than the average user-generated video, this becomes even more evident, and fining a short segment on a specific topic of interest often becomes intractable.

In this paper, we propose a system which tries to address this limitation by exploiting computer vision and machine learning techniques. In particular,

© Springer International Publishing AG 2017
C. Grana and L. Baraldi (Eds.): IRCDL 2017, CCIS 733, pp. 56–67, 2017.
DOI: 10.1007/978-3-319-68130-6_5

we rely on scene detection, a pattern recognition technique which enables the decomposition of a video into semantically coherent parts. In the case of scene detection, therefore, the objective is that of automatically segmenting an input video into meaningful and story-telling sequences, using perceptual and semantic features and exploiting editing rules or clustering algorithms. It is straightforward to see that scene detection can enhance video access and browsing, as it transforms a long video into a sequence of homogeneous parts. Also, it enables a fine-grained search inside the video itself, with which short sequences could be more easily retrieved with textual queries. Finally, it is worth to mention that sequences from the original video can also be exploited to create presentations or video lectures, thus enhancing the re-use of video collections.

In the case of broadcast edited videos, scenes represent one of the three levels at which the video can be decomposed. Edited videos are indeed made by sequences of shots, which in turn are frames taken by the same camera. Shots can then be grouped, according to their semantic meaning, into scenes. From this perspective, scene detection can be seen as the task of grouping temporally adjacent shots, with the objective of maximizing the semantic coherence of the resulting segments. The computer vision pipeline which will be described in the rest of this paper relies on this assumption, by creating an embedding space in which shots can be projected according to their relative semantic similarity, and exploiting a temporal clustering technique which is in charge of defining the final temporal segmentation of the video. We should also notice that using shots instead of the single frames as the basic unit of computation enables a reduction in computational complexity, and at the same time assures a quasi-optimal decomposition of the video, since shots usually have a uniform semantic content. This granularity level is also beneficial for visualization, since representative keyframes can be extracted from shots.

Using a scene detection algorithm that we have recently proposed in literature [6], and thanks to the application of Speech-to-Text techniques, it has been possible to automatically annotate a set of 500 educational broadcast videos taken from the large Rai Scuola archive[1]. Also, we developed a browsing and retrieval interface on top of a commercial ECMS, namely eXo Platform, from which the results of the automatic annotation can be browsed and manually refined. The interface has been developed as part of the Città Educante project, cofunded by the Italian Ministry of Education, with the aim of providing new technologies for education.

The rest of this paper is organized as follows: in Sect. 2 we give an overview of relevant works related to the topic of this paper; Sect. 3 describes the main algorithmic components of the system, by giving details on the scene detection approach and on the retrieval strategy we employ, while showing several examples and screenshots from the actual user interface. Finally, Sect. 4 draws the conclusion of the work.

---

[1] www.raiscuola.rai.it.

2   Related Work

In this section, we give a brief overview of the works related with the two main features of our system, namely video decomposition and video retrieval.

Video Decomposition. Since more than 15 years, automatic video decomposition has been categorized into three categories [9]: *rule-based methods*, that consider the way a video is structured in professional movie production, *graph-based methods*, where shots are arranged in a graph representation, and *clustering-based methods*.

Rule-based approaches consider the way a scene is structured in professional movie production. Of course, the drawback of this kind of methods is that they tend to fail in videos where film-editing rules are not followed, or when two adjacent scenes are similar and follow the same rules. Liu *et al.* [13], for example, propose a visual based probabilistic framework that imitates the authoring process. In [8], shots are represented by means of key-frames, clustered using spectral clustering and low level color features, and then labeled according to the clusters they belong to. Scene boundaries are then detected from the alignment score of the symbolic sequences, using the Needleman-Wunsch algorithm.

In graph-based methods, instead, shots are arranged in a graph representation and then clustered by partitioning the graph. The Shot Transition Graph (STG) [22] is one of the most used models in this category: here each node represents a shot and the edges between the shots are weighted by shot similarity. In [16], color and motion features are used to represent shot similarity, and the STG is then split into subgraphs by applying the normalized cuts for graph partitioning. Sidiropoulos *et al.* [18] introduced a STG approximation that exploits features from the visual and the auditory channel.

Clustering-based solutions assume that similarity of shots can be used to group them into meaningful clusters, thus directly providing the final story boundaries. With this approach, a deep learning based strategy has recently been proposed [4]. In this model, a Siamese Network is used together with features extracted from a Convolutional Neural Network and time features to learn distances between shots. Spectral clustering is then applied to detect coherent sequences.

Video Retrieval. Lot of work has also been proposed for video retrieval: with the explosive growth of online videos, this has become a hot topic in computer vision. In their seminal work, Sivic *et al.* proposed Video Google [20], a system that retrieves videos from a database via bag-of-words matching. Lew *et al.* [11] reviewed earlier efforts in video retrieval, which mostly relied on feature-based relevance feedback or similar methods.

More recently, concept-based methods have emerged as a popular approach to video retrieval. Snoek *et al.* [21] proposed a method based on a set of concept detectors, with the aim to bridge the semantic gap between visual features and high level concepts. In [3], authors proposed a video retrieval approach based on tag propagation: given an input video with user-defined tags, Flickr, Google Images and Bing are mined to collect images with similar tags: these are used to label each temporal segment of the video, so that the method increases the number of tags originally proposed by the users, and localizes them temporally. In [12] the problem of retrieving videos using complex natural language queries is tackled, by first parsing the sentential descriptions into a semantic graph, which is then matched to visual concepts using a generalized bipartite matching algorithm. This also allows to retrieve the relevant video segment given a text query. Our method, in contrast to [3], does not need any kind of initial manual annotation, and, thanks to the availability of the video structure, is able to return specific stories related to the user query. This provides the retrieved result with a context that allows to better understand the video content.

3   The System

The proposed system is comprises three main components: a scene detection algorithm, which is in charge of performing a temporal segmentation of the input video into coherent parts, an automatic tagging algorithm, and a retrieval module, with which users can search for scenes inside a video collection.

3.1   Scene Detection

The decomposition of a video into semantically coherent parts is an intrinsic multi-modal task, which cannot be solved by applying heuristic rules, or a-priori defined models due to the variety of boundaries which can be found in professionally edited video. The definition of a hand-crafted rules would indeed be very time consuming, and would probably lead to poor results in terms of localization accuracy. We therefore choose to rely on machine learning, and to build a deep learning architecture for temporal video segmentation which can learn the optimal way of segmenting the video by learning from examples annotated by different users. On a different note, to tackle the multi-modal nature of the problem, we employ a combination of multi-modal features which range from the frames and the audio track of the video, to the transcript of the speaker.

The video is firstly decomposed into a set of chunks taken by the same camera (i.e. shots), using an open source shot detector [1]. Given that the content of a shot is usually uniform from a semantic point of view, we can constrain scene boundaries to be a subset of shot boundaries, therefore reducing the problem of scene detection to that of clustering adjacent shots. This preliminary decomposition also reduces the computational efforts needed to process the entire video, given that few key-frames can be used as the representative of the whole shot. Similarly, features coming from other modalities can be encoded at the shot level by following the same homogeneity assumption. For each shot of the video, we extract different features, in order to take into account all the modalities present in the video.

Visual Appearance Features. We encode the visual appearance of a shot, and information about the timestamp and the length of a given shot. Visual appearance is extracted with a pre-trained Convolutional Neural Network which is shortened by cutting out the last fully connected layers. This extracts high level features from the input image, which can be a rich source of information to identify changes in visual content between one portion of the video and another. Given that a single key-frame might be too poor to describe a shot, we uniformly sample three key-frame from the input shot, and take the pixelwise maximum of the network responses.

Visual Concept Features. Using a part-of-speech tagger, we parse the transcript obtained with standard speech-to-text techniques, and retain unigrams which are annotated as *noun, proper noun* and *foreign word*. Those are then mapped to the Imagenet corpus by means of a skip-gram model [15] trained on the dump of the Italian Wikipedia. By means of this mapping we build a classifier to detect the presence of a visual concept in a shot. Images from the external corpus are represented using feature activations from pre-trained deep convolutional neural networks (CNN), which can extract rich semantic information from an input image [10]. In our case, we employ the VGG-16 model [19], which is well known for providing state-of-the-art results on image classifications, and for its good generalization properties [17]. Then, a linear probabilistic SVM is trained for each concept, using randomly sampled negative training data; the probability output of each classifier is then used as an indicator of the presence of a concept in a shot.

Keeping a shot-based representation, we build a feature vector which encodes the influence of each concept group on the considered shot. Formally, the visual concept feature of shot s, $\mathbf{v}(s)$, is a K-dimensional vector, defined as

$$\mathbf{v}(s) = \left[\sum_{t \in M(\mathcal{T})} \delta_{t,i} \cdot f_{M(t)}(s) e^{-\frac{(u_t - u_s)^2}{2\sigma^2}} \right]_{i=1,\dots,K} \tag{1}$$

where $\mathcal{T}$ is the multiset of all terms inside a video, $\delta_{t,i}$ indicates whether term t belongs to the i-th concept group, u_t and u_s are the timestamps of term t and shot s. M is the mapping function to the external corpus, and $f_{M(t)}(s)$ is the probability given by the SVM classifier trained on concept $M(t)$ and tested on shot s.

Textual Concept Features. Textual concepts are as important as visual concepts to detect story changes, and detected concept groups provide an ideal mean to describe topic changes in text. Therefore, a textual concept feature vector, $\mathbf{t}(s)$, is built as the textual counterpart of $\mathbf{v}(s)$

$$\mathbf{t}(s) = \left[\sum_{t \in \mathcal{T}} \delta_{t,i} \cdot e^{-\frac{(u_t - u_s)^2}{2\sigma^2}} \right]_{i=1,\dots,K} \tag{2}$$

We thus get a representation of how much each concept group is present in a shot and in its neighborhood.

Audio Features. Audio is another meaningful cue for detecting scene boundaries, since audio effects and soundtracks are often used to underline the development of a scene or a change in content. We extract MFCCs descriptors [14] over a 10 ms window. The MFCC descriptors are aggregated by Fisher vectors using a Gaussian Mixture Model with 256 components.

Multi-modal Fusion. The overall feature vector for a shot is the concatenation of all the previously defined features. A Triplet Deep Network is then trained on ground-truth decompositions by minimizing a contrastive loss function: at each training iteration, the network processes a triplet of examples, namely an anchor example, a positive and a negative example. The anchor example is randomly selected from the available shots in the database, the positive one is constrained to be part of the same scene of the anchor, and the negative sample is selected from a different scene. Each of the sample is embedded by the same function into a common, multimodal, embedding space. The contrastive loss function then forces the distance between the anchor and the positive shot to be smaller than the distance between the anchor and the negative. This, during training, promotes the creation of an embedding function suitable for the task.

At test time, the network has learned to distinguish similar and dissimilar shots, and can be therefore employed to perform scene detection. In particular, our clustering algorithm relies on the minimization of variances inside each scene. For further details, the reader is encouraged to read the paper in which the technique was proposed [6].

3.2   User Interface

While the temporal segmentation step is carried out off-line, and its results are saved into a database for browsing, we also build an appropriate user interface for visualization. In particular, we extend a popular Enterprise Content Management System (ECMS), namely eXo Platform, which is largely used to build enterprise intranets and dynamic portals. We exploit the extension capabilities of eXo Platform and develop an add-on which can visualize videos decomposed into scenes. Every time a video is uploaded on the platform, a remote web service is called to perform the automatic decomposition of the video into scene, and to extract key-frames for visualization. Each video can then be visualized in a time line fashion, were each is scene is presented by means of the key-frames it contains.

Figures 1 and 2 show two sample screenshot from the proposed interface. As it can be noticed, we built two different views, one showing the list of available videos, each presented with one of its keyframes, and one for the browsing of the video itself, in which the actual temporal segmentation is shown. It can also be noticed that the visualization of each scene is enriched by a set of tags. These

Fig. 1. Sample screenshot of the interactive visualization interface.

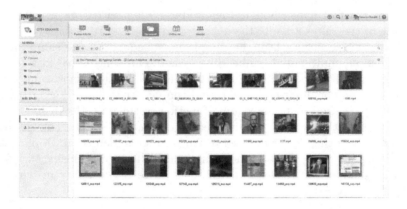

Fig. 2. Visualization of a collection of videos.

are obtained by parsing the transcript of the video, and extracting nouns and proper nouns with a NLP tagger trained for the Italian language.

Of course, even though generally precise, the automatic decomposition in scene might not always be correct, or appreciated by the final user, also considering the subjective nature of the task. Therefore, the output of the algorithm can not always be satisfactory for the user. For this reason, the interface allows the user to refine the automatic annotation, merging adjoining scenes together. Data collected from this manual annotation feature could be exploited in further works, both to extend the training set and to use it an a relevance feedback loop.

3.3 Retrieval

The ability to index parts of a video is an essential feature of a video browsing platform, as it enables a fine-grained search which is also important for video re-use. In developing this feature, we wanted video clips to be indexed at the

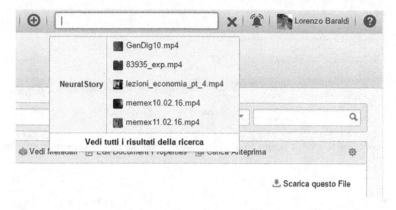

Fig. 3. eXo Platform search form, enhanced with results from the video collection.

Fig. 4. Screenshot of the results page.

scene level, so that users can search inside video clips and not only among video clips. Secondly, we constrained the indexing system to be fully automatic, and therefore chose to rely on the transcription solely, rather than exploiting user-generated annotations. This allows our retrieval strategy to be enough precise, and content oriented, as most of the extracted keywords will focus on the topics addressed during the video, rather than on what is actually shown in the video.

From an implementation point of view, we extended the built-in search capabilities of eXo, by developing a component which can search inside the video collection, given a textual query. This is done by building a Search Connector component, which is called by eXo itself every time a user performs a textual search. The Connector, in turn, searches for the given query inside the video database, and matches the query with the available tags. Of course, more sophisticated techniques could be used, even though they are outside the scope of this paper.

For each retrieved scene, a thumbnail is also selected among the key-frames of the video by using a semantic and aesthetic criterion [5], so that the user can be confident about the result of his research by simply looking at the provided

Fig. 5. Incorporation of a scene in a third-party extension (selection from the clipboard).

Fig. 6. Incorporation of a scene in a third-party extension.

thumbnails. Moreover, since results are presented in terms of scenes, the user is redirected directly to the video portion of interest for his query, without the need to search within the video of interest. Figures 3 and 4 show, respectively, the search interface and the results page.

3.4   Integration with Third-Party Add-Ons

One key feature of the system is the possibility to integrate our temporal segmentation, retrieval and visualization tools into third part components. This makes the developed system integrable with other software, which is a desirable property in most of the use cases, ranging from portals to project demonstrators.

Indeed, all the extensions which have been presented in the previous sections are designed to be naturally integrated with the underlying data structure of eXo, namely the Java JCR, and with third-party applications. In particular, full-length videos or portions of them can be retrieved from the database by any application inside the platform. Also, at an higher level, videos and scene managed by our application can be copied and pasted into the eXo Clipboard. This is a cross-application clipboard, which can be read an written across different applications and add-ons on the platform, and which provides an effective way to transfer content from one application to another.

Finally, for the purpose of demonstration, we developed a simple portlet which can showcase the benefit of using data provided by our algorithm outside the specific user interface we built for visualization. The demo portlet allows the insertion of video portions within a simple canvas, by exploiting the eXo Clipboard. A dialog shows the contents of the clipboard with the selected scenes by the user while navigating in the database: these can then be pasted on the canvas and displayed (Figs. 5 and 6).

Beside this simple example, the same extension capabilities showcased by our application can be used for integrating with other add-ons. In particular, this will also be beneficial in the context of the Città Educante project, in which the eXo Platform will be used as the enabling tool of the final demonstrator [2,7].

4   Conclusion

This paper has presented a video browsing and retrieval system for edited videos, which has been developed in the context of a national project, Città Educante. The main distinguishing feature of the system, with respect to other video browsing approaches, is that videos are automatically parsed and decomposed into meaningful segments (called scenes), by means of a novel scene detection algorithm which exploits state of the art multi-modal descriptors and machine learning techniques. In particular, it relies on a Triplet Deep Network which learns a multi-modal semantic embedding space in which shots from the input video can be projected, and on a temporal clustering algorithm which provides the final segmentation into scenes. The web-based interface enables the interactive visualization of a video, its automatic and semi-automatic annotation, as well as a keyword-based search inside a video collection. Finally, it is worth mentioning that using the proposed algorithm it has been possible to automatically annotate a set of 500 educational broadcast videos taken from the large Rai Scuola archive, which can be browsed and retrieved inside the internal portal of the Città Educante project. As a future work, it will also be possible to exploit the corrections and annotations provided by the users, as a source of additional training data, and to build a human-in-the-loop system which can possibly provide better temporal segmentation results.

References

1. Apostolidis, E., Mezaris, V.: Fast shot segmentation combining global and local visual descriptors. In: IEEE International Conference on Acoustics, Speech and Signal Processing, pp. 6583–6587 (2014)
2. Balducci, F., Grana, C., Cucchiara, R.: Affective level design for a role-playing videogame evaluated by a brain-computer interface and machine learning methods. Vis. Comput. **33**(4), 413–427 (2017)
3. Ballan, L., Bertini, M., Serra, G., Del Bimbo, A.: A data-driven approach for tag refinement and localization in web videos. Comput. Vis. Image Underst. **140**, 58–67 (2015)

4. Baraldi, L., Grana, C., Cucchiara, R.: A deep siamese network for scene detection in broadcast videos. In: Proceedings of the 23rd Annual ACM Conference on Multimedia Conference (MM 2015), pp. 1199–1202 (2015). http://doi.acm.org/10.1145/2733373.2806316

5. Baraldi, L., Grana, C., Cucchiara, R.: Scene-driven retrieval in edited videos using aesthetic and semantic deep features. In: Proceedings of the 2016 ACM on International Conference on Multimedia Retrieval (ICMR 2016), pp. 23–29 (2016). http://doi.acm.org/10.1145/2911996.2912012

6. Baraldi, L., Grana, C., Cucchiara, R.: Recognizing and presenting the storytelling video structure with deep multimodal networks. IEEE Trans. Multimed. **19**(5), 955–968 (2017)

7. Bolelli, F., Borghi, G., Grana, C.: Historical handwritten text images word spotting through sliding window HOG features. In: 19th International Conference on Image Analysis and Processing (2017)

8. Chasanis, V.T., Likas, C., Galatsanos, N.P.: Scene detection in videos using shot clustering and sequence alignment. IEEE Trans. Multimed. **11**(1), 89–100 (2009)

9. Hanjalic, A., Lagendijk, R.L., Biemond, J.: Automated high-level movie segmentation for advanced video-retrieval systems. IEEE Trans. Circ. Syst. Video Technol. **9**(4), 580–588 (1999)

10. Krizhevsky, A., Sutskever, I., Hinton, G.E.: Imagenet classification with deep convolutional neural networks. In: Advances in Neural Information Processing Systems, pp. 1097–1105 (2012)

11. Lew, M.S., Sebe, N., Djeraba, C., Jain, R.: Content-based multimedia information retrieval: state of the art and challenges. ACM Trans. Multimed. Comput. Commun. Appl. (TOMCCAP) **2**(1), 1–19 (2006)

12. Lin, D., Fidler, S., Kong, C., Urtasun, R.: Visual semantic search: retrieving videos via complex textual queries. In: IEEE International Conference on Computer Vision and Pattern Recognition, pp. 2657–2664, June 2014

13. Liu, C., Wang, D., Zhu, J., Zhang, B.: Learning a contextual/multi-thread model for movie/TV scene segmentation. IEEE Trans. Multimed. **15**(4), 884–897 (2013)

14. Logan, B., et al.: Mel frequency cepstral coefficients for music modeling. In: ISMIR (2000)

15. Mikolov, T., Sutskever, I., Chen, K., Corrado, G.S., Dean, J.: Distributed representations of words and phrases and their compositionality. In: Advances in Neural Information Processing Systems, pp. 3111–3119 (2013)

16. Rasheed, Z., Shah, M.: Detection and representation of scenes in videos. IEEE Trans. Multimed. **7**(6), 1097–1105 (2005)

17. Sharif Razavian, A., Azizpour, H., Sullivan, J., Carlsson, S.: CNN features off-the-shelf: an astounding baseline for recognition. In: Proceedings of the IEEE Conference on Computer Vision and Pattern Recognition Workshops, pp. 806–813 (2014)

18. Sidiropoulos, P., Mezaris, V., Kompatsiaris, I., Meinedo, H., Bugalho, M., Trancoso, I.: Temporal video segmentation to scenes using high-level audiovisual features. IEEE Trans. Circ. Syst. Video Technol. **21**(8), 1163–1177 (2011)

19. Simonyan, K., Zisserman, A.: Very deep convolutional networks for large-scale image recognition. arXiv preprint (2014). arXiv:1409.1556

20. Sivic, J., Zisserman, A.: Video google: a text retrieval approach to object matching in videos. In: IEEE International Conference on Computer Vision, pp. 1470–1477. IEEE (2003)

21. Snoek, C.G., Huurnink, B., Hollink, L., De Rijke, M., Schreiber, G., Worring, M.: Adding semantics to detectors for video retrieval. IEEE Trans. Multimed. **9**(5), 975–986 (2007)
22. Yeung, M.M., Yeo, B.L., Wolf, W.H., Liu, B.: Video browsing using clustering and scene transitions on compressed sequences. In: IS&T/SPIE's Symposium on Electronic Imaging: Science & Technology, pp. 399–413 (1995)

Text Line Extraction in Handwritten Historical Documents

Samuele Capobianco$^{(\boxtimes)}$ and Simone Marinai

Dipartimento di Ingegneria dell'Informazione,
Università degli Studi di Firenze, Florence, Italy
{samuele.capobianco,simone.marinai}@unifi.it
http://ai.dsi.unifi.it/

Abstract. We present a novel approach for the extraction of text lines in handwritten documents using a Convolutional Neural Network to label document image patches as text lines or separators. We first process the document to identify the most suitable patch size on the basis of an overall text line distance estimation. Using this information, we then extract several patches to train the CNN model. Finally, we use the trained model to segment text lines. We have evaluated this technique on the public database Saint Gall and on a private collection provided by the Ancestry company.

1 Introduction

Handwritten historical documents are widely available in Digital Libraries and archives. In particular, handwritten forms have been used in the past to record important personal facts. Significant examples are documents containing census information, birth records, and other public or private collections. The analysis of these documents is essential to reconstruct genealogies and to perform demographic studies. One first step to address the automatic transcription and information extraction from these documents is to localize and extract the text lines. Several techniques have been presented to address this task [1] and recent work focused on the use of artificial neural networks to find text lines in handwritten documents [2]. In this work we propose one solution to recognize the text lines and the separation between text lines using a Convolutional Neural Network. In the last few years, Convolutional Neural Networks [3] have been widely used to solve several tasks. In particular, these techniques have been used to segment [4] and localize objects [5] in Computer Vision as well as for page classification [6].

In our research we deal with documents having different layouts. However, one common feature is that in each page the distance between text lines is quite regular. We can use this prior to initialize the document analysis; subsequently by using a suitably trained neural model we can localize the text lines and the line separators. As in most training-based approaches, the solution is based on two main steps.

We first train a suitable CNN model. To this purpose, for each training page we estimate the average distance between text lines and use this information to

© Springer International Publishing AG 2017
C. Grana and L. Baraldi (Eds.): IRCDL 2017, CCIS 733, pp. 68–79, 2017.
DOI: 10.1007/978-3-319-68130-6_6

label random patches used to train the model. Subsequently, we design a text line separator. For each test page we estimate the average distance between text lines and use this information to extract dense patches that are classified using the trained model. The classified patches are then combined to obtain an overall page segmentation.

In the following sections we first describe in detail the initial step aimed at computing the adaptive patch dimension. We then analyze the proposed application scenario and discuss the experiments performed on two datasets.

2   Adaptive Estimation of Patch Dimension

The proposed approach to solve the line segmentation is based on a patch-wise representation of the document images. The patch is expected to cover an area of the image containing text and background. In the pre-processing phase we therefore need to estimate an average distance between text lines. As we can notice from the example in Fig. 1a in our data there is a certain regularity in the distance between lines in each page and this regularity can be used to adapt the patch dimension in the page. Subsequently, we can label the patch as text line separator (if it covers the space, or other separators, between text lines) or as text (if it contains text in the middle of the patch area).

2.1   Estimate Average Text Line Distance

To estimate the average text line distance we measure the vertical projection profile of the page and then compute the distribution of the distance between peaks in the profile. The distribution is fitted into two clusters and the smallest value is used as estimate for the distance between text lines.

In details the computation is composed by several steps. In the first step we remove black bands at the top and bottom borders of the page. Then, we compute the projection profile along the vertical dimension and find its local maxima. We then retain only the peaks larger than 20% of the maximum.

Considering these peaks, we can compute the distribution of the distance between pairs of neighboring peaks. This set of values can be fitted by two centroids using the k-means algorithm. At the end we take the minimum centroid which defines the average distance between lines. The main steps are depicted in Fig. 1 where we show one input image, the computed projection profiles, and the peaks used to define the distance distribution.

With this procedure it is possible to estimate the text line distance in each page. This distance is subsequently used to define the size of the patches extracted from the page.

2.2   Patch Definition

After the computation of the average text line distance, $\hat{h}$, we define the patch size (height, width) as $(\hat{h} \cdot \sqrt{2}, \frac{\hat{h}}{\sqrt{2}})$. The patch height is defined in order to

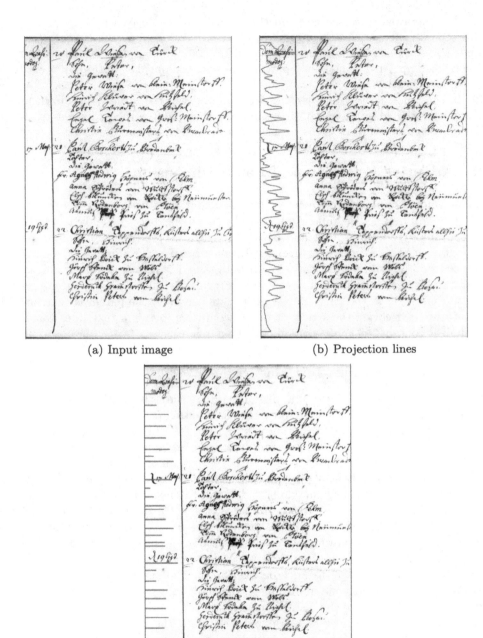

(a) Input image   (b) Projection lines

(c) Computed maximum peaks

Fig. 1. Steps to estimate the distance between text lines in one page.

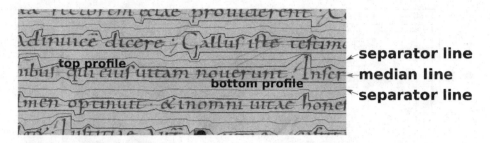

Fig. 2. Examples of separator and median lines and the corresponding top and bottom profiles.

capture almost two text lines with one separator (space or other) in between. The patch size has been chosen after some preliminary tests. In general we can observe that the classification of variable-size patches is a good option to be independent from the textline distance in the input image. A dense patch extraction with overlapping can cover all the lines providing a good hint on the presence of text line separators.

3   The Proposed Method

Taking into account the physical structure of the documents we can define two types of areas: the text line and the separator that is the area between two contiguous text lines. For the subsequent steps it is also useful to define the median line and the separator line. The median line is the middle line between the top profile of the text and the bottom profile. The separator line is the middle line between two consecutive median lines in the text area. We can see these lines in Fig. 2, in particular we show three text lines extracted from one page representing the top and bottom profiles with black lines, the separator and median lines in blue and red. These two types of lines can be used to label the extracted patches and subsequently train the CNN-based line segmentation. However, this information is not always available as groundtruth for the datasets. We therefore need to compute this representation from the available ground truth data.

For example, the ground truth of the *Saint Gall* dataset (more details in Sect. 4.1) is available as pixel-label images defining the text area. In this case we can compute the median line for each text line starting from the pixel level information. After that, we compute the separator line as the mid point between two consecutive median lines. In Fig. 6 we can see one example of the *Saint Gall* dataset and the corresponding ground truth information. Using this information we can compute the previously defined guidelines to label the extracted patches.

Unfortunately, sometimes the ground truth data does not contain this pixel-level labeling. In these cases we manually define only the separator lines and use this information to identify also text lines. More details on how to extract and label patches are described in Sect. 4. Using the document structure and

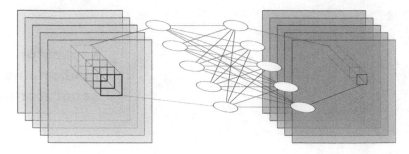

Fig. 3. The *mlpconv* layer is composed by three transformations, the first is a classic convolution followed by two inner products to map the results in the output feature maps.

the ground truth information, we can label each patch as separator, text, or background. The assigned class depends on the area covered by the patch on the document.

3.1   Network Architecture

Convolutional Neural Networks (CNN) are a particular type of Artificial Neural Networks that consist of alternated convolutional layers and spatial pooling layers [7]. The convolutional layers generate feature maps by linear convolutional filters followed by nonlinear activation functions (e.g. rectifier, sigmoid, tanh). In our work we extend the *Network in Network* (NIN) model proposed by Lin et al. [8]. This architecture (Fig. 4) consists of stacked blocks where each block is composed by a convolution operator followed by a Multi Layer Perceptron (MLP) (Fig. 3). This latter structure is called *mlpconv* layer.

The *mlpconv* maps the input area to the output feature vector with a multi-layer perceptron (MLP) consisting of two fully connected layers with nonlinear activation functions. The MLP is shared among all local receptive fields. The feature maps are computed by sliding the MLP over the input similarly to CNNs and are then fed into the next layer. We show one example of *mlpconv* layer in Fig. 3. This layer computes a convolutional transformation with a defined kernel dimension followed by two inner product transformations. Each transformation layer is followed by a ReLU [9] layer. The results are computed considering the same number of feature maps for each transformation in the *mlpconv*.

In this work we use a modified version of the original architecture. In the first *mlpconv* layer we have a convolutional layer with a kernel dimension of $3 \times 7 \times 7$ computing 96 feature maps with stride 2 and padding 3. In the second *mlpconv* layer we have a convolutional layer with a kernel dimension $96 \times 5 \times 5$ computing 256 feature maps with stride 1 and padding 2. In the third *mlpconv* layer we have a convolutional layer with a kernel dimension $256 \times 3 \times 3$ computing 384 feature maps with stride 1 and padding 1. After that, we have a dropout layer [10] which randomly selects 50% of input neurons during the training phase. In the fourth *mlpconv* layer we have a convolutional layer with a kernel dimension $384 \times 3 \times 3$

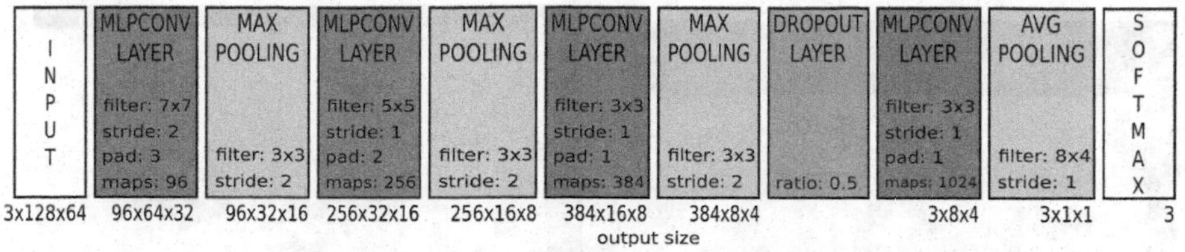

INPUT	MLPCONV LAYER	MAX POOLING	MLPCONV LAYER	MAX POOLING	MLPCONV LAYER	MAX POOLING	DROPOUT LAYER	MLPCONV LAYER	AVG POOLING	SOFTMAX
	filter: 7x7 stride: 2 pad: 3 maps: 96	filter: 3x3 stride: 2	filter: 5x5 stride: 1 pad: 2 maps: 256	filter: 3x3 stride: 2	filter: 3x3 stride: 1 pad: 1 maps: 384	filter: 3x3 stride: 2	ratio: 0.5	filter: 3x3 stride: 1 pad: 1 maps: 1024	filter: 8x4 stride: 1	
3x128x64	96x64x32	96x32x16	256x32x16	256x16x8	384x16x8	384x8x4		3x8x4	3x1x1	3

output size

Fig. 4. The architecture of the model. Different transformations are depicted with different colors. The *mlpconv* transformation is depicted in orange, the pooling undersampling in green and the input and output layer in white. The output result is composed by three classes. (Color figure online)

computing 1024 feature maps with stride 1 and padding 1. For the last *mlpconv* layer, we define the number of feature maps according to the number of classes in our task. We compute the global average pooling over the previous feature maps providing them to the softmax layer which models the distribution over the class labels. We use the stochastic gradient descent to train a model initialized with random weight values. The training is stopped on the best classification accuracy on a validation set. We use the Adam optimization algorithm [11] with a fixed learning rate 0.0001 with momentum (0.9, 0.999) for the training phase.

The overall architecture can be seen in Fig. 4. The model is composed by four *mlpconv* and pooling layers. In orange, we denote the *mlpconv* transformation, in green the pooling transformation layer. For the last *mlpconv* we compute 1024 feature maps until the second inner product, instead, for the last inner product we have the number of neurons according to the output classes.

4 Experiments

In this section we describe the experiments for localizing text lines using two different dataset.

4.1 Data Corpus

It is no easy to find public databases for the tasks addressed in this work. The HisDoc [12] project presents some datasets for developing handwriting recognition systems. In particular, we use the *Saint Gall* dataset that consists of 60 pages scanned from one medieval manuscript written in Latin (Fig. 5a). The ground truth information is gathered from the Hisdoc Divadia site[1]. The proposed approach has been tested also on handwritten documents from a private collection provided by the Ancestry company (the global leader in family history and consumer genomics). This database consists of 54 structured documents written in English by several writers (Fig. 5b). The line ground truth has been produced using one tool specifically developed to manually segment the lines. The images

---

[1] http://diuf.unifr.ch/main/hisdoc/divadia.

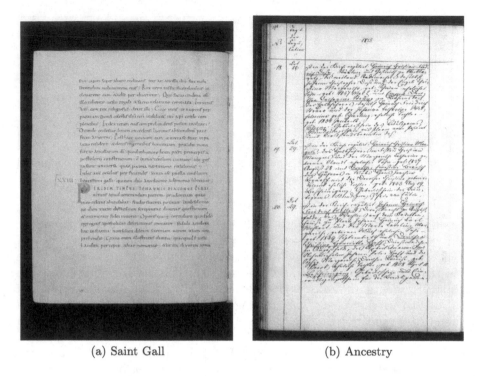

(a) Saint Gall   (b) Ancestry

Fig. 5. One example page for each dataset.

in this collection have been also used for performing experiments aiming at automatically counting the number of records in handwritten pages [13].

4.2 Extracted Patches

As previously mentioned, the first step is to extract the patches used to train the model. This extraction is based on the ground truth of the training set. As previously mentioned, for this research we consider two datasets with two different ground truth information.

In the *Saint Gall* dataset the ground truth is very detailed since it contains one XML file for each document. The XML file contains one pixel-wise representation for each text line. One example of this dataset is presented in Fig. 6 where we can see an input document, a pixel-wise representation of the ground truth for each text line, the computed median text line, and the text separator.

The ground truth produced for the Ancestry dataset defines only the separator line between two adjacent text lines. In Fig. 7 we can see one image example and its ground truth image.

Considering these labeled datasets we can build a large patch dataset to learn the CNN. We have seen how to compute the average distance between text lines; using this information we can define a patch with a suitable dimension

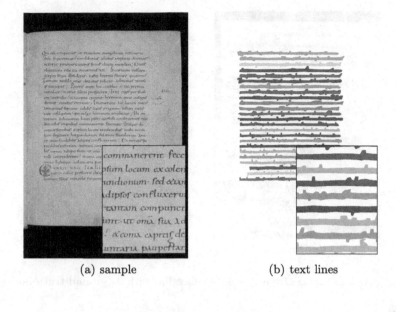

(a) sample   (b) text lines

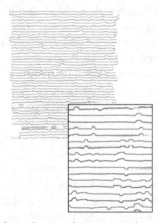

(c) median and separator lines

Fig. 6. In (a) one page from the *Saint Gall* dataset, in (b) the corresponding ground truth pixel-wise representation for each text line, in (c) the computed median text lines in red and the separator text lines in blue. (Color figure online)

to capture the document features. The creation of the image patches for the training set follows the ground truth guidelines, therefore in the first dataset we are able to define patches for three classes (text, separator and background) while only two classes can be considered for the second dataset. We can easily control the number of training patches for each class and we can therefore extract

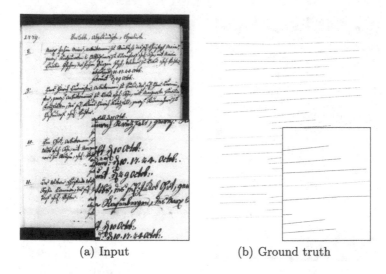

(a) Input   (b) Ground truth

Fig. 7. An input image from Ancestry collection with its ground truth image.

approximately the same number of patches for each class. We then scale each extracted patch to a fixed size of 128×64 pixels.

In the two experiments for each class we considered 100,000 training patches and 30,000 validation patches. The test patches are extracted from the test image as described in the following Section. For instance in the *Saint Gall* dataset the number of patches for each pages are around 600,000 (the number is not fixed, since the patches are extracted at random from background areas).

4.3 Textline Identification

The textline identification is made by extracting dense patches on the test images. Using a sliding window with the estimated dimensions, we classify the patches. The model used gives us an estimate of the probability for each class. This information can be used to infer the position of the lines in the image. We move the sliding window on the image with a stride size equal to 10% of the patch width and 1% of the patch height. In this way, we are able to compute several scores for the same position. We then compute the average probability along the horizontal direction with respect to the patch dimension. This approach is depicted in Fig. 8 where we describe the test procedure. In particular, we can see how we extract dense patches form the input image and also how we compute the probability score for the whole page.

4.4 Preliminary Results

We present in the following the preliminary results obtained for the two datasets.

In the Ancestry dataset, the ground truth defines only the text line separators, therefore we can consider only two classes: *text separator* and *no text*

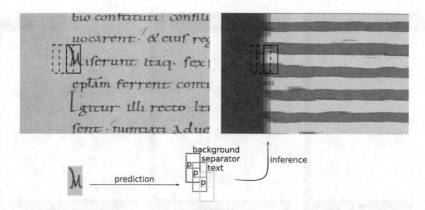

Fig. 8. Textline identification: for each patch one prediction is computed and results are combined to segment the page into three classes: background in blue, text line in green and separator in red. (Color figure online)

separator (background or text). The architecture used for this task is the same presented before. However, in the last *mlpconv* we have one output with only two feature maps. After the test step we can compute the results as we can see in Fig. 9. In the figure we present the results of the model considering only the probability value after the softmax function on the text line separator concept. The testing phase is made moving a window over the input image, therefore we have a probability score for each position. We are able to define the text areas computing the average probability score as we can see in Fig. 9b. This probability

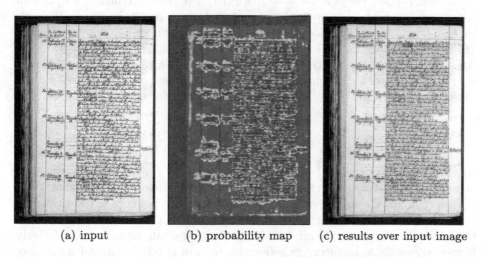

(a) input   (b) probability map   (c) results over input image

Fig. 9. Probability Map to localize text line separators. In (a) the input image, in (b) the probability map computed by our framework and in (c) the results after a threshold over the input image.

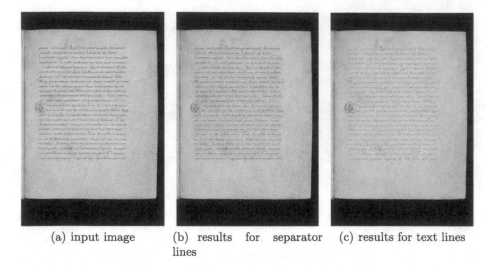

(a) input image   (b) results for separator   (c) results for text lines
                         lines

Fig. 10. Results obtained on the dataset with three classes. In (a) the input image, in (b) the results for separator lines and in (c) the results for text lines.

value represents the text line separator presence. The final result will be a probability map where we can discover the separator position. In this case, having only two classes, we want to discriminate better the result and using a threshold on this probability score, we can predict the text line separator as shown in Fig. 9c. In the figure, where we used a threshold of 0.7 to define the text line separators, we can see the probability map with the corresponding prediction results.

In the HisDoc project, we have more detailed ground truth where we can define median text lines and separator text lines. Using this information, we can use the proposed solution to predict three classes: text, separator and background. With this information, we can infer the text and separator line positions. An example of this approach is shown in Fig. 10 where we can see two different results, one for each class. In particular, in Fig. 10b we present the area for the separator class, while in Fig. 10c we present the area for the text line class.

5   Conclusions

In this paper we presented our preliminary work on the use of Convolutional Neural Networks to perform text line segmentation in historical documents. With these preliminary results we obtained a good starting point to extract the text lines in two different collections containing manuscript records. These results have been obtained considering a training made on small datasets and relatively homogeneous data. In future experiments, we will check the model with more data and we will investigate about possible changes in the model to improve the results.

Acknowledgments. This research is partially supported by a research grant from Ancestry.

References

1. Likforman-Sulem, L., Zahour, A., Taconet, B.: Text line segmentation of historical documents: a survey. Int. J. Doc. Anal. Recognit. **9**(2), 123–138 (2007)
2. Pastor-Pellicer, J., Afzal, M. Z., Liwicki, M., Castro-Bleda, M.J.: Complete system for text line extraction using convolutional neural networks and watershed transform. In: 12th IAPR Workshop on Document Analysis Systems, DAS 2016, Santorini, Greece, 11–14 April 2016, pp. 30–35 (2016)
3. LeCun, Y., Bottou, L., Bengio, Y., Haffner, P.: Gradient-based learning applied to document recognition. In: Proceedings of the IEEE, pp. 2278–2324 (1998)
4. Long, J., Shelhamer, E., Darrell, T.: Fully convolutional networks for semantic segmentation. In: CVPR 2015, pp. 3431–3440 (2015)
5. Sermanet, P., Eigen, D., Zhang, X., Mathieu, M., Fergus, R., LeCun, Y.: Integrated recognition, localization and detection using convolutional networks, Overfeat (2014)
6. Afzal, M.Z., Capobianco, S., Malik, M.I., Marinai, S., Breuel, T.M., Dengel, A., Liwicki, M.: DeepDocClassifier: document classification with deep convolutional neural network. In: 13th International Conference on Document Analysis and Recognition, ICDAR 2015, Nancy, France, 23–26 August 2015, pp. 1111–1115 (2015)
7. Goodfellow, I., Bengio, Y., Courville, A.: Deep Learning. MIT Press (2016). http://www.deeplearningbook.org
8. Lin, M., Chen, Q., Yan, S.: Network in network. CoRR, abs/1312.4400 (2013)
9. Glorot, X., Bordes, A., Bengio, Y.: Deep sparse rectifier neural networks. In: Gordon, G.J., Dunson, D.B. (eds.) Proceedings of the Fourteenth International Conference on Artificial Intelligence and Statistics (AISTATS-2011), vol. 15, pp. 315–323 (2011). Journal of Machine Learning Research - Workshop and Conference Proceedings
10. Hinton, G.E., Srivastava, N., Krizhevsky, A., Sutskever, I., Salakhutdinov, R.R.: Improving neural networks by preventing co-adaptation of feature detectors. CoRR, abs/1207.0580 (2012)
11. Kingma, D.P., Ba, J.: Adam: a method for stochastic optimization. CoRR, abs/1412.6980 (2014)
12. Fischer, A., Bunke, H., Naji, N., Savoy, J., Baechler, M., Ingold, R.: The HisDoc project. Automatic analysis, recognition, and retrieval of handwritten historical documents for digital libraries, vol. 38, pp. 91–106. De Gruyter (2014)
13. Capobianco, S., Marinai, S.: Record counting in historical handwritten documents with convolutional neural networks. CoRR, abs/1610.07393 (2016)

Data Management and Presentation

Using Formal Narratives in Digital Libraries

Carlo Meghini, Valentina Bartalesi[✉], and Daniele Metilli

Istituto di Scienza e Tecnologie dell'Informazione "Alessandro Faedo" – CNR,
Via G. Moruzzi 1, 56124 Pisa, Italy
{carlo.meghini,valentina.bartalesi,daniele.metilli}@isti.cnr.it

Abstract. Currently, Digital Libraries (DLs) provide simple search functionalities to respond to the user's queries, which return a ranked list of the resources included in the DLs. No semantic relation among the returned objects is usually reported that could help the user to obtain a more complete knowledge on the subject of the search. The introduction of the Semantic Web and in particular of the Linked Open Data has the potential of improving the search functionalities of DLs. In this context, the long-term aim of our study has been to introduce the *narrative* as new first-class search functionality of DLs. We intend *narratives* as semantic networks of events that are linked to the objects of the DLs and are endowed with a set of semantic relations that connect an event to another. In this paper, we report an overview of the main ontologies for representing events and of the tools developed in the Semantic Web field to visualize events and narratives. This overview is needed for achieving the first goal of our research, that is the development of an ontology for representing narratives and, on the top of this ontology, a tool to construct and visualize narratives using the digital objects included in DLs.

Keywords: Digital libraries · Narratives · Ontologies · Digital humanities · Semantic web

1 Introduction

Currently, Digital Libraries (DLs) provide simple search functionalities to respond to the user's queries, expressed in natural language. These functionalities return a ranked list of the resources included in the DLs. No semantic relation among the returned objects is usually reported that could help the user to obtain a more complete knowledge on the subject of the search. For example, consider as user a young woman wishing to know more about Dante Alighieri, the major Italian poet of the late Middle Ages. She may ask "Dante Alighieri" to a Web search engine and most likely she would get a list of ranked documents with the Wikipedia page about Dante within the top 5 results. Not willing to spend her time reading, the user tries other Web sites, where she hopes to find something quicker to consume than the typical textbook narrative. At some point, she tries to search on the Web page of a DL, e.g. Europeana[1]. However, the result

---

[1] http://www.europeana.eu.

C. Grana and L. Baraldi (Eds.): IRCDL 2017, CCIS 733, pp. 83–94, 2017.
DOI: 10.1007/978-3-319-68130-6_7

is a list of objects without any explicit semantic relations to each other. Each object offers a single view of Dante's life and works, but altogether incapable of providing an complete overview of Dante's life. This behavior, which generally characterizes DLs, is a consequence of seeing a digital library as a traditional library endowed with digital resources managed by software. The introduction of the Semantic Web [5], and in particular of the Linked Open Data[2], has the potential of improving the search functionalities of DLs. In this context, the long-term aim of our study has been to introduce the *narrative* as new first-class search functionality of DLs. As output of a query, the envisaged new search functionality should not only return a list of objects but it should also present one or more narratives, composed of events that are linked to the objects of the existing libraries and are endowed with a set of semantic relations connecting these events into a meaningful semantic network. As a necessary and preliminary step towards this direction, this paper presents an overview of the main developed ontologies for formally representing events, along with several tools for their construction and visualization in user-friendly forms, based on semantic models. Indeed, in order to introduce this new search functionality for DLs, we aim at developing: (i) a formal ontology for representing events and narratives, which reuses existing ontologies in order to maximize its interoperability; (ii) a tool that allows users to construct narratives but also to visualize them in an easy and useful way. Information about our project is available at http://narra.isti.cnr.it.

2   Ontologies for Representing Events

Narrative is a well-researched concept in several fields, ranging from literary studies to cognitive science. As a matter of fact, "narrative can be viewed under several profiles – as a cognitive structure or way of making sense of experience, as a type of text, and as a resource for communicative interaction" [16]. For the purposes of this research, a narrative is intended as a network of "temporally indexed representations of events" [32], that is events associated to time structures and related to one another and to the DL resources through semantic links.

The concept of *event* is a core element of the narratology theory and of the narratives. People conventionally refer to an *event* as an occurrence taking place at a certain time in a specific location.

In the following, we briefly describe some ontologies developed for representing events on the Semantic Web [4]. Ontologies can be divided into the following categories: upper ontologies and domain ontologies [37]. An upper ontology is a domain-independent ontology, from which more domain-specific ontologies may be derived. A domain ontology specifies concepts, which belong to a specific domain of interest.

---

[2] https://www.ted.com/talks/tim_berners_lee_on_the_next_web.

OpenCyc[3] is the open source version of the Cyc ontology. It is an upper ontology[4], which is used for representing human knowledge about the objects and events of everyday life. The Cyc knowledge base contains about five hundred thousand terms, including about seventeen thousand types of relations, and about seven million assertions relating these terms. OpenCyc distinguishes between static situations and events. The first ones are situations that are extended in time but do not change, whereas events are situations that are extended and change in time.

The *Suggested Upper Merged Ontology (SUMO)* [36] is a comprehensive upper ontology which is fully mapped to the WordNet lexical database [35]. The ontology has been successfully applied to the representation of narratives, in particular to automated story generation systems [7], and it is has also been used to model the cause-effect relations found in narratives [3].

DOLCE-Lite-Plus is the first module of the WonderWeb Foundational Ontologies Library [30]. DOLCE aims at representing the ontological categories underlying natural language and human common-sense. DOLCE is described as an "ontology of particulars" [30], which the authors explain as an ontology of instances rather than an ontology of universals or properties. Particulars are entities that cannot have instances; universals are entities that can have instances. In linguistics, proper nouns are normally considered to refer to particulars, while common nouns to universals. DOLCE+ is an extension of DOLCE containing some modules dedicated to core ontologies of contexts, time, space, plans etc. The current implementation of DOLCE+ is DOLCE-Lite-Plus. DOLCE-Lite-Plus has been used to align about 900 synsets from the noun hierarchies of the WordNet 1.6 English lexical database. This alignment makes it possible to put the entire 66,000 synsets from WordNet 1.6 (currently about 60,000 classes and 5,000 individuals) under DOLCE-Lite-Plus.

In DOLCE+, "Event" is a subclass of "Perdurant". "Classically, endurants (also called continuants) are characterized as entities that are in time, wholly present (all their proper parts are present) at any time of their existence. On the other hand, perdurants (also called occurrents) are entities that happen in time, which extend in time by accumulating different "temporal parts", so that, at any time t at which they exist, only their temporal parts at t are present. Events are called achievements if they are atomic, otherwise they are accomplishments".

The *CIDOC CRM*[5] (CRM for short) is a high-level ontology that allows to integrate the information contained in data of the cultural heritage domain along with their correlation with knowledge stored in libraries and archives [13]. The CRM is one of the most widely adopted ontologies in the domain of Cultural Heritage, where both digital libraries and narratives belong. CRM is also an ISO standard since 2006 (ISO21127:2006) and renewed 2014 (ISO21127:2014). Both these factors are crucial to attain semantic interoperability, based on sharing existing ontologies. In CRM, the class "Event", along with its subclass "Activ-

---

[3] http://opencyc.org.

[4] http://www.cyc.com.

[5] http://www.cidoc-crm.org.

ity", corresponds to the definition of Event in Event Calculus. In the CRM this class "comprises changes of states in cultural, social or physical systems, regardless of scale, brought about by a series or group of coherent physical, cultural, technological or legal phenomena".

The *Europeana Data Model* (EDM) [14] is a model that aims at structuring and representing data delivered to Europeana[6] by the various contributing cultural heritage institutions. Europeana is often presented as a portal giving access to millions of objects from all kinds of cultural heritage communities but in [6] it was explained that "Europeana is not so much a portal characterised by sheer volume, but that the core agenda of our endeavour is to make rich data and functionality available on an API basis. This would allow all kinds of external communities to make use of our rich (and numerous) representations of European cultural treasures for their own needs". In the EDM Primer[7] two approaches to provide contextual information about objects are reported: object-centric and event-centric. With the former, descriptive meta-data, such for example title or creator, are attached to the provided object. With the event centric approach, relations between different entities are described by means of Events, and metadata are attached to such events. For example, a piece of art can be related to its creator via a "creation" event, in which the author is specified as the event performer. The two approaches co-exist, so that duplicate and/or complementary information pieces can be provided in both ways.

The *Event Ontology* [38] was developed in the Center for Digital Music of the Queen Mary University of London. This ontology, which can be used in conjunction with other music-related ontologies, has not specific terms related to the music domain so it can be used in other domains as well. The top-level class in the Event Ontology is the class Event. The ontology defines event as "an arbitrary classification of a space/time region, by a cognitive agent. An event may have actively participating agents, passive factors, products, and a location in space/time" [38].

The *Linking Open Descriptions of Events* (LODE) ontology is a "minimal model that encapsulates the most useful properties for describing events" [40]. The aim of LODE is to permit interoperability when modeling the factual aspects of events. Those aspects are characterized in the four aspects: what happened, where did it happen, when did it happen, and who was involved. An event is described as a class that is defined as "something that happened".

The *Event-Model-F ontology* is mainly focused on the processing of events. The ontology is to be used in event based systems [39]. Its model is "based on the foundational ontology DOLCE+ DnS ultralight[8] and provides comprehensive support to represent time and space, objects and persons as well as mereological, causal, and correlative relationships between events" [39].

---

[6] http://www.europeana.eu.

[7] http://pro.europeana.eu/files/Europeana_Professional/Share_your_data/
Technical_requirements/EDM_Documentation/EDM_Primer_130714.pdf.

[8] http://www.loa.istc.cnr.it/ontologies/DUL.owl.

The *ABC ontology* is a basic model and an ontology to facilitate the development of a domain, role, or community specific ontologies, in particular "it is a basic Ontology, which provides a basic model for domain-related or community-related development" [43]. The ABC ontology was developed for modeling physical, digital and analogue objects contained in libraries, archives, and museums and on the Internet [17].

The *Simple Event Model (SEM)* [42] allows representing events in different domains, independently from the domain-specific vocabularies that can be used. An event in SEM is defined as everything that happens, even if fictional. SEM is developed with a minimum of semantic commitment to maximize its interoperability. The core classes of SEM are Event, Actor, Place and Time. These represent the main aspects of an event: what happens, who or what participated, where and when did it happen.

The *Drammar Ontology* is a semantic model for the representation of drama features, featuring a SRWL-based rule layer to provide automatic reasoning [25]. The Drammar model is based on *actions* carried out by *agents*. The core element driving the storyline is the *conflict*, which puts in motion an ordered sequence of actions linked together by causal relations. The actions are grouped in *units*, or narrative blocks. The Drammar ontology is also able to represent the characters' *emotions*. For the description of its terms, Drammar refers to the YAGO-SUMO ontology [12], i.e. an integration between SUMO and YAGO (Yet Another Great Ontology) [41].

3   Visualization of Narratives in DLs

Narratives have been recently proposed to enhance the information contents and functionalities of DLs, with special emphasis on information discovery and exploration.

For example, in the CultureSampo project [21] an application to explore Finnish cultural heritage contents on the Web, based on Semantic Web technologies was developed. This system uses an event-based model and makes links among events and digital objects. However it does not allow visualizing the event and the related digital objects as a semantic network provided with the semantic relations that connect events and objects but it presents nine "thematic perspectives" [20], e.g. (i) Maps Search and Browse Views, which presents four map views available using Google Maps, and displays, for example, any collection object with coordinate information on Google Maps, and shows the semantic relations of objects with the place, e.g. "place of acquirement", "place of subject"; (ii) for the Relational Search perspective the idea is not to search for objects but associative relation chains between objects. The user can indicate two names and CultureSampo shows how the persons or organizations are linked to each other by the social network based on some 50 different social roles (e.g., parent-of, teacher-of, patron-of etc.).

An extension of CultureSampo is WarSampo system [18] for publishing collections of heterogeneous data about the Second World War on the Semantic

Web. WarSampo is based on harmonizing different datasets using a event-based model and then, through a dedicated portal, allows historians to study war history from different interlinked perspectives. For example, an user could want to see how an event evolve in time and where it took place, or s/he could be interested in some persons and in their experiences in the war. Providing different perspectives to visualize the collected data allows this system to differ from other portals like Europeana that allows only a single view on its collection.

Narrative event structures and semantic event descriptions were used in end-user applications for searching and linking documents and other content about World War I [19]. Events are related to each others through narrative relations, e.g. sub event relationships that decompose events mereologically; succession relationships that order the events in time; causal relationships. The developed model allows representing multiple narratives that share same events, without mixing the story lines and the different causal relations among the same events cannot be represented, even if different authors may have different opinions about them. A World War I Web portal was developed to facilitate searching and browsing collection data by topics, people, places and time periods, and to visualize the collection metadata in an interactive ways.

Bletchley Park Text [33], a semantic application helping users to explore collections of museums. Visitors express their interests on some specific topics using SMS messages containing keywords. The semantic description of the resources is used to organize a collection into a personalized web site based on the chosen topics. The system relies on an ontology of story, taken from the Story Fountain project [34]. The stories represented in the system are exploited to create relations between the entities contained in the online collections, allowing the user to query the system for a semantic path between entities.

In the PATHS project [15] a system that acts as an interactive personalized tour guide through existing digital library collections was created. A path is a device for ordering, connecting and annotating a series of items of interest that have been collected in a Cultural Heritage digital library. In a path structure, (i) nodes representing items from an online collection or Web pages, which can have associated metadata; (ii) links that represent inherence relations between nodes allow the navigation across the path; (iii) annotations and external links can added by the path-creator to provide additional context and narrative.

Similar to the approach of PATHS project, within the CULTURA project [1] a tool to enrich the cultural heritage collections with guided paths in the form of short lessons called *narratives* was developed. The system is provided with automatic tools that simulate the research behavior of expert users when they interact with the multimedia application. The experimental results have been obtained using a multimedia application that manages the digital representation of historical manuscripts about botany.

DIVE [11] is a system that allows event-based browsing of cultural heritage objects from two heterogeneous historical Dutch collections (video and and radio news scripts). The collected data is modeled using the Simple Event Model (SEM). A Named Entity Recognition (NER) and Event extraction tools were adopted in order to retrieve a set of relevant concepts from the metadata and textual description associated to the collected data. In a second stage, crowd-sourcing approach was employed to to refine the results from Natural Language Processing tools. The results from the different tools and the crowdsourcing are translated into an RDF graph. Then, the graph can be explored using a browser that allows to visualize explicit relation between objects and events.

The Storyspace system [44] allows describing stories based on events that span museum objects. The system is focused on the creation of curatorial narratives from an exhibition. Each digital object has a linked creation event in its associated heritage object story. Kilfeather and McAuley (2003) [22] describe some tools which would facilitate the development of a meaningful story or narrative structure from existing or newly contents. The aim was to allow authors to establish semantic relations between different contents and to select and put them together. The ontology was based on existent taxonomies and thesauri related to Irish archaeology.

DECHO is a framework for the acquisition, ontological representation, and visualization of knowledge about archaeological objects [2]. The ontological component is based on the CIDOC CRM reference ontology. The visualization component has the ability to display narratives by linking together image or 3D representations of archaeological objects via *semantic hotspots* [31].

Another example is the CADMOS suite of applications, developed in conjunction with the Drammar ontology [26]. CADMOS adopts a computer-supported semantic annotation of narrative media objects (video, text, audio, etc.) and integrates with a large common-sense ontology (YAGO-SUMO) [29]. CADMOS also features a visualization tool, which gives a graphical representation of the basic aspects of the narrative [27].

Another ontology-based system for the visualization of narratives is the Labyrinth project [9]. The Labyrinth system allows users to explore digital cultural heritage archives by providing narrative relations among knowledge resources. Labyrinth is not tied to a specific collection of objects, but is instead an open system which allows the emergence of semantic connections among heterogeneous resources [8]. The exploration of the repository is mediated through a set of *cultural archetypes*, or narrative structures, which are modelled according to an Archetype Ontology [23]. More recently, the Labyrinth system has been extended with a three-dimensional interface [10].

A similar project is Invisibilia, which is focused on the domain of contemporary public art [28]. Invisibilia takes as input an ontological representation, constructed using a CRM-based ontology for intangible art [24], and outputs a 3D layout featuring the artworks.

4   Discussion

In order to introduce narratives as new search functionality in DLs and to develop an ontology for representing narratives, first we have analyzed the Artificial Intelligence (AI) literature, and in particular the Event Calculus theory, to identify the logical components of narratives (e.g. events, actions, fluents, physical object, agents), and give their formal definitions. Then, we studied the semantic models reported in the above Sections and we decided to map the identified logic components of narratives with the terms of two of the analyzed ontologies, the CIDOC CRM and DOLCE+, in order to evaluate if it would be possible to take one of them as reference vocabulary. We chose these ontologies since the first one is an ISO standard and the second one is a standard *de facto*. The above analysis shows that both DOLCE+ and the CRM are adequate to express the components of narratives. However, our choice has fallen on the CRM for the following main reasons:

- The CRM is an ISO standard since 2006 (ISO21127:2006) and renewed 2014 (ISO21127:2014). As such, it is widely known, it is regularly revised, and it is universally accessible.
- The CRM is specifically thought for the cultural heritage domain, and as such it is closer to the domain of narratives than DOLCE+. In fact, the CRM has been harmonized with the FRBR ontology (named as FRBRoo), a core ontology for bibliographic information, and therefore it provides fundamental notions to model text. Indeed, in many cases a narration represents a story expressed through a text.
- The Special Interest Group of the CRM continuously works for expanding the domain of applicability of the ontology, and a number of extensions have already been devised.

In order to define the factual components of the events, in particular we took into account the definitions reported in the LODE and SEM ontologies, where the main and necessary aspects that characterize an event are presented. A first version of the ontology, with descriptions of the classes and relations we used, is available online[9].

For the development of the tool to build narratives, we have taken into consideration several past projects. For instance, the PATHS projects has been a model for the integration of digital objects in a narrative. Unlike PATHS, our model of narratives revolves around events, but we are also interested in linking events to the objects found in digital libraries. PATHS has also given us ideas about the interface for the narrative construction, in particular by providing a feature to construct narratives through a simple drag-and-drop functionality. During the development of the visualization components of our tool, the "thematic perspectives" on the knowledge base provided by the CultureSampo project have been a useful inspiration. However, we also had to analyze the requirements of the users in order to identify the specific visualizations which were necessary to them, and adapt each view to these requirements. A first version of the tool is available online[10].

---

[9] http://narra.isti.cnr.it/ontology.
[10] http://narra.isti.cnr.it/tool.html.

5   Conclusions and Future Work

In this paper we have reported an overview of the main ontologies for representing events and of the tools developed in the Semantic Web field in order to visualize events and narratives. This overview has been useful for achieving the main goal of our research, that is the development of an ontology for representing narratives and, on the top of this ontology, a tool to construct narratives using the digital objects included in digital libraries. In this context, we intend narratives as semantic networks of events linked to each other and to digital objects by semantic relations. In particular, for developing an ontology for narratives, we have taken the CIDOC CRM as reference ontology and for defining the factual aspects of events we have referred to the LODE and SEM ontologies. For the development of the tool to construct narratives we took into consideration several existing projects, including PATHS and CultureSampo.

The long-term goal of our study is introducing the narrative as new first-class search functionality of digital libraries. As output of a query, this new search functionality should not only return a list of objects, as the current digital libraries do, but it should also present one or more narratives on the topic of the search.

References

1. Agosti, M., Manfioletti, M., Orio, N., Ponchia, C.: Enhancing end user access to cultural heritage systems: tailored narratives and human-centered computing. In: Petrosino, A., Maddalena, L., Pala, P. (eds.) ICIAP 2013. LNCS, vol. 8158, pp. 278–287. Springer, Heidelberg (2013). doi:10.1007/978-3-642-41190-8_30
2. Aliaga, D.G., Bertino, E., Valtolina, S.: DECHO–framework for the digital exploration of cultural heritage objects. J. Comput. Cult. Heritage (JOCCH) 3(3), 12 (2011)
3. Ang, K., Yu, S., Ong, E.: Theme-based cause-effect planning for multiple-scene story generation. In: Proceedings of the 2nd International Conference on Computational Creativity, Mexico City, Mexico, pp. 48–53 (2011)
4. Astrova, I., Koschel, A., Lukanowski, J., Martinez, J.L.M., Procenko, V., Schaaf, M.: Ontologies for complex event processing. Int. J. Comput. Inform. Sci. Eng. 8(5), 556–566 (2014)
5. Berners-Lee, T., Hendler, J., Lassila, O., et al.: The semantic web. Sci. Am. 284(5), 28–37 (2001)
6. Concordia, C., Gradmann, S., Siebinga, S.: Not just another portal, not just another digital library: a portrait of europeana as an application program interface. IFLA J. 36(1), 61–69 (2010)
7. Cua, J., Ong, E., Manurung, R., Pease, A.: Representing story plans in sumo. In: Proceedings of the NAACL HLT 2010 Second Workshop on Computational Approaches to Linguistic Creativity, pp. 40–48. Association for Computational Linguistics (2010)
8. Damiano, R., Lieto, A.: Ontological representations of narratives: a case study on stories and actions. In: OASIcs-OpenAccess Series in Informatics, vol. 32. Schloss Dagstuhl-Leibniz-Zentrum fuer Informatik (2013)

9. Damiano, R., Lieto, A., Lombardo, V.: Ontology-based visualisation of cultural heritage. In: 2014 Eighth International Conference on Complex, Intelligent and Software Intensive Systems (CISIS), pp. 558–563. IEEE (2014)

10. Damiano, R., Lombardo, V., Lieto, A.: Visual metaphors for semantic cultural heritage. In: 2015 7th International Conference on Intelligent Technologies for Interactive Entertainment (INTETAIN), pp. 100–109. IEEE (2015)

11. De Boer, V., Oomen, J., Inel, O., Aroyo, L., Van Staveren, E., Helmich, W., De Beurs, D.: Dive into the event-based browsing of linked historical media. Web Semant. Sci. Serv. Agents World Wide Web **35**, 152–158 (2015)

12. De Melo, G., Suchanek, F., Pease, A.: Integrating YAGO into the suggested upper merged ontology. In: 2008 20th IEEE International Conference on Tools with Artificial Intelligence, vol. 1, pp. 190–193. IEEE (2008)

13. Doerr, M.: The CIDOC conceptual reference module: an ontological approach to semantic interoperability of metadata. AI Mag. **24**(3), 75 (2003)

14. Doerr, M., Gradmann, S., Hennicke, S., Isaac, A., Meghini, C., van de Sompel, H.: The Europeana Data Model (EDM). In: World Library and Information Congress: 76th IFLA General Conference and Assembly, pp. 10–15 (2010)

15. Fernie, K., Griffiths, J., Archer, P., Chandrinos, K., de Polo, A., Stevenson, M., Clough, P., Goodale, P., Hall, M., Agirre, E., et al.: Paths: Personalising access to cultural heritage spaces. In: 2012 18th International Conference on Virtual Systems and Multimedia (VSMM), pp. 469–474. IEEE (2012)

16. Herman, D.: Basic Elements of Narrative. Wiley, New York (2011)

17. Hunter, J.: Enhancing the semantic interoperability of multimedia through a core ontology. IEEE Trans. Circuits Syst. Video Technol. **13**(1), 49–58 (2003)

18. Hyvönen, E., Heino, E., Leskinen, P., Ikkala, E., Koho, M., Tamper, M., Tuominen, J., Mäkelä, E.: WarSampo data service and semantic portal for publishing linked open data about the second world war history. In: Sack, H., Blomqvist, E., d'Aquin, M., Ghidini, C., Ponzetto, S.P., Lange, C. (eds.) ESWC 2016. LNCS, vol. 9678, pp. 758–773. Springer, Cham (2016). doi:10.1007/978-3-319-34129-3_46

19. Hyvönen, E., Lindquist, T., Törnroos, J., Mäkelä, E.: History on the semantic web as linked data-an event gazetteer and timeline for the world war i. In: Proceedings of CIDOC (2012)

20. Hyvönen, E., Mäkelä, E., Alm, O., Kurki, J., Ruotsalo, T., Takala, J., Puputti, K., Kuittinen, H., Viljanen, K., Tuominen, J., et al.: Culturesampo-finnish cultural heritage collections on the semantic web 2.0. In: Proceedings of the 1st International Symposium on Digital humanities for Japanese Arts and Cultures (DH-JAC-2009), Ritsumeikan. Citeseer (2009)

21. Hyvönen, E., Takala, J., Alm, O., Ruotsalo, T., Mäkelä, E.: Semantic kalevala – accessing cultural contents through semantically annotated stories. In: Proceedings of the Cultural Heritage on the Semantic Web Workshop at the 6th International SemanticWeb Conference (ISWC 2007), Busan, Korea. Citeseer (2007)

22. Kilfeather, E., McAuley, J., Corns, A., McHugh, O.: An ontological application for archaeological narratives. In: 14th International Workshop on Database and Expert Systems Applications, Proceedings, pp. 110–114. IEEE (2003)

23. Lieto, A., Damiano, R.: Building narrative connections among media objects in cultural heritage repositories. In: Koenitz, H., Sezen, T.I., Ferri, G., Haahr, M., Sezen, D., Ç atak, G. (eds.) ICIDS 2013. LNCS, vol. 8230, pp. 257–260. Springer, Cham (2013). doi:10.1007/978-3-319-02756-2_33

24. Lieto, A., Damiano, R., Michielon, V.: Conceptual models for intangible art. A formal modeling proposal. Mimesis J. Scritture della performance **3**(2), 70–78 (2014)
25. Lombardo, V., Battaglino, C., Pizzo, A., Damiano, R., Lieto, A.: Coupling conceptual modeling and rules for the annotation of dramatic media. Semant. Web **6**(5), 503–534 (2015)
26. Lombardo, V., Damiano, R.: Semantic annotation of narrative media objects. Multimedia Tools Appl. **59**(2), 407–439 (2012)
27. Lombardo, V., Damiano, R., Lieto, A., Pizzo, A.: Visualization of character's intentions in dramatic media. In: 2013 Seventh International Conference on Complex, Intelligent, and Software Intensive Systems (CISIS), pp. 582–587. IEEE (2013)
28. Lombardo, V., Guardini, N., Olivero, A.: Visualisation of contemporary public art. Mimesis J. Scritture della performance **3**(2), 79–89 (2014)
29. Lombardo, V., Pizzo, A.: Ontologies for the metadata annotation of stories. In: Digital Heritage International Congress (DigitalHeritage), vol. 2, pp. 153–160. IEEE (2013)
30. Masolo, C., Borgo, S., Gangemi, A., Guarino, N., Oltramari, A.: Wonderweb deliverable d18, ontology library (final). ICT project 33052 (2003)
31. Mazzoleni, P., Valtolina, S., Franzoni, S., Mussio, P., Bertino, E.: Towards a contextualized access to the cultural heritage world using 360 panoramic images. In: SEKE, pp. 416–419 (2006)
32. Meister, J.C.: Computing action: a narratological approach, vol. 2. Walter de Gruyter (2003)
33. Mulholland, P., Collins, T.: Using digital narratives to support the collaborative learning and exploration of cultural heritage. In: 13th International Workshop on Database and Expert Systems Applications, Proceedings, pp. 527–531. IEEE (2002)
34. Mulholland, P., Collins, T., Zdrahal, Z.: Story fountain: intelligent support for story research and exploration. In: Proceedings of the 9th International Conference on Intelligent User Interfaces, pp. 62–69. ACM (2004)
35. Niles, I., Pease, A.: Mapping wordnet to the sumo ontology. In: Proceedings of the IEEE International Knowledge Engineering Conference, pp. 23–26 (2003)
36. Pease, A., Niles, I., Li, J.: The suggested upper merged ontology: A large ontology for the semantic web and its applications. In: Working Notes of the AAAI-2002 Workshop on Ontologies and the Semantic Web, vol. 28 (2002)
37. Poli, R., Healy, M., Kameas, A.: Theory and Applications of Ontology: Computer Applications. Springer, Cham (2010)
38. Raimond, Y., Abdallah, S.: The event ontology. Technical report, Citeseer (2007)
39. Scherp, A., Franz, T., Saathoff, C., Staab, S.: F-a model of events based on the foundational ontology DOLCE+DnS ultralight. In: Proceedings of the Fifth International Conference on Knowledge Capture, pp. 137–144. ACM (2009)
40. Shaw, R., Troncy, R., Hardman, L.: LODE: linking open descriptions of events. In: Gómez-Pérez, A., Yu, Y., Ding, Y. (eds.) ASWC 2009. LNCS, vol. 5926, pp. 153–167. Springer, Heidelberg (2009). doi:10.1007/978-3-642-10871-6_11
41. Suchanek, F.M., Kasneci, G., Weikum, G.: YAGO: a core of semantic knowledge. In: Proceedings of the 16th international conference on World Wide Web, pp. 697–706. ACM (2007)

42. Van Hage, W.R., Malaisé, V., Segers, R., Hollink, L., Schreiber, G.: Design and use of the Simple Event Model (SEM). Web Semant. Sci. Serv. Agents World Wide Web **9**(2), 128–136 (2011)
43. Wenjun, W., Yingwei, L., Xinpeng, L., Xiaolin, W., Zhuoqun, X.: Ontological model of event for integration of inter-organization applications. In: Gervasi, O., Gavrilova, M.L., Kumar, V., Laganà, A., Lee, H.P., Mun, Y., Taniar, D., Tan, C.J.K. (eds.) ICCSA 2005. LNCS, vol. 3480, pp. 301–310. Springer, Heidelberg (2005). doi:10.1007/11424758_32
44. Wolff, A., Mulholland, P., Collins, T.: Storyspace: a story-driven approach for creating museum narratives. In: Proceedings of the 23rd ACM Conference on Hypertext and Social Media, pp. 89–98. ACM (2012)

The OpenAIRE Workflows for Data Management

Claudio Atzori$^{(\boxtimes)}$, Alessia Bardi, Paolo Manghi,
and Andrea Mannocci

Istituto di Scienza e Tecnologie dell'Informazione, "A. Faedo" - CNR, Pisa, Italy
{claudio.atzori,alessia.bardi,paolo.manghi,
andrea.mannocci}@isti.cnr.it

Abstract. The OpenAIRE initiative is the point of reference for Open Access in Europe and aims at the creation of an e-Infrastructure for the free flow, access, sharing, and re-use of research outcomes, services and processes for the advancement of research and the dissemination of scientific knowledge. OpenAIRE makes openly accessible a rich Information Space Graph (ISG) where products of the research life-cycle (e.g. publications, datasets, projects) are semantically linked to each other. Such an information space graph is constructed by a set of autonomic (orchestrated) workflows operating in a regimen of continuous data integration. This paper discusses the principal workflows operated by the OpenAIRE technical infrastructure in its different functional areas and provides the reader with the extent of the several challenges faced and the solutions realized.

Keywords: Aggregation · Workflows · e-Infrastructure · Metadata · Open science · Open access · De-duplication · Data mining · Information space

1   Introduction

The OpenAIRE initiative is the point of reference for Open Access in Europe [3, 4]. Its mission is to foster an Open Science e-Infrastructure that links people, ideas and resources for the free flow, access, sharing, and re-use of research outcomes, services and processes for the advancement of research and the dissemination of scientific knowledge. OpenAIRE operates an open, collaborative, service oriented infrastructure that supports (i) the realization of a pan-European network for the definition, promotion and implementation of shared interoperability guidelines and best practices for managing, sharing, re-using, and preserving research outcomes of different typologies; (ii) the promotion of Open Science policies and practices at all stages of the research life-cycle and across research communities belonging to different application domains and geographical areas; (iii) the provision of measurements of the impact of Open Science and the return of investment of national and international funding agencies; (iv) the development and operation of a technical infrastructure supporting services for the discovery of and access to research outcomes via a centralized entry point, where research outcomes are enriched with contextual information via links to objects relevant to the research life-cycle. This paper focuses on the workflows operated by the

C. Grana and L. Baraldi (Eds.): IRCDL 2017, CCIS 733, pp. 95–107, 2017.
DOI: 10.1007/978-3-319-68130-6_8

OpenAIRE technical infrastructure for the management of the OpenAIRE information space. The OpenAIRE technical infrastructure includes services dedicated to the aggregation of information about objects of the research life-cycle. In order to help repository managers to integrate their data with OpenAIRE, the guidelines (https://guidelines.openaire.eu) describe how to expose such information (publications, datasets, CRIS metadata) via the OAI-PMH protocol. Relationships between objects are collected from the data sources, but also automatically detected by inference algorithms [1] and added by users, who can insert links between publications, datasets and projects via the claiming procedure available from the OpenAIRE web portal. The Information Space is available for human and machine consumption via the OpenAIRE web portal and different kinds of APIs. Among the challenges emerging in this scenario, one is relative to the orchestration of the different workflows characterizing the OpenAIRE system. In fact, a key factor for its sustainability is represented by the system capability of being autonomic and extensible, i.e. the possibility to easily define and implement autonomous workflows. The OpenAIRE workflows orchestration is delegated to D-NET, a software toolkit for constructing and operating aggregative infrastructures in a cost-effective way as instances of service-oriented data infra-structures [6].

Outline. The following sections describe the OpenAIRE technical infrastructure by introducing the OpenAIRE data model (Sect. 2.1) and the general system architecture (Sect. 2.2). The remaining sections introduces the infrastructure workflows, intended as both automated and human activities aimed to (i) aggregate content (metadata and full-text) (Sect. 3), (ii) populate the OpenAIRE ISG (Sect. 4), (iii) de-duplicate it (Sect. 5), (iv) infer new valuable information from the full-text files (Sect. 6), (v) monitor and publish the ISG in order to make it available to both end users on the portal and third party services via the OpenAIRE API (Sect. 7).

2 OpenAIRE Technical Infrastructure

In this section, we introduce the OpenAIRE technical infrastructure by describing the OpenAIRE data model, and the general architecture of the system.

2.1 The OpenAIRE Data Model

The OpenAIRE technological infrastructure provides aggregation services capable of collecting content from data sources available on the web in order to populate the so-called OpenAIRE Information Space, a graph-like information space (ISG - Information Space Graph) describing the relationships between scientific articles, their authors, the research datasets related with them, their funders, the relative grants and associated beneficiaries. By searching, browsing, and post processing the graph, funders can find the information they require to evaluate research impact (i.e. return on investment, RoI) at the level of grants and funding schemes, organized by disciplines and access rights, while scientists can find the Open Access versions of scientific trends of interest. The ISG is then made available for programmatic access via several APIs (Search HTTP APIs, OAI-PMH, and Linked Open Data), for search, browse and statistics consultation via the OpenAIRE portal, and soon for data sources with the

Literature Broker Service [8]. The graph data model is inspired by the standards for research data description and research management (e.g. organizations, projects, facilities) description provided by DataCite and CERIF, respectively. Its main entities are Results (datasets and publications), Persons, Organizations, Funders, Funding Streams, Projects, and Data Sources:

Results are intended as the outcome of research activities and may be related to Pro-jects. OpenAIRE supports two kinds of research outcome: *Datasets* (e.g. experimental data) and *Publications* (other research products, such as Patents and Software will be introduced). As a result of merging equivalent objects collected from separate data sources, a Result object may have several physical manifestations, called instances; instances indicate URL(s) of the payload file, access rights (i.e. open, embargo, restricted, closed), and a relationship to the data source that hosts the file (i.e. provenance).

Persons are individuals that have one (or more) role(s) in the research domain, such as authors of a Result or coordinator of a Project.

Organizations include companies, research centers or institutions involved as project partners or that are responsible for operating data sources.

Funders (e.g. European Commission, Wellcome Trust, FCT Portugal, Australian Research Council) are Organizations responsible for a list of Funding Streams (e.g. FP7 and H2020 for the EC), which are strands of investments. Funding Streams identify the strands of funding managed by a Funder and can be nested to form a tree of sub-funding streams (e.g. FP7-IDEAS, FP7-HEALTH).

Projects are research projects funded by a Funding Stream managed by a Funder. Investigations and studies conducted in the context of a Project may lead to one or more Results.

Data Sources, e.g. publication repositories, dataset repositories, journals, publishers, are the sources on the web from which OpenAIRE collects the objects populating the OpenAIRE graph. Each object is associated to the data source from which it was collected. More specifically, in order to give visibility to the contributing data sources, OpenAIRE keeps provenance information about each piece of aggregated information. Since de-duplication merges objects collected from different sources and inference enriches such objects, provenance information is kept at the granularity of the object itself, its properties, and its relationships. Object level provenance describes the origin of the object consisting of the data sources from which its different manifestations were collected. Property and relationship level provenance tells the origin of a specific property or relationship when inference algorithms derive these (e.g. algorithm name).

2.2 General Architecture

The OpenAIRE system depicted in Fig. 1 illustrates the system architecture from a high-level perspective, highlighting the data flows occurring within the subsystem, conceived as decoupled components. The aggregator is intended as the set of services responsible for the collection, validation, semantic and structural transformation of the metadata records, and the collection of the full-texts relative to the Open Access publications. The data provision pipeline consists of (i) a mapping layer used to populate the ISG, and (ii) the Action Manager Service, the implementation of a framework responsible for the management of the enrichments introduced to the ISG. They can be new nodes of the graph, property of existing nodes, or relationships among nodes. Such *Actions* and are organized in *Action Sets*, a logical container for all the *Actions* produced by a given process. The system associates dedicated Action Sets to the processes contributing at the ISG enrichment, such as deduplication, and the different mining algorithms described in the followings. All the components described in Fig. 1 are defined as decoupled subsystem, and in order to realize the data management workflows OpenAIRE relies on, the orchestration mechanism is provided by the D-NET software toolkit.

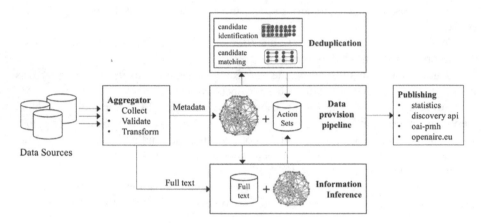

Fig. 1. High level architecture.

3   Content Aggregation Workflow

OpenAIRE aggregates metadata and full-texts according to a well-defined content acquisition policy: metadata records and full-texts of open access publications, metadata records of publications funded by EC projects or national funding schemes, metadata records about datasets that are outcomes of a funded research project or related to a publication already in the OpenAIRE ISG [12]. To ensure a minimum level of quality of the aggregation, OpenAIRE requires data sources to comply with the OpenAIRE guidelines. The OpenAIRE aggregation services support the OpenAIRE data managers in implementing the content acquisition policy and in supervising the content aggregation activity. This consists of (i) registration of a new data source, (ii) validation of its content with respect to the OpenAIRE guidelines, (iii) configuration of existing data sources in terms of access parameters and workflow scheduling, (iv) configuration of the rules for transforming input objects according to the OpenAIRE data model, (v) monitor and tracking the history of workflow executions.

3.1 Metadata Aggregation

Objects and relationships in the OpenAIRE ISG are extracted from information pack-ages, i.e. metadata records, collected from data sources of the following kinds:

Institutional or thematic repositories (aggregated 543). Information systems where scientists upload the bibliographic metadata and PDFs of their articles, because of either obligations from their organization or community practices (e.g. ArXiv, Europe PMC).

Open Access Publishers and journals (aggregated 6676). Information system of open access publishers or relative journals, which offer bibliographic metadata and PDFs of their published articles.

CRIS (aggregation starting by end of 2017). Information systems adopted by research and academic organizations to keep track of their research administration records and relative results; examples of CRIS content are articles or datasets funded by projects, their principal investigators, facilities acquired thanks to funding, etc.

Data archives (aggregated 59). Information systems where scientists deposit descriptive metadata and files about their research data (also known as scientific data, datasets, etc.); data archives are in some cases supported by research and academic organizations and in some cases supported by research communities and/or associations of publishers.

Aggregator services (aggregated 16). Information systems that, like OpenAIRE, collect descriptive metadata about publications or datasets from multiple sources in order to enable cross-data source discovery of given research products; aggregators tend to be driven by research community needs or to target the larger audience of researchers across several disciplines; examples are DataCite for all research data with DOIs as persistent identifiers, BASE for scientific publications, DOAJ for OA journals publications.

Entity Registries (aggregated 13). Information systems created with the intent of maintaining authoritative registries of given entities in the scholarly communication, such as OpenDOAR for the institutional repositories or re3data for the data repositories.

As of December 2016, OpenAIRE aggregates about 21 million of information pack-ages describing publications and datasets. OpenAIRE features three workflows for metadata aggregation: (i) for the aggregation from data sources whose content is known to comply with the OpenAIRE content acquisition policy, (ii) for the aggregation of content that is not known to be eligible according to the policy, (iii) for the aggregation of information packages from entity registries.

Workflow for OpenAIRE compliant data sources. This workflow is for data sources that comply with the OpenAIRE guidelines and thus it is executed for the majority of data sources. The workflow consists of three phases: collection, validation, and transformation. The collection phase collects information packages in form of XML metadata records from an OAI-PMH endpoint of the data source (as the OpenAIRE guidelines mandate) and stores them in a metadata store. The validation phase is an optional phase that can be enabled to validate the collected metadata records according to the OpenAIRE guidelines. Finally, the transformation phase transforms the collected records according to the OpenAIRE data model and stores them in another metadata store, ready to be read for populating the OpenAIRE ISG.

Workflow for data sources with unknown compliance. This workflow applies to data sources that are registered into OpenAIRE but are not known to be OpenAIRE compliant. This is the typical case for aggregators of data repositories (e.g. Datacite). According to the content acquisition policies, OpenAIRE can include a dataset into the ISG only if it has a link to an object (project or publication) already in the ISG. Therefore, OpenAIRE collects all metadata records and transforms them according to the OpenAIRE data model, but the records are marked so that the ISG population workflow will not use them for the creation of the ISG. In fact, the inference workflow (see Sect. 6) will use those objects and will add to the ISG only those that have been detected as eligible according to the content acquisition policy.

Workflow for entity registries. This workflow applies to data sources offering authoritative lists of entities. The workflow consists of two phases: collection and transformation. The collection phase collects information packages in the form of files in some machine-readable format (e.g. XML, JSON, CSV) via one of the supported exchange protocols (OAI-PMH, SFTP, FTP(S), HTTP, REST). The transformation phase transforms the packages according to the OpenAIRE data model and stores them into a metadata store ready to be read for populating the OpenAIRE ISG.

3.2   Full-Text Aggregation

The full-text aggregation workflow has a twofold goal: (i) collect and store the files described by publication metadata records, and (ii) extract their full-texts so that they can be used by full-text mining algorithms (Sect. 6). When collecting a file, it is crucial to preserve the association between the file and the corresponding metadata record. This association plays a crucial role in the inference workflow as it determines the possibility to correctly associate the inference results produced by mining a given full-text, to the corresponding object in the OpenAIRE ISG. While in case of metadata records describing publications the aggregation system can rely on well-established formats and exchange protocols such as Dublin Core [7] and OAI-PMH [8] respectively, in case of full-text files the aggregation system often needs to crawl the landing page referred in a metadata record to discover the link to the actual file. The full-text collection system is therefore designed to be extensible with new plugins, capable to manage specific html page structures or to be configured to recognize specific URL patterns.

The large majority of full-texts collected by the system are PDF files, a for-mat well suited for printing and human reading, but less tractable by machines. For this reason, the full-text collection workflow includes a final phase designed to automatically extract structured metadata from such PDF files using CERMINE [2]. The extracted full-texts are then stored in dedicated caches that are accessible by the OpenAIRE Information Inference System. As of December 2016, OpenAIRE collects about 4.5 million of full-text files responding to different formats: PDF, JATS, HTML.

4   Information Space Graph Population

An information package collected from a data source is a file in some machine-readable format (e.g. XML, JSON, CSV), which contains a data source-assigned identifier (mandatory) and information (e.g. properties) relative to one or more primary object. Beyond the primary object, an information package may contain information (but not necessarily the identifier) relative to other entities, called derived objects, which must be directly or indirectly associated with the primary object. Such association represents a link between the objects, which collectively form the OpenAIRE Information Space Graph. For example, a Dublin Core bibliographic metadata record describing a scientific article will yield one OpenAIRE result object (of Publication typology) and a set of OpenAIRE person objects (one per author) with relationships between them. In OpenAIRE we opted for representing the ISG with an adjacency list, as we believe this choice can cope well with a large class of scenarios. The storage system identified to persist the ISG is Apache HBase [17]. By supporting horizontal scalability and featuring full support for the Hadoop MapReduce framework, its columnar storage system is well suited to persist and process the adjacency list exploiting the parallelism offered by the MapReduce framework.

As of December 2016, the OpenAIRE ISG counts about 21 million publications, 600,000 projects, 30,000 datasets, 80,000 organizations, 16 million persons, 18,000 data sources and more than 90 million of relationships.

5   Information Space De-duplication

The OpenAIRE ISG possibly contains, by construction, different objects representing the same publication. In fact, metadata about one publication can be collected from different data sources. For the disambiguation of publications in the graph, OpenAIRE features a de-duplication system based on the GDup software [16] implementing a workflow in three phases: (i) candidate identification: considering the number of publication objects participating to the graph (about 21 million), matching all pairs of publications to identify the duplicates is by no means feasible: heuristics are needed to compare only publications that are likely to be duplicates; (ii) candidate matching: once the candidates are identified, their properties are compared and a similarity mark assigned; (iii) graph disambiguation: groups of duplicates are identified and, for each group, one unique publication is created to represent all members. In the following paragraphs, the three phases are explained in details with respect to the challenges posed by the de-duplication of publications. However, the system is configured to treat the same problem also for the organization entities, aggregated from different sources, and suffering from the same duplication issue.

5.1   Candidate Identification

Matching all possible pairs of 21 million publications is by no means tractable. To address this issue, candidate identification is the phase entitled of providing the heuristics and technological support necessary to avoid such "brute force" solution.

Candidate identification is solved using clustering techniques based on functions that associates to each publication one or more key values, out of its properties, to be used for clustering. The idea is that publications whose keys fall in the same cluster are more likely to be similar than across different clusters. This action narrows down the number of pairwise matches to perform within the clusters of publications, thereby reducing the complexity of the problem. Ideally, the definition of a good clustering function for de-duplication should avoid false negatives (i.e. making sure that obvious duplicates fall in the same cluster), avoid false positives (i.e. making sure that clearly different publications do not fall in the same cluster), and make the number of matches to be tractable for the technology at hand. The definition of a good clustering function for de-duplication of publications starts from the properties available in the publications metadata. From the analysis of the publication properties, the only always present and informative enough is the title. Clustering publications starting from their title may be done according to different strategies, which avoid or tolerate minor differences in the values, typically caused by typos or the partial or full presence of words. Some examples are: removing stop words, blank spaces, etc.; lower-casing all words; using combination of prefixes or postfixes of title words; using n-grams of relevant words; using hashing functions. Using any of these strategies has implications that depend on the features of titles in the ISG. For example, the heavy presence of short titles (consisting at most of a few short words) may find in the hashing function a better solution than using prefixes of words. On the other hand, the adoption of high performance technologies may allow for a greedier approach, which allows for more matches to be performed hence avoid false negatives.

The OpenAIRE ISG is very heterogeneous as both data sources and disciplines behind publications are of different kinds. As a consequence, the preferred approach is the one that combines the first letters of words (like an acronym) into a clustering key and the last letters of words into another clustering key. The approach is quite typo-safe and proves to exclude the majority of false negatives, on the other hand it includes false positives, which shall be excluded with the subsequent detailed similarity match.

5.2   Candidate Matching

The method described above is well known in record linkage literature as Blocking. It is well suited to address the de-duplication problem in large datasets [14, 15], and to further narrow the number of pairwise comparisons can be followed by the so-called Sliding Window method. The sliding window is based on the idea that publications in the cluster are ordered according to a defined function, to maximize the probability that similar publications are as close as possible. Publications in the cluster are then pairwise matched only if they are part of the same sliding window of length K. When all the publications have been matched, the sliding window is moved to the next element of the ordering and a new set of pairs is matched. Sliding windows introduce false negatives, since they exclude from the match publications in the same cluster, but control performance (especially in terms of memory and execution time) by setting an upper bound to the number of matches in each cluster. In order to define a solid candidate matching function, we need to identify which properties are most influential in the matching process, i.e. those that best contribute to establish publication equivalence introducing lower computational cost, while allowing clear cut decisions, and are often present in the publications. As in the previous phase of candidate identification, the title is again a good choice: it is present in (almost) all objects and consists of a relatively short text, which can be fast and reliably processed by known string matching functions. In general, if the titles of two publications are not similar "enough" (according to a given threshold) then no other property-to-property match may revise this decision. Conversely, sufficient similarity in titles (or even equivalence) alone is not enough as one of the following cases may occur: (i) very short titles, composed of few, commonly used words may lead to obvious equivalence; e.g. the title "Report on the project XYZ" may be recurrent, the only difference being the name "XYZ" of the project; (ii) recurrent titles; e.g. the title "Introduction" of some chapters is very common and introduces ambiguity in the decision, and (iii) presence of numbers in titles of different published works; e.g. the title "A Cat's perspective of the Mouse" is likely referring to a publication different from "A Cat's perspective of the Mouse v2", but not different from "A Cat perspective of the Mouse"; As a consequence, the decision process must be supported by further matches that may strengthen the final conclusion, possibly based on one or more of the following publication properties: author names, date of acceptance, abstract, language, subjects, PID. Those are all features that could contribute to the matching on different levels, however their contribution mostly depends on data quality. In OpenAIRE case, PIDs are significantly contributing to the matching process. Unluckily they are present only in a subpart of our publication objects (between 30–40%), but on the bright side they contribute allowing to take strong decisions on the equivalence of two publications: if two publications provide the same DOI they are indeed duplicates. Therefore, a similarity function, based on the availability of certain properties can take straightforward decisions on equivalence or difference between publications, while in other cases can only come up with a rank of confidence that depends on the availability and weights of the properties above.

5.3 Graph Disambiguation

Duplicate identification terminates providing a set of pairs of duplicate publications. In order to disambiguate the ISG, duplicates should be hidden and replaced by a "representative object" that links to the duplicates it represents (and vice versa). The representative publication becomes the hub of all incoming and outgoing relationships relative to the publications it hides. As a result, the graph is disambiguated but still keeps track of its original topology, hence allowing data managers to measure the duplicates percentage for a given data source. The graph disambiguation phase consists of two steps: duplicates grouping and duplicates merging. Grouping duplicates requires the identification of the connected components formed by the equivalence relationships identified by duplicate identification. Merging the groups of duplicates requires instead the creation of a representative publication for each connected component (or group of duplicates) and the propagation towards this new object of all incoming and outgoing relationships of the object it merges. Both actions have serious performance implications, which depend on the topology of the graph (e.g. fragmentation and density of graph, edge distance of publications in the graph, number of the duplicates). For example, the number of duplicated publications depends on the replication of the publication across different data sources, e.g. institutional repository of the author, thematic repository, and a number of aggregators, but it is in general not very high (e.g. co-authors, each depositing in their respective institutional repositories which are in turn harvested by OpenAIRE).

6 Information Inference Workflow

The OpenAIRE information inference system (IIS) is based on an instantiation of the Information Inference Framework (IIF) [1]. The IIS is responsible for enriching the ISG with new information produced by various types of data mining algorithms. The inference workflow has been designed to work on a snapshot of the entire ISG, in this sense the IIS is a stateless subsystem, whose outcome can be regenerated from scratch on each run. Each IIS inference algorithm is associated to an Action Set, i.e. a logical container that stores and versions the inference results. Such results consist of new objects (publications and datasets), new properties that enrich existing objects (such as document classification properties and citation lists), and semantically typed relationships among objects in the ISG. The IIS results versioning supported by Action Sets allows, in case of regressions in one or more mining algorithms, to reuse previously generated results without requiring to (i) rollback an algorithm to one of its previous versions, (ii) reintegrate it in the IIS, (iii) re-execute it to obtain consistent results. The inference workflow has been divided in two distinct phases: pre-processing and primary. The pre-processing phase supports the implementation of the OpenAIRE acquisition policy [12], according to which (i) a non-Open Access publication can be included into the ISG if it is funded by a project already in OpenAIRE; (ii) a dataset can be included into the ISG only if it is related to a publication already in OpenAIRE. To this aim the pre-processing phase includes the algorithms tailored to infer links between publications and projects, and between publications and datasets. The IIS main phase instead, operates over the ISG and executes all the full-text mining algorithms described in the Table 1 below, which summarizes the inference results produced in November 2016.

Table 1. Summary of IIS results, Nov 2016.

Phase	Description	Count
Pre-processing	Dataset references found in publications	88.592
Primary	Dataset references found in publications	78.086
	Publications enriched by protein data bank references	43.586
	Protein data bank references	196.462
Pre-processing	Project references found in publications	88.978
Primary	Project references found in publications	351.302
Primary	Citation references	15.319.346
	Publications enriched by citation references	2.632.059

(continued)

Table 1. (*continued*)

Phase	Description	Count
Primary	Software references	21.481
	Publications enriched by software references	15.592
Primary	Similarity references	164.602.477
Primary	Publications enriched by document classes ArXiv, Mesh, ACM	2.405.869

7 Information Publishing

The result of the workflows described in previous sections (content aggregation, ISG population, de-duplication and inference) are materialized by the data publishing workflow into four ISG projections: (i) a full-text index to support search and browse queries from the OpenAIRE Web portal and to expose subsets of the ISG on the OpenAIRE search API, (ii) a E-R database and a dedicated key-value cache for statistics, (iii) a NoSQL document storage in order to support OAI-PMH bulk export of subsets of the ISG in XML format, and finally (iv) a triple store in order to expose the ISG as LOD via a SPARQL endpoint. Every time the data publishing workflow executes, four new ISG projections are generated and persisted in a "pre-public status" before being accessible from the general public. The switch from pre-public to public, meaning that the currently accessible ISG projections and statistics will be dismissed and the new versions will take their place, is still manual for safety reasons. Whenever new pre-public ISG projections (pre-public ISG) are created, it is important to verify some constrains in order to evaluate whether the switch to public can be performed or some regressions in the overall data quality needs to be addressed first. Some constraints to be ensured regard the control of quality metrics extracted from the different projections of the ISG and may involve one or more projections (e.g. threshold checks, alignment of different ISG projections); other conditions regard instead the trend throughout time of such quality metrics (e.g. whether a certain trend is monotonic increasing/decreasing or not) and may involve one or more trends extracted from different projections.

The number of quality metrics that has to be extracted to ensure the quality of the ISG is large (about a hundred metrics) and cannot be covered here for the sake of brevity. However, it is important to notice that, since the processes for the generation of the four projections run in parallel, the aforementioned quality metrics will be evaluated in different time, as soon as it is possible; hence to enable a correct comparison among them a synchronization routine takes place in order to align them to the same "epoch".

The data publishing workflow of the OpenAIRE's production environment has been monitored since 2015 by a monitoring system implemented utilizing MoniQ [15], a data flow quality monitoring system resulting from an enhancement of the solution proposed in [10]. Despite the switch to public is still triggered manually, the collection and inspection of the quality metrics from ISG projections is performed automatically via MoniQ, hence dramatically decreasing the operational cost of the control phase.

8 Conclusions

The mission of OpenAIRE is to foster an Open Science e-infrastructure supporting the advancement of research by means of interlinking and disseminating scientific knowledge. Thanks to its growing network composed of different scholarly communication stakeholders (e.g. institutional repositories, data repositories, OA journals, libraries, and funders) and to its mature technological infrastructure, OpenAIRE makes openly accessible a rich Information Space Graph (ISG) where objects of the research life-cycle (e.g. publications, datasets, projects) are semantically linked to each other. The management of the OpenAIRE ISG is a complex operation realized by means of different types of workflows orchestrated by the D-NET framework: the content aggregation, the population of the ISG and its de-duplication, the mining of inferred knowledge from publications full-texts, the publication of the ISG and the monitoring of its quality metrics. The workflow automation represents an important advantage for the data managers work, who can focus on supervising the workflow executions, monitoring the data quality, and limiting their intervention only when necessary.

Acknowledgments. Research partially supported by the EC H2020 project Open-AIRE2020 (Grant agreement: 643410, Call: H2020-EINFRA-2014-1).

References

1. Kobos, M., Bolikowski, Ł., Horst, M., Manghi, P., Manola, N., Schirrwagen, J.: Information inference in scholarly communication infrastructures: the OpenAIREplus project experience. Procedia Comput. Sci. **38**, 92–99 (2014). doi:10.1016/j.procs.2014.10.016
2. Tkaczyk, D., Szostek, P., Fedoryszak, M., Dendek, P.J., Bolikowski, Ł.: CERMINE: automatic extraction of structured metadata from scientific literature. Int. J. Doc. Anal. Recognit. (IJDAR) **18**(4), 317–335 (2015)
3. Manghi, P., Bolikowski, L., Manola, N., Schirrwagen, J., Smith, T.: OpenAIREplus: the European scholarly communication data infrastructure. D-Lib Magaz. **18**(9), 1 (2012)
4. Manghi, P., Manola, N., Horstmann, W., Peters, D.: An infrastructure for managing EC funded research output – the OpenAIRE project. Int. J. Grey Lit. **6**, 31–40 (2010)
5. Manghi, P., Artini, M., Atzori, C., Bardi, A., Mannocci, A., La Bruzzo, S., Candela, L., Castelli, D., Pagano, P.: The D-NET software toolkit: a framework for the realization, maintenance, and operation of aggregative infrastructures. Program **48**(4), 322–354 (2014)
6. Weibel, S., Kunze, J., Lagoze, C., Wolf, M.: Dublin core metadata for resource discovery (No. RFC 2413) (1998)
7. Sompel, H.V.D., Nelson, M.L., Lagoze, C., Warner, S.: Resource harvesting within the OAI-PMH framework. D-Lib Magaz. **10**(12), 1082–9873 (2004)
8. Artini, M., Atzori, C., Bardi, A., La Bruzzo, S., Manghi, P., Mannocci, A.: The OpenAIRE literature broker service for institutional repositories. D-Lib Magaz. **21**(11), 3 (2015)
9. Príncipe, P., Schirrwagen, J.: OpenAIRE guidelines for data source managers: aiming for metadata harmonization. In: CERN Workshop on Innovations in Scholarly Communication (OAI9) (2015)
10. Mannocci, A., Manghi, P.: DataQ: a data flow quality monitoring system for aggregative data infrastructures. In: Fuhr, N., Kovács, L., Risse, T., Nejdl, W. (eds.) TPDL 2016. LNCS, vol. 9819, pp. 357–369. Springer, Cham (2016). doi:10.1007/978-3-319-43997-6_28

11. Kolb, L., Thor, A., Rahm, E.: Parallel sorted neighborhood blocking with mapreduce. arXiv preprint (2010). arXiv:1010.3053
12. McNeill, N., Kardes, H., Borthwick, A.: Dynamic record blocking: efficient linking of massive databases in mapreduce. In: Proceedings of the 10th International Workshop on Quality in Databases (QDB) (2012)
13. Jaro, M.A.: Advances in record-linkage methodology as applied to matching the 1985 census of Tampa, Florida. J. Am. Statist. Assoc. **84**(406), 414–420 (1989)
14. Fellegi, I.P., Sunter, A.B.: A theory for record linkage. J. Am. Statist. Assoc. **64**(328), 1183–1210 (1969)
15. Mannocci, A.: Data Flow Quality Monitoring in Data Infrastructures (2017)
16. Atzori, C.: gDup: an integrated and scalable graph deduplication system (2016)
17. George, L.: HBase: The Definitive Guide: Random Access to Your Planet-Size Data. O'Reilly Media, Inc., Sebastopol (2011)

Crowdsourcing for Film-Induced Tourism: An Approach to Geolocation

Daniel Zilio, Andrea Micheletti$^{(\boxtimes)}$, and Nicola Orio

Department of Cultural Heritage, University of Padua,
Piazza Capitaniato, 7, 35139 Padua, Italy
{daniel.zilio,andrea.micheletti,nicola.orio}@unipd.it

Abstract. This paper presents an initial proposal for the development of a crowdsourcing platform aimed at gathering information about audiovisual productions. Our goal is to foster the task of identifying movie excerpts that are filmed in a given location and of manually geolocating these excerpts. In this way it is possible to link audiovisual content to a geographical area. The information is used to populate a database system that is the core component for designing novel *film-induced tourism* offers. The task of identifying the locations of movies, TV and web series, spots and music videos is carried out by a community of non experts, using a crowdsourcing approach where participation and engagement are promoted by a *reputation* mechanism. The paper presents a multilevel approach to geolocation and discusses its motivations and initial results.

Keywords: Crowdsourcing · Film-induced tourism · Reputation · Geolocation

1 Introduction

Film-induced tourism regards the interest towards destinations motivated by a connection with audiovisual content. Film-induced tourism has been defined by Sue Becton as "visitation to sites where movies and TV programmes have been filmed as well as to tour to production studios, including film-related theme parks" [2]. It may be very helpful for destination management and destination marketing: it attracts new visitors and also tourists who have already seen the area for a different reason; it is largely independent of seasonal trends; it might convey tourists from overcrowded sites to new and less explored ones; and it can be suitable for a substantial re-branding of a certain area. A number of film-induced tourism related initiatives has been already undertaken at the international level by public and private bodies, which developed movie maps and movie tours or exploited the success of a particular movie as a tool for destination branding [5].

Visit Britain, the tourism office of the UK, was one of the first agencies to use movies for attracting tourists: since the nineties it designed movie tours and developed tools such as movie maps, that is maps representing locations of movies and TV series. Another interesting case is related to *The Lord of the*

© Springer International Publishing AG 2017
C. Grana and L. Baraldi (Eds.): IRCDL 2017, CCIS 733, pp. 108–116, 2017.
DOI: 10.1007/978-3-319-68130-6_9

Rings saga (Jackson, 2001–2003), which is still attracting masses of tourists in New Zealand, thanks to a thoughtful policy by the local government. Also Italy has a number of relevant cases, including *The Passion of the Christ* (Gibson, 2004) that doubled the number of tourists visiting Matera in Basilicata and a number of fictions such as *Inspector Montalbano* in Sicily, *Carabinieri* and *Don Matteo* in Umbria [9].

Tourism effectiveness can be improved through the access to a rich collection of structured data, which is the starting point for designing an exhaustive and attractive tourism offer and for developing ICT tourism tools. Unfortunately, the creation of a structured collection of multimedia items is a time-consuming task, which may require a huge quantity of individuals involved in a boring and unsatisfying activity. In this paper, we address this problem using crowdsourcing and reputation principles. Since these tools showed their effectiveness in a variety of fields, we believe that they can be a viable solution to the task of geolocating a large number of audiovisual excerpts.

2   Motivation

Our interest towards film-induced tourism applications dates back to 2014 [10]. The goal was the creation of a database to represent the relationship between movie excerpts and locations. The project had a double goal: promoting film-induced tourism and raising interest towards audiovisual productions, their language and their relation with the landscape. Although the focus was on locations in Padua and its Province, the in-depth description even for a relatively small geographical area showed to be a time-consuming task. One critical aspect was that a restricted number of users – e.g. scholars in film studies – were involved in providing all the information, from film analysis to location identification. Yet, only part of this information required the competences of trained experts while most of the time was spent in the less specialized task of annotating multimedia items with geographical information. These considerations suggested a crowdsourcing approach.

The term *crowdsourcing* was coined in 2006 [8] as a variant of the term (and the practice of) outsourcing: an institution asks that a given function is undertaken by an undefined, and possibly large, group of individuals. The term is applied to situations where individuals receive a payment for their work, but it is also used when participation is voluntary. Amazon Mechanical Turk[1] and Crowd-Flower[2] are well-known crowdsourcing platforms, which have been exploited also for multimedia research. Relevant research projects that are based on crowdsourcing include the segmentation of ancient Maya hieroglyph-blocks [4], the assessment of Internet video quality [7] and the teaching in cinematography field [1].

In order to encourage participation to a crowdsourcing activity, we envisage an interaction with a simple and intuitive interface, which implements a

---

[1] http://www.mturk.com.
[2] http://crowdflower.com.

reputation mechanism. The latter is likely to be part of a more complex process that is an investment in social capital. In this contest, "social capital is the actual or potential resources which are linked to a durable network of institutionalized relationships of mutual acquaintance or recognition" [3]. The quest for gaining a social capital requires a continuous search for consensus [12] and sharing with the group what we know is becoming a pleasure without the expectation of reciprocity.

This identification with a group, based on sharing just for the pleasure of it with no hidden agenda, is one major aspect of new digital media also because digital objects (e.g. recordings in a music digital library) can be replicated and shared an infinite number of times without losing quality. Moreover, sharing with the group both what we have and what we know is becoming a pleasure without the expectation of reciprocity, an openness based on selfless approach. This sense of belonging, which is shared also by on-line communities that have been called *emotion communities*, is balanced by an opposite drive: consumption and participation as a narcissistic act of exhibitionism in order to be socially recognized [6,11].

2.1   Crowdsourcing for Film-Induced Tourism

Our goal is to develop a web portal where registered users can contribute to data gathering in all the forms that can be useful for film-induced tourism applications. The main functions that will be available are the following.

- Discover, and insert into the database system, metadata related to multimedia content – from now on called *MOVIE* – that is relevant for film-induced tourism: movies, TV and web series, advertisements, documentaries, music videos.
- Identify the excerpts of a given MOVIE that are relevant for a given geographical area or a particular location. We define these excerpts *MOI*, from Moment Of Interest.
- Geolocate the MOIs, that is associate to the excerpts one or more geographical locations; geolocation can have different resolutions, from a wide area to a precise place with given spatial coordinates. We define these locations *SOI*, from Site of Interest as an extension of the well-known concept of Point Of Interest (POI).
- Vote the activities carried out by the other users, in particular geolocation, in order to create a community of users based on the concept of reputation.

The next section focuses on the geolocation task, providing a first case study.

3   Geolocation Model

We define a MOI m as a portion of a MOVIE defined by the time interval $[t_1, t_2]$ with $t_1 < t_2$. Considering the set M of the MOIs of a MOVIE, geolocation consists in the association of geographical information to each $m \in M$. Given U the set of users, the outcome of geolocation can be described by

$$\bar{v}_{u,m}^l = <\bar{s}_{u,m}^l, \bar{g}_{u,m}^l> \tag{1}$$

which represents the operation carried out by user $u \in U$ for MOI $m \in M$; l is the index of the SOI. Although it is possible that two different geographical areas are relevant for the same movie excerpt, for instance because they are the result of film editing, for simplicity of notation we assume that a single SOI is associated to a MOI and hence we omit the index l in the following discussion. The outcome of geolocation can thus be represented in two, not exclusive, forms:

- $\bar{s}_{u,m}$ represents the symbolic description of a geographical area, such as the name of a region, a province, a city, and so on.
- $\bar{g}_{u,m}$ represents the geographical coordinates, usually in the form of latitude and longitude. Symbolic information is strictly required, at least defining a wide area such a country or a region, geographical information is not mandatory.

Let us define V as the set of all insertions for a given SOI, and $\bar{v}_{o,m}$ the ground truth. In this case, we assume that the ground truth can be obtained by an expert in film-induced tourism who has a perfect knowledge about both the MOVIE and the SOIs. In our context, the ground truth represents the optimal position for a tourist to fully appreciate the connection between the audiovisual content and the physical location. We assume that the ground truth is described with the maximum available accuracy for associating a SOI to a MOI. The goal is to find $\bar{v}^* \in V$ that minimizes the distance with the ground truth, providing that each user of the system can provide an incomplete, imprecise or even incorrect estimate of a SOI. Thus, a distance function needs to be defined between $\bar{v}$.

The choice of the distance function depends on how $\bar{v}$ is represented. The computation of a distance between two SOIs that include geographical information $\bar{g}$ is straightforward but, in a crowdsourcing environment, the requirement of providing precise geographical coordinates may discourage users, who may not be able to geolocate MOI at this level of detail. Yet, users may contribute some relevant information, because they are aware of the geographical area, the city, or even the neighbors of a MOI.

Distance Between Symbolic Descriptions. In order to overcome this problem, we propose to use the symbolic representation $\bar{s}$ of a SOI. Formally, the insertion made by user u about MOI m is defined as

$$\bar{s}_{u,m} = <\alpha_{u,m}^0, \alpha_{u,m}^1, ..., \alpha_{u,m}^V> \tag{2}$$

while the ground truth for MOI m is defined as

$$\bar{s}_{o,m} = <\alpha_{o,m}^0, \alpha_{o,m}^1, ..., \alpha_{o,m}^N> \tag{3}$$

where elements have an increasing level of accuracy, and $V \leq N$ that is the information provided by a user is at most as accurate as the ground truth.

A practical example may help describing the approach. Let us consider as MOI m the first four minutes of the MOVIE *Galileo* (Cavani, 1968), that have been filmed inside the Anatomical Theatre of the Palazzo Bo, the main building of the University of Padua, located in Via VIII Febbraio. Two SOIs, with different level of detail, could be inserted by users u and w:

$$\bar{s}_{u,m} = \langle \textit{Italy, Veneto, Province of Padua} \rangle$$

$$\bar{s}_{w,m} = \langle \textit{Italy, Veneto, Province of Padua, Padua, Via VIII Febbraio} \rangle$$

where the second represents also the ground truth, which has the highest level of accuracy according to film scholars. It is important to note that the different levels need to be consistent, but this can be obtained through the user interface that computes whether the insertion corresponds to a real location or not.

We propose to measure the difference between two symbolic descriptions through a binary similarity. Starting from α_0 the two arrays are paired until a difference is found or it is reached the end of the shortest one: the longest the common subsequent the highest the similarity. Moreover, it is possible to give a weight ρ^k to each level of α^k, with $\rho^0 \leq \rho^1 \leq \cdots \leq \rho^N$ in order to penalize very short common subsequences. A conceptual algorithm that outputs the difference between SOIs $\bar{s}_{u,m}$ and $\bar{s}_{w,m}$, with respective length Lu and Lw is the following:

```
Δ ← MAX_DIST // maximum distance between SOIs
L ← min{Lu, Lw}
for i ← 0 to L do
    if α^i_{u,m} = α^i_{w,m} then
        Δ ← 1/ρ^m
        i←i+1
    else
        return Δ
    end if
end for
return Δ
```

3.1 SOI Insertion

Users are completely free to insert new SOIs, and each new contribution is also managed as a reinforcement of similar records that are already present in the system. For instance in the case of MOI m, user u can insert the array $\bar{s}_{u,m} = \langle \alpha^0_{u,m}, \dots, \alpha^V_{u,m} \rangle$. If another user w has already inserted array $\bar{s}_w = \langle \alpha^0_{w,m}, \dots, \alpha^N_{w,j} \rangle$, with $N \geq M$ and with the same first M elements, his/her contribution automatically obtains a reinforcement. For instance, if for the first four minutes of *Galileo* a user already inserted the array $\bar{s}_{w,m}$ that has an accuracy until the street number, the insertion of $\bar{s}_{u,m}$ with same location but a lower accuracy gives automatically a positive weight to $\bar{s}_{w,m}$. In case of SOIs having the geographical component $\bar{g}$ they are consider equal only if the distance is within a given threshold. Since we want to encourage participation, the user is asked to give his/her contribution also by voting the quality of the existing contributions, without inserting new SOIs.

3.2   Evaluation of Users' Insertions

As described in Sect. 2, users need to be motivated to contribute to geolocation and in general to the different crowdsourcing tasks. This can be based on the fact that each contribution is evaluated by other users, providing an indirect judgment about user's knowledge about audiovisual content and the geographical areas. Users participate to the activity to gain reputation as experts in the subject. We propose the following evaluation mechanism.

Starting from the SOI $\bar{v}_{w,m} = <\bar{s}_{w,m}, \bar{g}_{w,m}>$, each user $u \in U$ with $u \neq w$ can provide a negative, neutral, or positive judgment to all the elements that constitute $\bar{v}_{w,m}$. Being $\bar{g}_{w,m}$ the most accurate description, a positive judgement is inherited by all the elements of $\bar{s}_{w,m}$. On the contrary, a negative judgement to any of the α^i of $\bar{s}_{w,m}$ is propagated to all $\alpha^k \in \bar{s}$, with $k < s$, and to $\bar{g}_{w,m}$ if present. The possibility to provide a partial judgement to a SOI allows us to highlight the potentially correct symbolic components, encouraging the community to cooperate inserting new SOIs that refine existing and incomplete information. Using again the example of the movie *Galileo*, if $\bar{s}_{w,m} = \langle$*Italy, Veneto, Province of Padua, Padua, Via VIII Febbraio*$\rangle$ receives positive judgements to the component *Province of Padua* and negative judgements to *Padua*, it is likely that the real location is within the province but outside the city of Padua.

Judgements are weighted by user's reputation, which in turns depends on the number positive and negative judgements received by the user. It is likely that reputation can be split in *general reputation*, which takes into account the general reliability of a user, and in *local reputation*, which is related to the ability of a user to carry out correct and precise identification in a given geographical area. The way reputation is computed is part of our future work.

3.3   Experiments

We are carrying out a first test of the proposed approach, to verify the feasibility of a crowdsourcing approach. We developed a web portal that is currently used by about 100 undergraduate students of *Design and Management of Cultural Tourism*, who do not have a background in film studies. Participation is not mandatory, although students were encouraged to carry out the activities in order to gain points which could be added to the final grade for the course in *Computer Tools for the Organization of Tourism Offer*. We assigned the following tasks, to be completed in subsequent steps.

1. Identify and insert in the system audiovisual productions that have been filmed in Veneto, specifying the source of information and describing the reason of the insertion.

2. Confirm the insertions made by other students, also in this case describing the reason of the confirmation (to this end, the reason of the insertion was not available to other students).
3. Geolocate on GoogleMaps interface the MOIs of the already inserted movies, specifying start and end time of the MOI; geolocation was possible only for audiovisual content available on YouTube.

• Figure 1 shows a screenshot of the portal homepage. Figure 2 shows the web interface, divided in three vertical parts, that is used for geolocation. In the first part, the user can insert a YouTube URL and select the starting and ending points of the MOI; in the second one, the user geolocates the MOI using the Google Maps interface; and in the last part a summary of the current activity is provided.

The first two tasks started together, while the third one started three weeks later. Students inserted 125 audiovisual productions – including movies, TV and web series – and provided 108 confirmations of already inserted productions. After one week from the beginning of task three students inserted 60 SOIs.

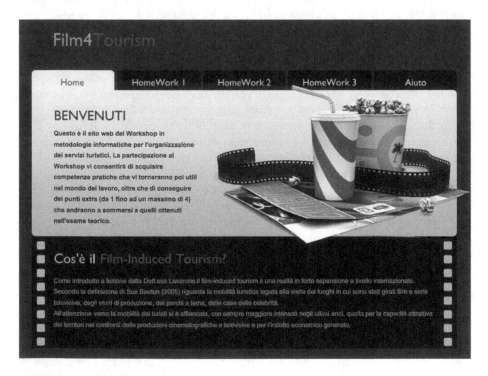

Fig. 1. Screenshot of the homepage of student's workshop on film-induced tourism

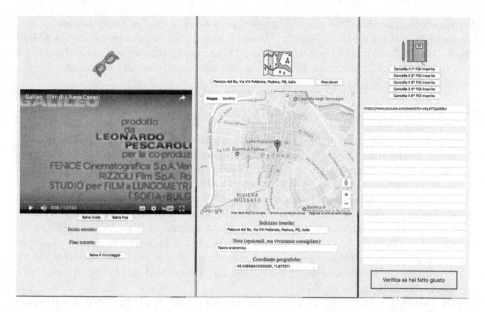

Fig. 2. Screenshot of the geolocation page of student's workshop on film-induced tourism

The reputation mechanism has not been introduced yet, mainly because our primary goal was to test the effectiveness of the web interface. Nevertheless the initial results are encouraging and we believe that the crowdsourcing mechanism can be extended also to general users. Students feedback was very important for the improvement of the system interface and to refine the model described in Sect. 3.

4   Conclusions and Future Developments

This paper described the main ideas behind the design and development of a crowdsourcing portal aimed at gathering information for film-induced tourism. Among the different tasks, the geolocation of audiovisual excerpts plays a central role for film-induced applications and it thus should be carried out reliably also when non expert users are involved. This goal can be achieved by reinforcing user engagement through the concept of reputation, that is the social status of being acknowledged as an expert by a social community. The case study presented in Sect. 3.3 showed that the approach is feasible: the information gathered during this initial step are the basis for the development of the crowdsourcing portal that will be starting point for the development of the crowdsourcing platform.

Our future activities will address the complete definition of the reputation mechanism. Moreover, we envisage to include a number of gamification tools to increment users' involvement in the crowdsourcing effort.

Acknowledgements. The research project presented in this paper is funded by the European Social Fund (FSE projects, Veneto Region). We thank our colleagues Farah Polato, Giulia Lavarone of the Department of Cultural Heritage and Sandro Savino of the Department of Information Engineering, both at the University of Padua.

References

1. Bares, W., Schwartz, D.: Film ties: crowd-sourced teaching of cinematography using intelligent example galleries. In: Proceedings of the 19th ACM Conference on Computer Supported Cooperative Work and Social Computing Companion (CSCW 2016 Companion), pp. 229–232, NY, USA. ACM, New York (2016)
2. Beeton, S.: Film-Induced Tourism. Channel View Publications, Clevedon (2005)
3. Bourdieu, P.: The forms of capital. In: Richardson, J.C. (ed.) Handbook of Theory and Research for the Sociology of Education. Greenwood, New York (1985)
4. Can, G., Odobez, J.M., Gatica-Perez, D.: Is that a jaguar? Segmenting ancient maya glyphs via crowdsourcing. In: Proceedings of the 2014 International ACM Workshop on Crowdsourcing for Multimedia (CrowdMM 2014), pp. 37–40, NY, USA. ACM, New York (2014)
5. Di Cesare, F., Rech, G.: Le produzioni cinematografiche, il turismo, il territorio, pp. 45–88. Carrocci, Roma (2007)
6. Fabris, G.: La società post-crescita: consumi e stili di vita. Egea, Milano (2010)
7. Figuerola Salas, O., Adzic, V., Shah, A., Kalva, H.: Assessing internet video quality using crowdsourcing. In: Proceedings of the 2nd ACM International Workshop on Crowdsourcing for Multimedia (CrowdMM 2013), pp. 23–28, NY, USA. ACM, New York (2013)
8. Howe, J.: The rise of crowdsourcing. Wired Magaz., June 2006
9. Lavarone, G.: Cinema, media e turismo. Esperienze e prospettive teoriche del film-induced tourism. Padova University Press, Padova (2016)
10. Lavarone, G., Orio, N., Polato, F., Savino, S.: Modeling the concept of movie in a software architecture for film-induced tourism. In: Calvanese, D., De Nart, D., Tasso, C. (eds.) IRCDL 2015. CCIS, vol. 612, pp. 116–125. Springer, Cham (2016). doi:10.1007/978-3-319-41938-1_13
11. Micheletti, A.: Motivating and involving users through gamification: a proposal. In: Agosti, M., Bertini, M., Ferilli, S., Marinai, S., Orio, N. (eds.) IRCDL 2016. CCIS, vol. 701, pp. 20–30. Springer, Cham (2017). doi:10.1007/978-3-319-56300-8_3
12. Wellman, B., Wortley, S.: Different strokes from different folks: community ties and social support. Am. J. Sociol. **96**(3), 558–588 (1990)

Cultural Heritage

Dating the Historical Documents from Digitalized Books by Orthography Recognition

Darko Brodić[1][(✉)] and Alessia Amelio[2]

[1] Technical Faculty in Bor, University of Belgrade, V.J. 12, 19210 Bor, Serbia
dbrodic@tfbor.bg.ac.rs
[2] DIMES, University of Calabria, Via Pietro Bucci Cube 44, 87036 Rende, CS, Italy
aamelio@dimes.unical.it

Abstract. This paper introduces a new method for automatically dating Serbian and Croatian historical documents. It is based on the concept that the documents in a certain script or language evolving in different historical periods are characterized by differences in orthography rules. Accordingly, we propose three stages of script coding, texture analysis and classification for capturing such a difference. Hence, the input document is transformed into a sequence of numerical codes, each representing an intensity value, determining an image. Then, texture analysis extracts features from the image to create a feature vector. Finally, it is classified for orthography recognition. Results obtained on two databases of historical documents in angular Glagolitic script and Slavonic-Serbian and Serbian languages extracted from digitalized books demonstrate the efficacy of the proposed method.

Keywords: Orthography recognition · Historical documents · Image processing · Digital book · Classification

1 Introduction

Digital libraries include the creation of digital counterparts of the original historical analog books and document materials. This digitization process has a few benefits: (i) digital preservation of the original analog material, (ii) easy way of accessing it through the Internet, (iii) creation of collections, which are previously not known, and (iv) additional potential of researching historical materials.

Documents are written in a certain language, incorporating different orthography rules. Orthography as a word has a background from the Greek words ($\acute{o}\rho\theta\acute{o}\zeta$) and ($\gamma\rho\acute{\alpha}\phi\epsilon\iota\nu$), which means "correct writing". Hence, it is deeply connected to the written language. Among the others, it takes care of capitalization, emphasis, hyphenation, punctuation and word breaks style [13]. In this way, it includes all methods and rules of correct writing. Accordingly, it is a sub-part of natural language processing. On the other side, linguistics sees the orthography as the methodology of writing a language. It considers the orthography as a standardization, which is given as a spectrum of conventions, i.e. set of rules. Some

© Springer International Publishing AG 2017
C. Grana and L. Baraldi (Eds.): IRCDL 2017, CCIS 733, pp. 119–131, 2017.
DOI: 10.1007/978-3-319-68130-6_10

languages incorporate non-consistent orthography such as the English language, while the others such as Serbian language have remarkably consistent orthography. In the example of the Serbian language, it means that one letter in the written language has the equivalence of one sound in the spoken language. Also, it is worth noting that any language during a certain historical period has been evolved under different influences. Accordingly, its orthography was changed, too. Sometimes, the orthographic rules were so changed that they have acknowledged the new historical era of the language. In such cases, the differentiation between the orthographic rules can be used to correctly evaluate the historical period of the analyzed document or book. Basically, the differentiation of documents by their orthography can, in many cases, clearly identify documents' dating and printing origin.

In previous works about orthography, authors mainly tried to establish a link between the discrimination of some tokens during the transformation of the language [18] or among different languages [4]. Hence, they used typical linguistic tools like bi-grams, tri-grams, probabilistic mapping and variation in tokens and vocabulary [24]. The main limitation of these works is that they analyze orthography changes in the same language or among different languages. In this study, we overcome this limitation by proposing a new method for orthography discrimination inside the same language and during the evolution of the written language. In this way, we propose a system for recognition of the historical period of the Serbian and Croatian documents according to the use of the orthographic rules present inside the document. In such a context, the document is analyzed and further processed in its digital format, which is essential for the cultural heritage preservation. To the very best of our knowledge, it is the first time that a similar approach has been introduced in the literature. For evaluating the proposed approach, we conduct two quite different experiments: (i) on digitalized printed documents written by angular Glagolitic script dated between XIV and XIX century, which are written in Croatian language, and (ii) on digitalized printed documents written by Cyrillic script dated between XVIII and XIX century, which are written in Slavonic-Serbian and Serbian languages. In the first experiment of the angular Glagolitic script, the writing of the same script is changed, i.e. evolved over time. Hence we are talking about script evolving rules based on the orthography. In the second experiment, the change of the orthography is used as a change of the language and not only of script writing rules. Basically, the transformation of Slavonic-Serbian to modern Serbian language is established by more means: (i) change of the Cyrillic alphabet (differences in letters), (ii) change of language, i.e. rapid evolvement of the language, and (iii) change of the orthographic rules.

Printed medieval documents were written in the angular Glagolitic script by the Croatian recension of the Church Slavonic language. Angular Glagolitic was mainly used in the regions along the east, i.e. Croatian side of Adriatic coast. Up to XV century, the holy books were written by hand printing. After inventing printing machine by Gutenberg, the printed books spread over Europe. Up to 1561, the printing offices were opened along Croatian Adriatic coast, i.e. in

Senj (from 1491 to 1508) and Rijeka (from 1530 to 1531) [16]. Accordingly, many books were printed by the angular Glagolic script, but using the old orthographic rules [2]. These rules incorporate the writing of capital letters as descendent ones, which is typical for hand printed Glagolitic medieval books. Hence, the use of the old Glagolitic orthography was linked with the printing offices in Rijeka, Senj, Kosinje or Venice, if the editors were Croats. Outside Croatia, the Glagolitic books were mainly printed in Venice, Rome [20], Urach, Tubingen and Prague [3] around and after 1535. However the editors, who were mainly Italians, did not know the old orthography rules. Instead, they used Latin-based orthography in Glagolitic books. This means the use of capital letters as ascending ones. Hence, the change of orthography rules was clearly limited by the historical period before and after 1535.

Slavonic-Serbian language was the literary language used in Habsburg Empire by the Serbs. In the beginning, the Habsburg Empire tried to assimilate the Serbian population by changing their culture and heritage. Accordingly, it wanted to change the Serbian alphabet from Cyrillic to Latin one. Serbian Church opposed to this change by asking help to Russian Empire. Consequently, in that period, all books, especially liturgical ones, as well as literary, were printed in the Russo-Slavonic language. During the XVIII century, the writers began to blend Russo-Slavonic with Serbian language resulting with a mixed language, which is called Slavonic-Serbian. In 1818, Vuk Stefanović Karadžić with the help of Jernej Kopitar and Sava Mrkalj concluded his book Serbian Dictionary in Vienna. This book was the beginning of reforming the Slavonic-Serbian language with its old orthography according to the widespread modern language of the Serb population. It reformed the Slavonic-Serbian language by Cyrillic alphabet using strict phonemic principles. In this way, the modern Serbian language was distanced from Slavonic-Serbian language in different alphabet and new orthography rules. In the meantime, the last notable work in Slavonic-Serbian was published in 1825 [19]. After that, the modern Serbian language with the new orthography style spread in printed books.

To identify orthography changes defining old and new orthography, the proposed approach uses our previous method for language and script discrimination [5–8]. Then, obtained results are subjected to classification by Naive Bayes. In both examples, recognition of different orthography rules used in the digital documents can distinctively identify the printing date of these documents.

The paper is organized as follows. Section 2 introduces the methodology for the orthography differentiation. Section 3 presents the experiments. Section 4 gives the results of the experiments and makes a discussion. Section 5 draws conclusions and outlines future work directions.

2   Methodology

The methodology for orthography recognition is composed of the following steps: (i) script coding, (ii) texture analysis, and (iii) classification.

In script coding, a document is transformed into a sequence of four numerical codes. It is based on character classification in four script types according to their height in the text line area. Hence, the obtained coded text is considered as a 1-D image, where each code represents an intensity level. Then, the texture analysis is employed on the 1-D image for feature extraction. It performs successfully because characters height and their disposition in the text may change according to the orthography rules. Codes envelope the height information. Linear patterns of codes detected by texture analysis capture the characters disposition. For this reason, extracted features exhibit a discriminant capability. At the end, the document represented as a feature vector is classified as given in old or new orthography by Naive Bayes approach. Next, we describe the main steps of the method.

2.1 Script Coding

Script coding represents the first and crucial stage in the proposed methodology. It converts each letter according to its position in the text-line into different script types. The given letters are mapped to a certain script type based on their horizontal energy profiles. In this way, all letters are grouped into: (i) the base letters, (ii) the ascender letters, (iii) the descendent letters, and (iv) the full letters [29]. Figure 1(a) illustrates this grouping.

| (a) | (b) | (c) |

Fig. 1. The basis of the script mapping: (a) initial text, (b) script coding, and (c) transformation into image

Furthermore, this mapped text is coded. The coding is performed as follows: (i) the base letter to 0, (ii) the ascender letter to 1, (iii) the descendent letter to 2, and (iv) the full letter to 3 [7,8]. Figure 1(b) shows the coding. In this way, the initial text is coded into a string corresponding to a combination of the set of codes {0, 1, 2, 3}. The final coded text can be seen as an image $\mathbf{I}(1,j)$ with the pixel values taken from the set {0, 1, 2, 3}. Figure 1(c) shows the transformation to the image. The given transformation enables the reduction of variables from the number of letters in the alphabet to 4. Still, because of the specific transformation, additional information is added such as differentiating between capital and small letters. Furthermore, the transformation of coded text into a 1-D image allows a wide variety of additional analyses to be performed.

Orthography. In the following, we present an example of orthography differentiation by using script coding. Old style Glagolitic orthography implicates the writing of the capital letters as descendent letters. On the contrary, new Glagolitic orthography follows the rule of writing a capital letter as ascender one like in Latin alphabet. Coding will be performed on the old style orthography used in hand printed and printed Glagolitic documents as well as on the new style Glagolitic orthography used in the newer printed Glagolitic books. Figure 2 illustrates hand printed and printed excerpts in old orthography and their coding. Figure 3 depicts an excerpt using the new orthography style and its coding. Figure 4 shows the distribution of the script types of the hand printed and printed Glagolitic documents written with the old orthography rules, and printed Glagolitic document written with the new orthography rules. The graphical results show that differentiation between old and new orthography in Glagolitic documents is clearly visible at the level of use of base, descendent and full letters.

On the contrary, Slavonic-Serbian and Serbian languages are related to different alphabet, different evolving language and according to that, different words in use.

(a) hand printed (dated 1368)

```
000 001 10 10 30 21102 03
100000 3 3000200 10 222 2000
100 0201200 000 3 20101 01
0010 0 100
0022 00000
01000 010 100
00000 0020000000
00 00000 000010
000 0000013010
000000 010000
30 000 30010 030000 0103
101 03010000 300000 3
20010 0100000010 3020 00
```

(b) coding

(c) printed (dated 1493)[2]

```
31000 0100
30100 010 010100100 00200100 0300
0 0000 000 012100 2010 0030 00 301000
300000000 120 0010001011110 200 3 310
310000000 220 0100 0101 22 000
30001 1210100001201010 3101 0 0101
```

(d) coding

Fig. 2. Glagolitic hand printed and printed excerpts written in the old orthography and their equivalent coding

(a) printed (dated 1862)[3]

```
100 20010000 0000001000 1010 000000
310 000 010020000 000100000 000001000
100 0 0001002 1000 000000 00 01001
00100
10000 0100000 00 200000
```

(b) coding

Fig. 3. Glagolitic printed excerpt written in the new orthography and its equivalent coding

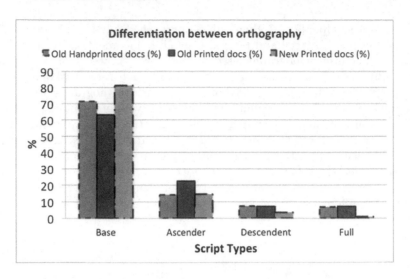

Fig. 4. Distribution of the script types in old and new Glagolitic orthography

2.2   Texture Analysis

Texture analysis is employed on the 1-D image obtained by the script coding phase, and representing the codified document. Texture envelopes information of spatial positioning of intensities in the image, determining the features. Two typical methods adopted for texture feature extraction are: (i) run-length statistics, and (ii) (A)LBP. Texture features extracted from these methods are the input to the classification algorithm.

Run-length statistics is based on the concept of run. It is a sequence of consecutive pixels of the same intensity in a certain direction of the texture. Let $\mathbf{I}$ be the image with M intensity levels, and N be the maximum run length. A matrix $\mathbf{p}$ is computed from the runs in $\mathbf{I}$ along an established direction. Position (i, j) of $\mathbf{p}$ contains the number of runs of intensity level i and of run length j. From matrix $\mathbf{p}$, 11 features are computed: (i) Short run emphasis (SRE), (ii) Long run emphasis (LRE), (iii) Gray-level non-uniformity (GLN), (iv) Run length non-uniformity (RLN), (v) Run percentage (RP) [17], (vi) Low gray-level run emphasis (LGRE) and (vii) High gray-level run emphasis (HGRE) [10], (viii) Short run low gray-level emphasis (SRLGE), (ix) Short run high gray-level emphasis (SRHGE), (x) Long run low gray-level emphasis (LRLGE), and (xi) Long run high gray-level emphasis (LRHGE) [15].

Figure 5 shows a 1-D image with the corresponding numerical codes, and the associated run-length matrix $\mathbf{p}$. For example, element at position $(1, 1)$ has a value of 11, which indicates that the number of runs, i.e. consecutive pixels, of intensity level 1 and length 1 in the 1-D image is 11.

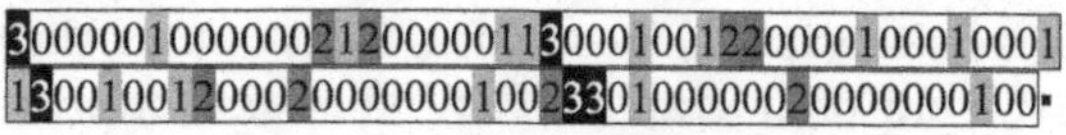

3000001000000212200000113000100122000010001000113001001200020000000100233010000002000000010 0■

(a) 1-D image pattern (a unique sequence, ■ marks the end of the text)

$p(i,j)$ j

i

	1	2	3	4	5	6	7
0	1	5	4	1	2	2	2
1	11	2	0	0	0	0	0
2	6	1	0	0	0	0	0
3	3	1	0	0	0	0	0

(b) run-length matrix

Fig. 5. Run-length matrix computed on 1-D image

For each center pixel of the 1-D image, Local Binary Pattern (LBP) examines its neighbor pixels (left and right pixels) to find if their intensity is above or below the center pixel intensity and thresholds them according to this intensity. Then, it creates binary numbers and generates a histogram of the corresponding decimal labels for the overall image [23]. However, LBP determines in our case only 4 different elements, which are not enough to be employed for discrimination [22]. Consequently, the extension to Adjacent LBP (ALBP) is performed [9]. Considering the two horizontal pixels in the neighborhood (LBP(+)), a binary number is created from LBP(+) and adjacent LBPs(+) are combined to create ALBP. This combination creates 4-bit binary numbers between '0000' and '1111' representing 16 features [22].

Figure 6 shows the thresholding procedure for two center pixels of intensity levels 1 and 2 (in gray) of the 1-D image (on the top left), the adjacent LBP(+) combination determining the 4-bit binary number '0111' (on the top right), and the resulting histogram of the decimal labels computed for the overall image, realizing the 16 features (on the bottom).

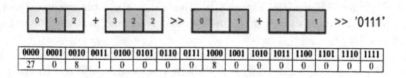

0000	0001	0010	0011	0100	0101	0110	0111	1000	1001	1010	1011	1100	1101	1110	1111
27	0	8	1	0	0	0	0	8	0	0	0	0	0	0	0

Fig. 6. ALBP features computed from 1-D image

3   Experiment

The experiment includes two different parts of the orthography test.

In the first part of the experiment, the text written in the Glagolitic script by old and new orthography style is analyzed. It is performed on a database of thirteen Glagolitic printed documents. Five out of thirteen documents are written using the old orthography. They are text excerpts from pages of the book entitled *Missale Romanum Glagolitice* dated from 1483 [20,21]. Figure 7(a) shows a sample excerpt from the book. It represents the first printed Glagolitic book and the most beautiful of all printed Glagolitic books at all. Eight of thirteen documents are written in the new orthography. Six of them are text excerpts from pages of the book entitled *The Confession and Knowledge of the True Christian Faith* dated from 1564 [20]. The last two documents are text excerpts from pages of the book entitled *Foundations of the Old Slavic language* dated from 1862 [3]. Figure 7(b) illustrates a sample excerpt from the book.

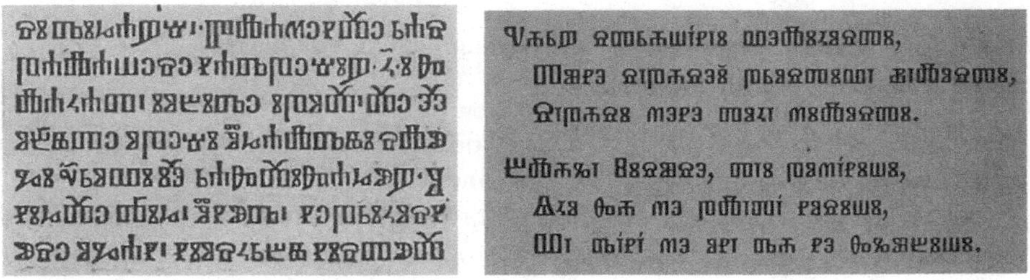

(a)   (b)

Fig. 7. Documents written in: (a) old Glagolitic and (b) new Glagolitic orthography

The second part of the experiment covers the documents written in Slavonic-Serbian and Serbian languages. A database of fifteen documents is analyzed. Five out of fifteen documents are written in Slavonic-Serbian language, while ten out of fifteen documents are written in modern Serbian language. The documents written in Slavonic-Serbian language are text excerpts from pages of the book entitled *Fisika* by Atanasije Stojković dated from 1802 [27]. Figure 8(a) shows a sample excerpt from the book *Fisika*. The rest of the ten documents is a collection of text excerpts from pages of the book *Zabavnik* dated from 1826 by Vuk Stefanović Karadžić. Figure 8(b) illustrates a sample excerpt from this book. These documents are written in so-called reformed Serbian language, i.e. modern one [26].

Historical Glagolitic books are available in their digital format at National Library of Zagreb[1]. On the contrary, serbian books are collected in their digital format at National Digital Library of Serbia[2]. Hence, documents have been selected from the digital books and processed in digital format.

---

[1] http://stari.nsk.hr/home.aspx?id=24.

[2] http://digitalna.nb.rs/.

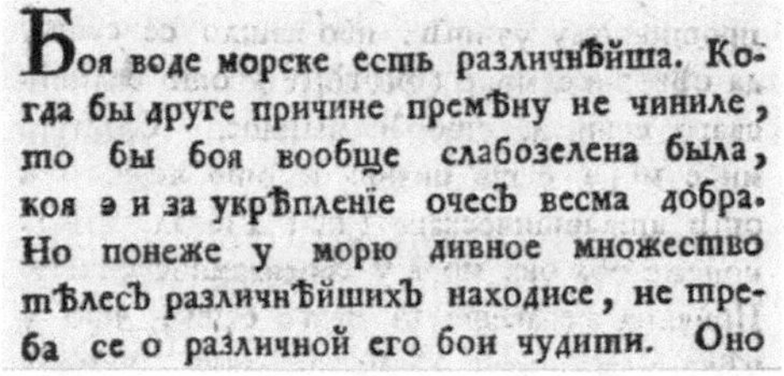

Боя воде морске есть различнѣйша. Ко-
гда бы друге причине премѣну не чиниле,
то бы боя вообще слабозелена была,
коя э и за укрѣпленїе очесь весма добра.
Но понеже у морю дивное множество
тѣлесь различнѣйшихь находисе, не тре-
ба се о различной его бои чудити. Оно

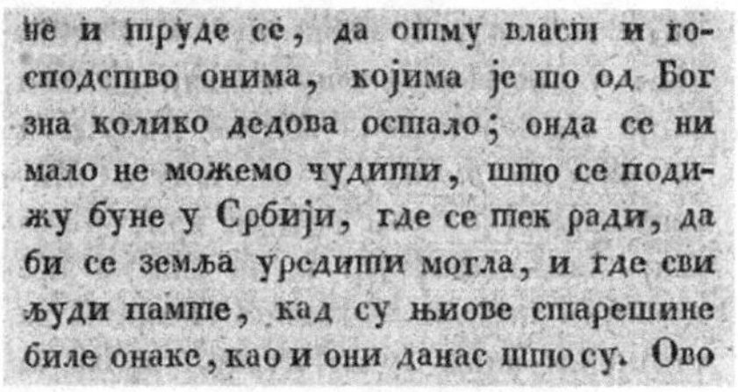

ће и труде се, да отиму власти и го-
сподство онима, којима је то од Бог
зна колико дедова остало; онда се ни
мало не можемо чудити, тито се поди-
жу буне у Србији, где се тек ради, да
би се земља уредити могла, и где сви
људи памте, кад су њиове старешине
биле онаке, као и они данас тито су. Ово

(a)   (b)

Fig. 8. Documents written in (a) Slavonic-Serbian and (b) Serbian

4   Results and Discussion

Experiment has been performed in Matlab R2015a on a laptop computer with
Quad-Core CPU at 2.2 GHz, 16 GB RAM and UNIX operating system. Our aim
is to recognize the historical period of the digitalized printed documents.

Firstly, each document in the Serbian and Croatian databases is represented
as a feature vector derived from the aforementioned feature coding. In particular,
documents in Serbian database are represented as 27-dimensional feature vectors
of run-length (the first 11 features) and ALBP (the last 16 features) statistics.
Documents in Croatian database are given as 11-dimensional feature vectors of
run-length statistics. In fact, we found that they perform considerably better
than ALBP in the classification process of Glagolitic documents.

Secondly, Naive Bayes classifier is employed on each database for solving
the binary recognition problem of documents as given in new or old orthography [25]. Because adopted run-length and ALBP features determine numerical
values, the classifier uses the normal distribution for probabilities computation.
Different classifiers, i.e. K-Nearest Neighbors (KNN) [1] and Support Vector
Machine (SVM) [12] have also been tested on the databases for solving the classification task. Because Naive Bayes performs considerably better than the other
classifiers, it has been definitively adopted in this context.

Document feature vectors for each database have been normalized before
the classification process. In particular, we normalize every value x_i^k of k-th
feature for the i-th document feature vector x_i in a certain database by using
the following min-max approach:

$$\overline{x_i^k} = \frac{x_i^k - min_k}{max_k - min_k},$$
(1)

where min_k is the minimum value of the k-th feature and max_k is the maximum
value of the k-th feature in that database.

Confusion matrix for the binary classification problem (new and old orthography) is used for performance evaluation, from which precision, recall and
f-measure are computed [11]. Evaluation is performed by dividing each database into training and test sets. To make the evaluation process independent

from the selected training and test sets, we adopt the K-fold cross validation strategy [14]. Accordingly, performance measures are computed K times, and the average value together with the standard deviation are reported. In our case, the K value is fixed to 5 and 10.

Table 1 shows the classification results obtained by our approach on the database of Glagolitic documents using old and new orthography, and on the database of Slavonic-Serbian and Serbian documents. In the case of Glagolitic database, it is worth noting that f-measure is very high, reaching a value of 0.9333 for both classes in 5-fold and a peak of 0.9667 for new orthography recognition in 10-fold. In the case of Serbian database, our approach perfectly recognizes the new (modern Serbian) and old (Slavonic-Serbian) orthography in 5 and 10-folds, with an f-measure value of 1.

To confirm the efficacy of our method, a comparison is performed with bi-gram and tri-gram language models. In particular, documents in Slavonic-Serbian and Serbian languages are represented by bi-gram and tri-gram frequency vectors [28], on which the same Naive Bayes classifier is employed. Because Glagolitic documents are in the same language but in different script, comparison with bi-grams and tri-grams is not possible. It is a clear limitation of the methods which is overcome by our approach. Table 2 shows the classification results obtained by bi-gram and tri-gram language models. We can observe that our approach outperforms both the competitor methods in terms of f-measure. In fact, bi-gram language model performs poorly in old orthography (Slavonic-Serbian) recognition, with an f-measure of 0.20 in 5-fold and 0.60 in 10-fold. In any case, the f-measure is always below 0.90. On the other hand, tri-gram language model totally misses the old orthography (Slavonic-Serbian) recognition, with an f-measure value of 0 in 5-fold and 0.50 in 10-fold. Also, the f-measure value for new orthography (modern Serbian) recognition is always below 0.85. Again, standard deviation values are pretty high, demonstrating that the methods do not obtain a stable solution.

Table 1. Classification results of our method for old and new orthography recognition

Class		Glagolitic database			Serbian database		
		Precision	Recall	F-Measure	Precision	Recall	F-Measure
5-fold	*new orth.*	0.9500	1.0000	0.9714	0.9600	1.0000	0.9778
		(0.1118)	(0.0000)	(0.0639)	(0.0894)	(0.0000)	(0.0497)
	old orth.	1.0000	0.9000	0.9333	1.0000	0.9000	0.9333
		(0.0000)	(0.2236)	(0.1491)	(0.0000)	(0.2236)	(0.1491)
10-fold	*new orth.*	0.9667	1.0000	0.9800	0.9667	0.9500	0.9467
		(0.1054)	(0.0000)	(0.0632)	(0.1054)	(0.1581)	(0.1167)
	old orth.	0.9000	0.9000	0.9000	0.8500	0.9000	0.8667
		(0.3162)	(0.3162)	(0.3162)	(0.3375)	(0.3162)	(0.3220)

Table 2. Classification results of n-gram language model for old (Slavonic-Serbian) and new (modern Serbian) orthography recognition in Serbian language

Class		Bigram features			Trigram features		
		Precision	Recall	F-Measure	Precision	Recall	F-Measure
5-fold	new orth.	0.7500	0.6167	0.6500	0.9333	0.5667	0.7010
		(0.4330)	(0.4394)	(0.4183)	(0.1491)	(0.0913)	(0.0984)
	old orth.	0.0667	0.2000	0.1000	0.4000	0.6000	0.4800
		(0.1491)	(0.4472)	(0.2236)	(0.3651)	(0.5477)	(0.4382)
10-fold	new orth.	0.5500	0.5500	0.5500	0.6000	0.5000	0.5333
		(0.4972)	(0.4972)	(0.4972)	(0.4595)	(0.4082)	(0.4143)
	old orth.	0.2500	0.3000	0.2667	0.4500	0.5000	0.4667
		(0.4249)	(0.4830)	(0.4389)	(0.4972)	(0.5270)	(0.5018)

Finally, our method is computer time non-intensive, taking 1 s for processing a document of 2 K characters. Differently, bi-gram method takes 4 s and tri-gram method takes 5 s on the same document of 2 K characters. Hence, our method clearly showed its advantage.

5 Conclusions

This paper presented a new method for dating Serbian and Croatian documents from historical books by orthography recognition, overcoming the limitations of the current methods. It considered that text written in a script or language evolved through different historical periods is characterized by difference in orthography rules. Such a difference is captured by script coding, mapping the document characters to four numerical codes. If each code is considered as intensity level, codified text represents an image, subjected to texture analysis for feature extraction. Document features are classified by Naive Bayes approach for recognition of old or new orthography. Results on two databases of historical documents demonstrated that our method obtains very accurate results and very good performances when compared with other state-of-the-art methods.

Future work will extent the databases with a much larger collection of documents from multiple sources. Also, it will test the robustness of the method by using a set of noisy documents. Finally, it will provide a test set of documents from unknown sources for extending the experiment.

References

1. Altman, N.S.: An introduction to kernel and nearest-neighbor nonparametric regression. Am. Stat. **46**(3), 175–185 (1992)
2. Baromic's Breviary, Venice (1493)

3. Berčić, I.: Foundations of the Old Slavic language written by Glagolitic scripts to read the church books, Prague (1862)
4. Biller, O., El-Sana, J., Kedem, K.: The influence of language orthographic characteristics on digital word recognition. In: The 11th IAPR International Workshop on Document Analysis Systems, Tours, pp. 131–135 (2014)
5. Brodić, D., Amelio, A., Milivojević, Z.N.: Clustering documents in evolving languages by image texture analysis. Appl. Intell. **46**(4), 916–933 (2017)
6. Brodić, D., Amelio, A., Milivojević, Z.N.: An approach to the language discrimination in different scripts using adjacent local binary pattern. J. Exp. Theor. Artif. Intell. **29**(5), 929–947 (2017)
7. Brodić, D., Amelio, A., Milivojević, Z.N.: Identification of Fraktur and Latin Scripts in German historical documents using image texture analysis. Appl. Artif. Intell. **30**(5), 379–395 (2016)
8. Brodić, D., Amelio, A., Milivojević, Z.N.: Language discrimination by texture analysis of the image corresponding to the text. Neural Comput. Appl., 1–21 (2016)
9. Brodić, D., Maluckov, Č.A., Milivojević, Z.N., Draganov, I.R.: Differentiation of the script using adjacent local binary patterns. In: Agre, G., Hitzler, P., Krisnadhi, A.A., Kuznetsov, S.O. (eds.) AIMSA 2014. LNCS (LNAI), vol. 8722, pp. 162–169. Springer, Cham (2014). doi:10.1007/978-3-319-10554-3_15
10. Chu, A., Sehgal, C.M., Greenleaf, J.F.: Use of gray value distribution of run lengths for texture analysis. Pattern Recogn. Lett. **11**(6), 415–419 (1990)
11. Confusion   Matrix.   http://www2.cs.uregina.ca/~dbd/cs831/notes/confusion_matrix/confusion_matrix.html
12. Cortes, C., Vapnik, V.: Support-vector networks. Mach. Learn. **20**(3), 273–297 (1995)
13. Coulmas, F.: The Blackwell Encyclopedia of Writing Systems, p. 379. Blackwell, Oxford (1996)
14. Cross Validation (1997). https://www.cs.cmu.edu/~schneide/tut5/node42.html
15. Dasarathy, B.R., Holder, E.B.: Image characterizations based on joint gray-level run-length distributions. Pattern Recogn. Lett. **12**(8), 497–502 (1991)
16. Febvre, L., Martin, H.J.: The Coming of the Book: The Impact of Printing 1450–1800, Verso (1976)
17. Galloway, M.M.: Texture analysis using gray level run lengths. Comp. Graph. Im. Proc. **4**(2), 172–179 (1975)
18. Garrette, D., Alpert-Abrams, H.: An unsupervised model of orthographic variation for historical document transcription. In: The 15th Annual Conference of the North American Chapter of the Association for Computational Linguistics: Human Language Technologies, San Diego, pp. 467–472 (2016)
19. Ivić, P.: Overview of History of the Serbian Language, Novi Sad (1998)
20. Lipovčan, S.: Discovering the Glagolitic Script of Croatia. Erasmus Publisher, Zagreb (2000)
21. Missale Romanum Glagolitice, Kosinje (1483)
22. Nosaka, R., Ohkawa, Y., Fukui, K.: Feature extraction based on co-occurrence of adjacent local binary patterns. In: Ho, Y.-S. (ed.) PSIVT 2011. LNCS, vol. 7088, pp. 82–91. Springer, Heidelberg (2011). doi:10.1007/978-3-642-25346-1_8
23. Ojala, T., Pietikainen, M., Harwood, D.: A comparative study of texture measures with classification based on featured distributions. Pattern Recogn. **29**(1), 51–59 (1996)
24. Reffle, U., Ringlstetter, C.: Unsupervised profiling of OCRed historical documents. Pattern Recogn. **46**, 1346–1357 (2013)

25. Russell, S., Norvig, P.: Artificial Intelligence: A Modern Approach, 2nd edn. Prentice Hall, Egnlewood Cliffs (1995, 2003)
26. Stefanović Karadžić, V.: Građa za Srpsku Istoriju našega vremena. Štamparija Kraljevskog Univerziteta, Budim (1828)
27. Stojković, A.: Fisika. Štamparija Kraljevskog Univerziteta, Budim (1803)
28. Turney, P.D., Pantel, P.: From frequency to meaning: vector space models of semantics. J. Artif. Intell. Res. **37**(1), 141–188 (2010)
29. Zramdini, A., Ingold, R.: Optical font recognition using typographical features. IEEE Trans. Pattern Anal. Mach. Intell. **8**(20), 877–882 (1998)

An Adaptive Cross-Site User Modelling Platform for Cultural Heritage Websites

Maristella Agosti[1][✉], Séamus Lawless[2], Stefano Marchesin[1], and Vincent Wade[2]

[1] Department of Information Engineering, University of Padua, Padua, Italy
maristella.agosti@unipd.it, stefano.marchesin@dei.unipd.it
[2] Department of Computer Science and Statistics, Trinity College Dublin, Dublin, Ireland
{seamus.lawless,vincent.wade}@scss.tcd.ie

Abstract. This paper discusses an adaptive cross-site user modelling platform for cultural heritage websites. The objective is to present the overall design of this platform that allows for information exchange techniques, which can be subsequently used by websites to provide tailored personalisation to users that request it. The information exchange is obtained by implementing a third party user model provider that, through the use of an API, interfaces with custom-built module extensions of websites based on the Web-based Content Management System (WCMS) Drupal. The approach is non-intrusive, not hindering the browsing experience of the user, and has a limited impact on the core aspects of the websites that integrate it. The design of the API ensures user's privacy by not disclosing personal browsing information to non-authenticated users. The user can enable/disable the cross-site service at any time.

Keywords: Cross-site information needs · Cross-site user modelling · Web information exchange · User model provider

1 Introduction and Motivations

The exponential increase in Web usage has allowed modern societies to access, create, manage and distribute massive amounts of information. This fact has led to an increase in the rate at which information is created and consequently uploaded to the Web. The phenomenon is known as 'information explosion' and results in an increased difficulty in organising digital information to meet users' information needs.

A variety of systems have been created to try to address the problem by assisting users' information needs. These systems include, among other tools: keyword-based search engines, recommender systems, and web personalisation techniques, which adapt different aspects of the web experience to the needs and preferences of the individual user. Techniques like personalised information

© Springer International Publishing AG 2017
C. Grana and L. Baraldi (Eds.): IRCDL 2017, CCIS 733, pp. 132–141, 2017.
DOI: 10.1007/978-3-319-68130-6_11

retrieval, where the search result list is re-ranked based on the user's individual search history, or social graphs[1] have been widely adopted.

Within this context, however, most current approaches are unable to assist users in more complex conditions than just providing results for simple information needs, such as providing recommendations for a retail website. For example, a user's information needs that span different subject domains from different independently hosted websites represent a challenge which these "traditional" techniques cannot answer. In addition, the cross-site browsing process carries with it two phenomena that are known as 'lost in hyperspace' and 'information overload', which can both negatively affect the fulfilment of a user's information needs [1,2]. Therefore, to support the user and prevent them from being affected by these phenomena, a browsing experience is required that in a unified manner exploits all the content of the different websites the user is browsing/has browsed to tailor the content to be provided. In this way, although the traditional method of browsing is left unchanged, i.e. when a user browses individual websites across the Web moving from one to another, the conceptual vision of the browsing experience can be redefined as a unified and seamless browsing experience, not simply within, but also across different websites. Even websites, and consequently web publishers, would benefit from this new way of seeing the browsing experience, by gaining more insight on each individual user that landed on them and therefore being able to provide better content to users, thus prolonging their stay in the website.

Clearly there is a need for a consistent cross-site support mechanism that ensures effective assistance to users in the websites they browse across. A concrete representation of such a cross-site support mechanism, which is presented in this paper, is a third party cross-site user modelling service. This service is based on a user model provider, held and maintained by a single website, that is able to take specific aspects of each user together from different websites in order to provide cross-site information to target websites which can subsequently use it for personalisation. In addition, it has to ensure that the user is able to freely browse without any limitation or control, by implementing non-intrusive (implicit) tracking methods and allowing the user to decide when to activate the information exchange mechanism. Moreover, it is also necessary to investigate limited-impact techniques allowing information exchange mechanisms to be introduced to websites with a limited effort. Furthermore, the service should limit the flow of user's information from the third party user model provider to target websites, thus honouring users' privacy needs.

The paper is organized as follows. Section 2 reports on related work. Section 3 presents the proposed cross-site user modelling approach. Section 4 presents the service architecture. Finally, Sect. 5 reports on conclusions and future work.

---

[1] Social graphs 'socially connect' users with content and products that 'peers' like [3].

2   Related Work

Web personalisation can be defined as any action that tailors the web experience to a particular user, or set of users, by providing the information users want or need without expecting them to ask for it explicitly, as described in [7].

Therefore, it is clear that a key challenge lies in providing web personalisation techniques that assist users across the Web and not only on isolated websites. To address this problem, web personalisation methods have to balance the needs of both website users and web publishers. For website users, the web personalisation techniques have to provide assistance across different websites, but in doing so honour the user's privacy needs and browsing freedom [6]. For the web publisher, the web personalisation techniques have to ensure simple and cost effective integration of web personalisation to existing websites and honour the website owner's control over the website as argued in [9], which has been a work of interest from which this project differs in some fundamental aspects highlighted in Sect. 4. Figure 1 sketches the concept of Cross-Site Personalisation (CSP). Based on this, it can be argued that a cross-site approach requires influencing both areas simultaneously and in real-time by creating a *state of equilibrium* in which the needs of the user and the web publisher are balanced.

In order to integrate a cross-site approach to websites, limiting the integration impact to websites, information exchange techniques at run-time can be investigated. Such techniques have their main challenges in understanding the interdependencies within a website. To address this integration challenge Web Information Systems (WIS) can be used, which allow the implementation of an entire website as out-of-the-box deployment [5]. However, WIS are traditionally proprietary software products that limit extensibility without the vendors

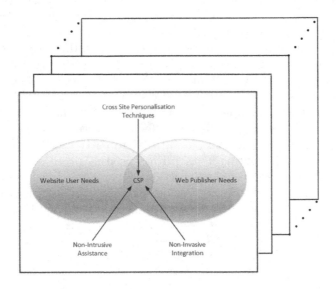

Fig. 1. Cross-site personalisation concept.

help and/or approval. Therefore, to overcome this limitation Web-based Content Management Systems (WCMS) can be used instead, which allow a simple and more flexible implementation based on their open source nature. The main feature of WCMS is the extendible framework, which allows external modules to influence different levels of the functional layer of the website without the need for re-design or re-deployment. This pluggable nature of WCMS allows for low impact personalisation approaches in the form of external modules that can be enabled/disabled by web publishers at ease. Furthermore, applying the cross-site service to WCMS provides the additional benefit of giving web publishers control in deciding which area(s) of the website should be affected by the cross-site user modelling platform and also in deciding how much the extension should influence the overall website look and feel. For example, a web publisher may decide to make the service visible in the homepage or only in specific sections of the website, depending on their needs.

Regarding the research area of 'user modelling', which is a wide and complex area, the following discussion is mainly focused on implicit user models in order to comply with the non-intrusiveness notion adopted for the cross-site service presented in this paper [4]. Within this area, user models that allow high-level abstraction are often referred to as user profiles. User profiles can be defined as a subclass of user modelling, less sophisticated and more suited for applications that require a more general abstraction of information needs [8].

To allow the user to gain a deep understanding in the meaning of the extracted terms and to overcome the problem of polysemy semantic, term networks can be used. Semantic networks usually consist of a term structure, which entails an order or relationship.

3 Cross-Site User Modelling Approach

The domain chosen for the use-case presented in this paper is cultural heritage. Within this domain the Virtual Research Environment (VRE) for the Digital Humanities of the CULTURA[2] project has been investigated. This VRE supports users with different levels of experience to use a variety of tools to interact with a number of cultural heritage collections. The study of this work inspired us to envisage a parallel and complementary approach. This approach provides relevant information to users that attempt to answer cross-site information needs within its browsing space. In those situations where the user's need spans topics that are not confined to a single website, the introduction of the proposed cross-site service might improve the effectiveness of the website personalisation, along with the user's level of satisfaction. An example of this could be an overarching user's interest in the living conditions of the Irish middle class during Irish rebellions, which cannot be addressed by a single website of the CULTURA VRE but requires the user to navigate across different websites of the VRE browsing space. Hence, with the introduction of the cross-site service the user model could gain a higher precision in those topics that are more relevant to the user and,

---

[2] http://www.cultura-strep.eu/.

therefore, the website the user is browsing might be able to provide more tailored personalisation to help address the user's cross-site information needs.

The use-case process identified is as follows: (1) The user lands on a website related to an information gathering task in the cultural heritage domain; (2) The user authenticates a first time with the third party service; (3) The website tracks all user activities in the webpages along with the relevant text entities identified by a term identification component; (4) The user triggers the information exchange function, in anticipation of subsequent personalisation by the target website, which provides relevant user data (based on the selected communication pattern) to the website and newly tracked user information to the service; (5) The user surfs to a second website and, depending on whether they are already authenticated or not, authenticates or directly triggers the information exchange function, which should provide more tailored information to the website; (6) Steps (1)–(5) can then be re-iterated many more times, without a strict order of execution (Fig. 2).

The use-case approach described above requests the following features in order to be applied: (1) websites enable/allow third party sign-in/authentication by using OAuth[3]; (2) the website needs to communicate with the user model provider. The communication includes: (a) sending of content browsed by users for term identification to a third party service, (b) enable/allow browsing behaviour tracking, (c) sending tracked user activities and extracted text entities to the user model provider; (3) the website has to use custom-built WCMS module

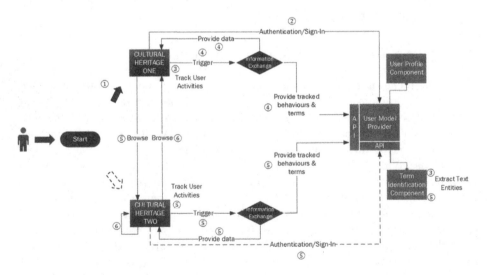

Fig. 2. High-level possible use-case process.

---

[3] http://tools.ietf.org/html/rfc5849.

extensions in order to access the cross-site information exchange service REST-ful API; (4) user authentication with the third party service is required in order to enable the information exchange mechanism and to protect users from unregulated treatment of their data.

The following section introduces the architecture of the proposed cross-site user modelling platform.

4   Cross-Site User Modelling Architecture

According to the components depicted in Fig. 3, the high-level service architecture is presented below, highlighting, where necessary, the differences from the work in [9].

Term Identification Component: The main purpose of the term identification component is to identify text entities related to the body of the current webpage the user is viewing. Text entities indicate the meaning of the underlying content from websites belonging to the cross-site browsing space. A text entity can be considered any set of useful information connected to an extracted content-related term. Examples of this term-connected information can be the topic, the confidence level (which is the probability that the extracted term refers to the connected topic) and the resource reference. Text entities are retrieved through an external term extraction tool. An additional responsibility of the term identification component is to ensure the creation of a shared conceptualisation of the user's cross-site browsing space. The shared conceptualisation is represented as a text entity space and it is based on the contents the user has browsed within the websites of the cross-site browsing space. In this sense, taxonomies and ontologies used by external term identification tools play a fundamental role in defining the characterisation of the shared conceptualisation.

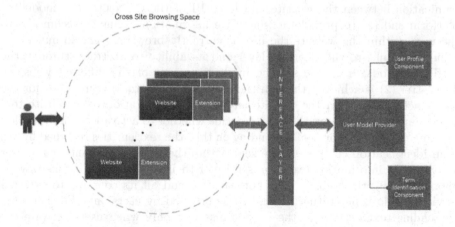

Fig. 3. High-level service architecture.

Generic ontologies, like DBpedia[4], will lead to a shallower shared conceptualisation than specific domain ontologies. Therefore, depending on the domain of
application, different ontologies have a different impact over the granularity and
quality of the conceptualisation. However, in order to extract terms and create
such a shared conceptualisation, the term identification component needs access
to the openly accessible contents on the different websites. Within the interface
layer of this architecture, it is proposed that the website sends at run-time the
contents the user is currently browsing to the term identification component.
Hence, the external tool returns to the website the text entities extracted.

User Profile Component: The user profile consists of text entities related to
the current task of the user and that were identified by the term identification
component. In addition, activities the user has conducted on the content are also
stored, helping to understand which of the contents browsed by the user, and
therefore which of the topics inferred by text entities, are more relevant. These
activities can include mouse clicks, scrolls, cut & paste operations etc.

Interface Layer: The interface layer provides an abstraction from the specific
implementation of the different websites within the user's cross-site browsing
space. It does so by implementing a RESTful API (Representational State Transfer[5]) that facilitates the communication between the user model provider and the
websites the user is browsing. A key responsibility of the API is to ensure that
the interface with the user model provider is browser independent and does not
depend on a specific technology stack. Furthermore, it should ensure fast and
accurate interconnectivity between the interfacing websites and the cross-site
information exchange platform.

Web-based Content Management System Module Extensions: WCMS
module extensions allow a simple and limited-impact integration of cross-site
information exchange techniques into existing website implementations. The
responsibility of the WCMS module extensions is twofold: (1) To facilitate communication between the website and the API of the cross-site user modelling
platform and (2) to provide non-intrusive information exchange techniques to
the user, within the website the user is currently browsing. The former (1) is
achieved thanks to the interface layer and its ability to abstract, through the
HTTP methods, from the specific implementations of the different websites.
The latter (2) is achieved through the use of implicit tracking methods for the
user's activities within the website and the implementation of a website tool
(i.e. a button) that allows the user to decide whether to activate the information
exchange mechanism or not. Depending on this, the text entities returned by the
term identification component are kept within the website until either the user
activates the information exchange service or their session ends. In this way, as
opposed to [9], the website does not have to send all its contents to external
services a priori, but rather to send those browsed by users only. Furthermore,
by sending text entities to the cross-site service only when users activate the

---

[4] http://wiki.dbpedia.org/.
[5] http://www.ics.uci.edu/~fielding/pubs/dissertation/rest_arch_style.htm.

information exchange mechanism, the approach can be considered the basis for *'personalisation on demand'*. This allows websites (i.e. web publishers) to better preserve their contents and therefore to more easily accept the introduction of a third party cross-site user modelling service.

Cross-Site Browsing Space: The application of information exchange techniques to independently hosted websites introduces a cross-site browsing space, an example of which has been presented in Sect. 3. Within the browsing space target websites receive user data through information exchange techniques. The information exchange techniques are enabled through the aforementioned WCMS module extensions. Based on the back-end integration of the user model provider with the website, the user can enable/disable the information exchange service whenever they want. This allows the user to control the mechanism and ensures the user's privacy is honoured. The enabling/disabling of the service passes through the service's authentication system, in fact the user has to authorise the website to interface with the service via third party sign-in authentication with it. Hence, the website sends the cross-site service user's credentials and authorises the third party service to receive and send relevant cross-site information. In this way, the only authentication required is the one with the cross-site user modelling service, thus avoiding multi-log problems and not burdening the browsing experience of the user too severely.

Regarding information exchange techniques, several different methods have been designed. The techniques range from highly generic to highly specific, providing different levels of information enrichment for both the websites and the service. The former tend to be more satisfactory from a web publisher perspective, allowing a massive flow of user's information to leak from the service, thus ignoring or not sufficiently considering the user's privacy concerns. The latter, on the other hand, are more focused on preserving the user's privacy, thus avoiding the provision of huge amounts of information to websites or, in extreme cases, not providing it at all, tend to be more satisfactory both for the user, who sees their privacy more respected, and the service itself, as it doesn't give away the only real value it holds – user data.

For each technique, pros and cons related to privacy concerns were pointed out along with a technical review focusing on the effectiveness of the exchange. However, no claim was made regarding an ideal or optimal solution: all the techniques present both advantages and shortcomings that might be relevant depending on the context and the scope of the application that deploys them. Table 1 summarises the comparison of the exchange techniques in relation to their effectiveness. Hence, for each technique three aspects related to effectiveness are considered: volume, quality and granularity. Volume refers to the amount of data returned to the target website by each information exchange technique. Quality refers to the ability of each information exchange technique to provide tailored information to target websites, therefore exchange techniques that return huge amounts of information tend to have a lower quality in the information they provide. Granularity refers to the level of detail of the information returned to the target website, therefore information exchange techniques that return only

Table 1. Effectiveness comparison.

Information Exchange Techniques	Volume	Quality	Granularity
Privacy Insensitive Technique	High	Low	Low
Threshold Technique	Medium	Low	Low
Top-Feature Selection Technique	High/Medium/Low	Low/Medium	Low
Ranking Technique	Medium	Medium	Low
Entity-Oriented Technique	Medium	Medium	Medium
Activity-Oriented Technique	Low	Medium	Low
Knapsack Technique	Low	Medium	Low
Semantic Technique	Low	High	Low/Medium
Suggestion-Oriented Technique	Low	High	High

entities or informed decisions tend to have a higher level of granularity. Each aspect can take on the values "High", "Medium" and "Low", keeping in mind that a "Low" granularity refers to a high level of detail.

5   Conclusion and Future Work

This paper presented a cross-site user modelling platform for information exchange techniques. The approach introduced serves as a starting point to address a gap between current web personalisation services and what should be a seamless browsing experience for users across independently hosted websites. Thus, the approach fits in the CSP context, through the use of a third party user model provider and WCMS extensions. Therefore, the main contribution of the research described in this paper is the enhancement of user profiles through the usage of a shared conceptualisation, which results from the aggregation of the text entities extracted from the websites belonging to the cross-site browsing space. In addition, the integration of limited-impact information exchange techniques at run-time contributed to the area of web engineering.

The architecture presented in this paper serves for the implementation of a service prototype which is still in progress and will be the subject of future work. The evaluation of this preliminary prototype focused on the effectiveness of the information exchange techniques designed. The first results extracted are encouraging and motivate the following two areas to be addressed in future work.

First, the natural direction this research work should take, in order to evolve, is the implementation of personalisation techniques. Hence, due to the semantic nature of the information stored in the third party user model, i.e. the text entities extracted by the term identification component, personalisation techniques that are able to understand and handle semantic data, such as semantic recommender systems, could be used. Second, user profile management and user scrutiny could be considered in order to enhance the user's trust and control over their needs. Therefore, to allow users to actively engage with their user profile, the cross-site service has to: (1) allow users to view terms relating to their cross-site information needs (model scrutiny); (2) enable users to add and delete terms within the user profile; (3) provide insight on where the information was collected and used. The CULTURA project provided an initial form of model scrutiny, allowing the user to visualise their interests as a word-cloud where the terms could be enlarged or diminished by the user depending on the relevancy that the user gave them [10,11] and this can be considered as a starting point for future work.

Acknowledgements. Stefano Marchesin would like to thank Trinity College Dublin for the use of facilities during his stay in 2016. We thank the reviewers for their insights and comments on the earlier version of the manuscript.

References

1. Ahn, J.W., Brusilovsky, P., He, D., Grady, J., Li, Q.: Personalized web exploration with task models. In: Proceedings of the 17th International Conference on World Wide Web, pp. 1–10. ACM (2008)
2. Berghel, H.: Cyberspace dealing with information overload. Commun. ACM **40**(2), 19–24 (2000)
3. Dieberger, A., Dourish, P., Höök, K., Resnick, P., Wexelblat, A.: Social navigation: techniques for building more usable systems. Interactions **7**(6), 36–45 (2000)
4. Gauch, S., Speretta, M., Chandramouli, A., Micarelli, A.: User profiles for personalized information access. In: Brusilovsky, P., Kobsa, A., Nejdl, W. (eds.) The Adaptive Web. LNCS, vol. 4321, pp. 54–89. Springer, Heidelberg (2007). doi:10. 1007/978-3-540-72079-9_2
5. Isakowitz, T., Bieber, M., Vitali, F.: Web information systems. Commun. ACM **41**(7), 78–80 (1998)
6. Kay, J.: Scrutable adaptation: because we can and must. In: Wade, V.P., Ashman, H., Smyth, B. (eds.) AH 2006. LNCS, vol. 4018, pp. 11–19. Springer, Heidelberg (2006). doi:10.1007/11768012_2
7. Keenoy, K., Levene, M.: Personalisation of web search. In: Mobasher, B., Anand, S.S. (eds.) ITWP 2003. LNCS, vol. 3169, pp. 201–228. Springer, Heidelberg (2005). doi:10.1007/11577935_11
8. Koch, N., Wirsing, M.: Software engineering for adaptive hypermedia applications. In: 8th International Conference on User Modeling, Sonthofen, Germany (2001)
9. Koidl, K., Conlan, O., Wade, V.: Cross-site personalization: assisting users in addressing information needs that span independently hosted websites. In: Proceedings of the 25th ACM Conference on Hypertext and Social Media, pp. 66–76. ACM (2014)
10. Sweetnam, M., Siochru, M., Agosti, M., Manfioletti, M., Orio, N., Ponchia, C.: Stereotype or spectrum: designing for a user continuum. In: The Proceedings of the First Workshop on the Exploration, Navigation and Retrieval of Information in Cultural Heritage, ENRICH (2013)
11. Sweetnam, M.S., et al.: User needs for enhanced engagement with cultural heritage collections. In: Zaphiris, P., Buchanan, G., Rasmussen, E., Loizides, F. (eds.) TPDL 2012. LNCS, vol. 7489, pp. 64–75. Springer, Heidelberg (2012). doi:10.1007/ 978-3-642-33290-6_8

SACHER: Smart Architecture for Cultural Heritage in Emilia Romagna

Fabrizio Ivan Apollonio[1], Francesca Rizzo[1], Silvia Bertacchi[1],
Giorgio Dall'Osso[1], Andrea Corbelli[2(✉)], and Costantino Grana[2]

[1] Alma Mater Studiorum Università di Bologna, 40136 Bologna, BO, Italy
{fabrizio.apollonio,f.rizzo,silvia.bertacchi,g.dallosso}@unibo.it
[2] Università degli Studi di Modena e Reggio Emilia, 41125 Modena, MO, Italy
{andrea.corbelli,costantino.grana}@unimore.it

Abstract. The current Cultural Heritage management system lacks of ICT platforms for the management and integration of heterogeneous and fragmented data sources and interconnection between private and public subjects involved in the process. The SACHER project intends to fill this gap, working both on a technological level and on a business model level: firstly providing a platform based on an open-source distributed cloud-computing environment for the management of the complete data lifecycle related to cultural assets; moreover providing new models based on participatory design for Cultural Heritage data directed towards social entrepreneurship. This paper presents the first implementation of a system for managing data based on the 3D model of the cultural object, with a focus on the process for cultural assets management and the interface design for cultural services.

Keywords: 3D model · Cultural heritage · ICT platform · Service design

1 Introduction

The current Cultural Heritage management system lacks of ICT platforms that are able to manage the complete data lifecycle, integrate heterogeneous and fragmented data sources and interconnect the different private and public subjects involved.

The SACHER Project goal is to fill this gap, working both on a technological level and on a business model level. On the technological level, the SACHER Project will provide a platform capable of managing the complete data lifecycle associated with cultural assets based on an open-source, distributed cloud-computing environment. The platform will be based on the Active Digital Identity paradigm and will also take care of hardware and software integration between private and public partners. The SACHER platform will make collaborations between different public and private groups involved in Cultural Heritage management easier.

© Springer International Publishing AG 2017
C. Grana and L. Baraldi (Eds.): IRCDL 2017, CCIS 733, pp. 142–156, 2017.
DOI: 10.1007/978-3-319-68130-6_12

On the business model level, SACHER will provide new models based on participatory design for Cultural Heritage data directed towards social entrepreneurship.

The SACHER platform will be tested on physical Cultural Heritage assets restoration projects in the Palazzo del Podestà area in collaboration with the Comune di Bologna.

The final purpose of the SACHER platform is not only to quickly produce a system that works in a real Cultural Heritage context and can be easily transferred to different cities, but also to create an environment of services and actors capable of enhancing the values of the Cultural Heritage business processes.

2   Management of Cultural Heritage

At present, the protection and enhancement of Cultural Heritage, particularly when dealing with significant monumental complexes, is supported by a series of digital devices not only used for reliable documentation, but also for carrying out in-depth scientific analysis on the work of art or monument and, further, to facilitate programmed maintenance activities.

Within this scope, the idea to use ICT platforms for managing data is not new anymore [1–3], but it becomes more and more necessary to design a platform providing support to the whole process related to cultural assets – actually missing – and, moreover, capable of gathering fragmented and incomplete data of different nature and from various sources. This fact has relevant implications for the efficiency of the platform in the long term and to assure an actual usability of the information system for the collection of all information about the cultural asset and the surviving of the data during the whole lifecycle.

In fact, when operating on Cultural Heritage, the amount of records resulting from the research phase is generally huge and heterogeneous [15]. As a matter of fact, a monument or building usually dates back to several centuries and it is necessary to carry out a very careful historical analysis before taking action with restoration or any other activity [11]: documents gathered include historical descriptions and drawings/paintings, graphic materials, analogue/digital pictures, existing technical and financial reports, construction site records filled out during previous interventions, etc. All the available information helps to reconstruct the evolution in time and consequently to design a correct approach to restoration and maintenance activities.

During the effective intervention phase, the documentation supplied by the operators is various and should be stored in a system which meets the requirements of easy sharing and storage, with reduced search times and preventing any possibility of errors or data loss. Furthermore, with reference to the importance of making the complete documentation available in real-time to experts and professionals in the field, the same applies to monitoring operations and in case of routine/emergency or planned preventative maintenance, as shown in Fig. 1.

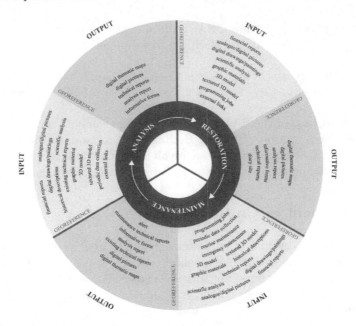

Fig. 1. Process of management of a cultural asset organised in three main phases: analysis of the current state of preservation and collection of existing documentation; restoration activities including intervention project, scientific analysis on materials and structures; maintenance and monitoring activities.

In recent decades the spread of digital and ICT tools in the various areas related to the cultural assets has supported, and now almost largely replaced, traditional methods of data-gathering, organization and management of information relating to Cultural Heritage. For this reason, there exist numerous studies aimed at developing software and web-based platforms for the collection of a multitude of heterogeneous data from the field of architecture and more particularly concerning the history of the restoration of monumental buildings, interesting from the historical and artistic point of view [13].

With regards to the management of Cultural Heritage data and IT solutions for documentation, since 2003 several national projects have been promoted with the collaboration of external partners and coordinated by the Italian Ministry of Culture. Among the various projects, ARTPAST[1] (*Applicazione informatica in Rete per la Tutela e Valorizzazione del Patrimonio culturale nelle aree sottoutilizzate*) had very fruitful outcomes. The project, coordinated by the Superintendence of Pisa and promoted by the General Directorate for Technological Innovation and Promotion, has been founded by CIPE for the years 2004–2008. Its purpose was to gather data for the SIGECweb (*Sistema Informativo Generale del Catalogo*) national database [12, 14] and to digitize the heritage of historical-

---

[1] More information at ARTPAST - *Progetto per la digitalizzazione del Patrimonio*: http://www.artpast.iccd.beniculturali.it.

artistic and ethno-anthropological interest according to the standards laid down by the ICCD (*Istituto Centrale per il Catalogo e la Documentazione*) cataloguing system [7]. The project allowed an online consultation of databases by the Superintendence (nearly two millions forms containing photographs), in order to improve the control on works of art. Thanks to the collaboration between universities and ICT companies, two free and web-based software packages dedicated to the restoration have been implemented: ARISTOS [4] and SICAR [6].

As a result of multi-year studies, such as the RE.ARTE[2] project (*Restauri in Rete*), further contributions were given to the work started in previous years, both for data entry and user training. In this framework, the SICAR[3] Information System (*Sistema Informativo per la documentazione di Cantieri di Restauro*) has been implemented as an open-source platform paying specific attention to restoration [5]. The software has been developed by Liberologico as an implementation of an existing platform called Akira GIS Server [8,9], which was created specifically for the restoration of the Leaning Tower in Pisa.

The SICAR platform is a web-based GIS designed for managing the restoration work and characterized by the possibility to georeference vectors, rasters and alphanumeric documentation, from the earlier design phase until the restoration site phase and further intervention. It is a large archive based on forms relating different typologies of data: 2D geometric information (vector data) and alphanumeric ones (text documents, hypertext and semi-structured text in different categories, external data attached to system forms). Raster images can be the reference background (on an appropriate scale) on which it is possible to map 2D georeferenced polygons. The application is multi-user (with a lock system to avoid data inconsistency due to simultaneous modification by different users) and accessible via the web, both for data-entry and consultation by means of cross-searches.

The software has been officially adopted by MiBACT in 2008, becoming the official IT platform for the management of documentation concerning restoration sites, freely available for use by the ministerial employees in museum and public bodies. In 2011 its application has become mandatory for all the work promoted and financed by the Ministry, especially in case of intervention on protected objects, with the intention of computerizing procedures[4], simplifying the documentation delivery and sharing the process with the Superintendence, entrusted with collecting the available documentation on the restoration activities[5].

Recent updates of the SICAR software for its use in different domains are described in [20].

---

[2] See at http://www.sbappsae-pi.beniculturali.it/index.php?it/212/progetto-rearte.

[3] Details about the project at http://sicar.beniculturali.it:8080/website/.

[4] Italian legislative decree n. 82, 07/03/2005, "*Codice dell'amministrazione digitale*", in particular art. 42.

[5] The Circular n. 31, 22/12/2011 by the Directorate-General for Landscape, Fine Arts, Architecture and Contemporary Art provides for the compulsory use of the SICAR application for all restoration activities promoted and financed by the Ministry.

This paperless approach (also called "dematerialisation") is a common practice in Italian public administration since the introduction in 2005 of the requirement of a progressive increase in the computerized document management within the public administration and the replacement of traditional media for the administrative documentation in favour of IT documents. According to national regulations, this objective has been included as a matter of priority in recent strategies designed for gradual elimination of the paper, through the digitization of processes, towards a complete use of digital media for storage of written sources. The goal of dematerialisation in the restoration process is twofold: on one hand to avoid – or significantly reduce – the creation of new paper documents necessary by current procedures; on the other hand, to digitize the existing paper documents in the archives, replacing them with appropriate IT records. The main advantages are saving money and storage space, speed up sharing information and data, besides reducing the environmental impact.

2.1   3D Web Platforms for CH

Recently, thanks to further research in the domain, advanced novel solutions can include a detailed 3D model in latest-generation web-based information systems, providing additional and reliable information on the current state of preservation of the cultural object before restoration and on its possible modification during/after the restoration activity.

Many online platforms such as Sketckfab[6] or ARIADNE[7] allow community users to upload 3D digital contents for visualisation and web-based widespread dissemination.

Lately, it is increasingly common that researchers develop specific tools for information analysis and sharing results in Cultural Heritage. An example of this is CHER-Ob[8] (CULTURAL HERITAGE-Object) [19], an open source platform developed by the Computer Graphics Group of Yale University, which was tested on a section of the case study serving as a physical test of the SACHER project, the Palazzo del Podestà in the city centre of Bologna (Fig. 2). The system allows easy annotation on the model on the basis of some categories related to documentation, materials and analysis with possible upload of photographs and report generation of the collected material; however, heavy 3D models are not supported under the standard configuration, which can be an issue when dealing with complex architectures. More flexible platforms have been created for publishing high-resolution 3D contents with smart user interface [18] and in the latest times these have been used as web-based viewer by restorers with excel-

---

[6] Sketchfab - Your 3D content online and in VR: https://sketchfab.com/.

[7] ARIADNE - Visual media service: http://visual.ariadne-infrastructure.eu/.

[8] CHER-Ob: An Open Source Platform for Shared Analysis in Cultural Heritage Research, Computer Graphics Group, Yale University: http://graphics.cs.yale.edu/site/cher-ob-open-source-platform-shared-analysis-cultural-heritage-research.

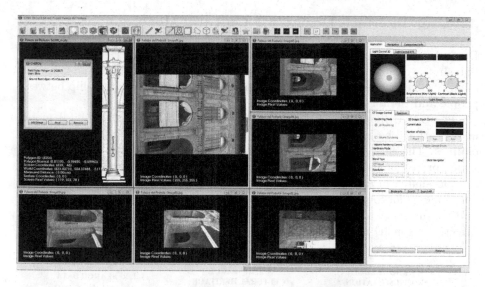

Fig. 2. The 3D model of the porticoed ground floor of the Palazzo del Podestà (5th column) and some reference pictures inside the CHER-Ob platform.

lent results for the Information System of the Neptune Fountain in Bologna[9], on the occasion of its recent restoration (started in 2016 and still in progress).

In this sense, web-based ICT systems can offer increasingly updated tools for the Cultural Heritage management, mainly for querying and storing work site documentation, but also for integrating public and private archives, connecting professionals to public bodies in a quicker and easier way and, if available, providing a smart 3D navigation system, always accessible to the users via the Internet. This results in a significant simplification in managing, and the number of domains where those applications can be profitably used is increasingly broad.

Since one of the objective of the SACHER project consists also in an active, widespread and free fruition by users, an open-source and distributed cloud-computing environment is considered the most appropriate tool for the SACHER platform.

The definition of operational protocols about cultural assets with an in-depth study on the process of the Cultural Heritage management – still an ongoing research activity – will provide a suitable data modelling in order to define data requirements needed to efficiently support activities and the information system. The analysis work done so far has involved academics, ICT experts, public bodies and final users working in this field. This useful collaboration provided suggestions and information on the ongoing project.

---

[9] Il Nettuno di Bologna. Il Sistema Informativo del restauro (Visual Computing Lab, ISTI - CNR): http://vcg.isti.cnr.it/activities/nettuno/.

3   User Interface Design for Cultural Heritage

Designing user interface services in the domain of Cultural Heritage is a hot issue in the current debate on Information Technologies, that more and more frequently generates new application dynamics to support the relationship between people and Heritage.

The SACHER project is based on the use of a textured 3D digital model as operational heart of a system that connects data pertaining to different disciplines. Therefore, the three-dimensional model represents the mean through which professionals in the sector can access and retrieve multidisciplinary information shared in a joint database and uploaded in a chronological order. The core concept for SACHER is the visualization and usability of contents and information thanks to an interactive exploration of the cultural object, linking data directly to the 3D model.

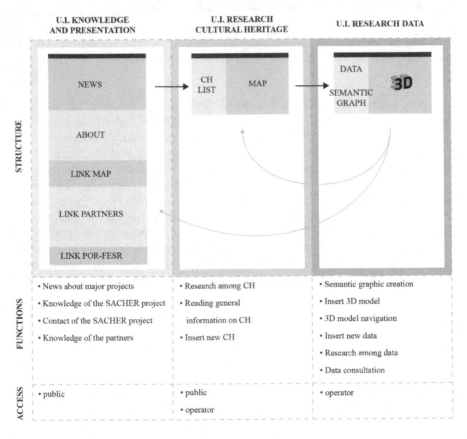

Fig. 3. SACHER platform, navigation: interfaces, levels of access and hierarchy.

On the basis of this idea, the development of the SACHER user interface exploits the 3D model and integrate three different design layers:

- the workflow of model of interaction between the users and the system;
- the organisation of the space of the interface with respect to the different tasks the users can perform;
- the graphics style of the interface.

In the SACHER platform, navigation is marked by three interfaces, with three different levels of access and hierarchy (Fig. 3):

- UI for introduction and presentation;
- UI for Cultural Heritage catalogue search;
- UI for information retrieval and data entry.

The first user interface (Fig. 4) is accessible to any user, and has the function of presenting and providing general information about the SACHER project, its partners' contacts, and a slideshow. The slideshow plays a relevant role in the platform, since it showcases the most important projects managed by SACHER, and it promotes the companies and professionals who work there.

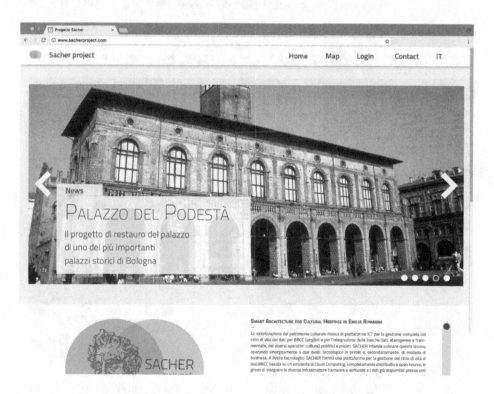

Fig. 4. UI for introduction and presentation.

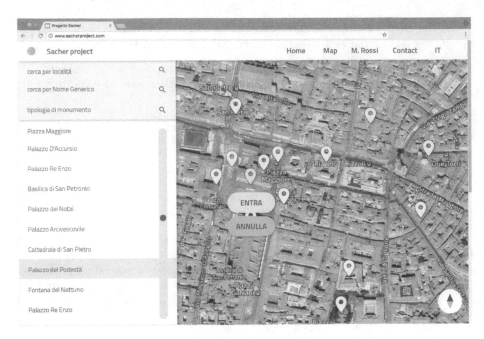

Fig. 5. UI for Cultural Heritage catalogue search.

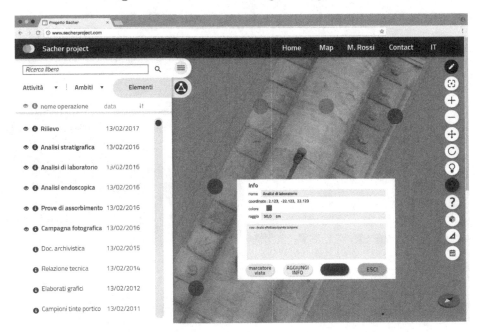

Fig. 6. UI for information retrieval and data entry.

Through this page, access is granted to the Cultural Heritage catalogue search interface (Fig. 5), where the SACHER Cultural Heritage catalogue can be explored through the search field or through navigation on an interactive map.

If the user level allows it, new Cultural Heritage items can also be registered. By selecting a specific item on the map, its presentation window can be opened. Through this window, access to the data management page of the item will be available (Fig. 6).

The professionals' work is focused mainly on the last UI, for information retrieval as well as data entry. This page shows a 3D model of the Cultural Heritage item, and its division into semantic areas. Beside the model, a graph that reflects the semantic distribution of the item can be used as guidance. Data can be consulted by navigating the 3D model, and isolating the single elements of interest.

If the user level allows it, it is possible to enter new data, indicating the relevant position on the 3D model, and attaching pictures or other documents. The windows that allow these operations are designed to save time, and to prevent users from becoming disoriented during interactions with the 3D model. The graphic style of the interface is inspired by the "Material Design" guidelines developed by Google, to improve usage and effectiveness of the digital tools, and to ensure compatibility on whichever device is used to access the platform. The colours are part of the coordinated image of SACHER, and due care has been used to avoid altering the perception of the 3D textures.

4   System Prototype

As previously suggested by Cucchiara et al. [10], the goal of this system is to bridge the gap between two different worlds, multimedia technologies and the arts, which can benefit from each other contributions We plan to bridge this gap by creating a reusable, practical and open-source tool to manage restoration processes of Cultural Heritage assets with the clear intention of building a common and shared work methodology for the operators of both fields.

For this project we decided to rely only on open-source software tools. The main reason is to avoid vendor lock-in and to create a system that is completely independent from proprietary tools and formats and that can be easily adopted by anyone. A secondary but still very important aspect to consider is the cost reduction due to lack of software licenses needed to run open-source software.

We propose an architecture based on a web platform, which is easily accessible and does not require the users to install any kind of technical 3D modeling software to visualize the models.

The prototype of the system is based on a web platform called "eXo Platform", which is an open-source social collaboration software aimed at the creation of corporate intranets. Out of the box this platform provides everything that is needed to run a corporate social network, with features such as wikis, forums, calendars, documents management and private spaces.

The eXo platform is based on J2EE (Java2 Enterprise Edition), the portlet technology and on the GateIn portal manager. The platform is able to run on Tomcat or JBoss, two well known web application servers. The platform data is managed through the Java JCR API (Java Content Repository), an API that allows access to data repositories in a uniform manner, hiding the actual storage strategy. eXo Platform requires a database in order to work properly but is not tied to a specific RDBMS, in its default configuration it uses HSQLDB, a DBMS engine written in Java that is also able to use the filesystem to store the data and does not require a server application.

The strength of the eXo platform lies in its customization capabilities and in this project the platform has been widely customized to be able to host all the data needed to manage many Cultural Heritage restoration projects. By default, the website is accessible only to registered users, so a public homepage with "Login" and "Register" buttons has been added, in order to allow new users to request access to the platform. By logging in a user is able to browse the social area of the platform which shows the latest activities from the user's connections in a dashboard, as shown in Fig. 7.

The most interesting and useful feature offered by the eXo platform is called "Spaces". A space is a private area of the website in which subscribed users are able to share documents, wikis, forums and calendar events. In this project the concept of a space has been used to create private areas dedicated to different restoration projects, each of them with its own models and documents, such as images, technical reports and analysis, etc. In Fig. 8 the private document area reserved for a space is shown. The documents uploaded in this section are not available to those users who are not part of the space.

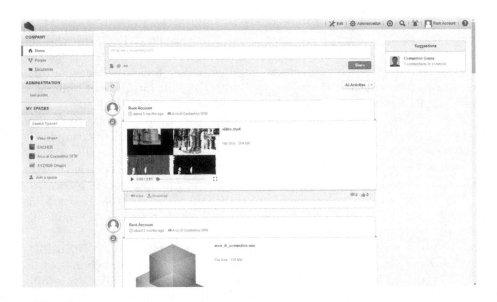

Fig. 7. eXo platform main social dashboard.

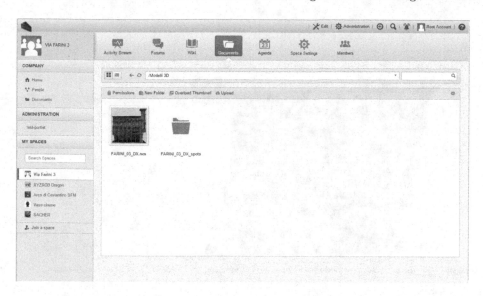

Fig. 8. The document area inside a private space, in this case called "Via Farini 3".

The main custom feature added to the platform concerns the 3D models visualization. Since the eXo platform provides an extensible mechanism to display specific file types in the browser, such an extension has been created based on a visualizer called 3DHOP (3D Heritage Online Presenter) [17]. 3DHOP is an open-source 3D model visualizer created by CNR (Consiglio Nazionale delle Ricerche) specifically designed to show Cultural Heritage 3D models in a web browser. It has been completely developed in Javascript and is ready to be used and integrated in a website.

3DHOP is able to show 3D models in the well known PLY format and also provides all the tools needed to take advantage of a different format called Nexus [16], created by the 3DHOP developers, which allows for fluid download and visualization of models of sizes ranging from a few kilobytes to a few gigabytes.

The Nexus format provides a multi-resolution representation of the model, allowing for a selective download of the 3D data through the HTTP protocol using the "range" parameter used to download only the parts of the model that are needed.

The 3DHOP visualizer capabilities have been extended in order to provide an annotation feature for the final user, allowing him to associate a point on the model, called "spot", to any kind of data uploaded on the server. All the spots are visible on the models as semi-transparent blue spheres and by clicking on them the user can edit the spot's properties, deleting it, changing its name or its size. In Fig. 9 is shown an example of an editing popup. Each spot is associated with a folder in the space's private documents area in which all the files associated with the spot can be stored. The folder is accessible directly from the spot's editing popup by clicking on a link, an example of such a folder is shown in Fig. 10.

Fig. 9. The annotation editing popup. The user has the possibility to delete the spot or to change some of its parameters, such as its name or size. (Color figure online)

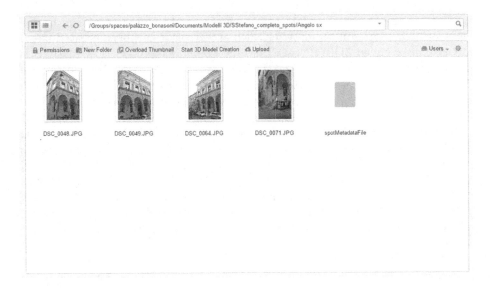

Fig. 10. The folder associated with a spot may contain images, documents and other data. The folder hierarchy can be extended based on the need of each restoration project.

The annotation feature is possible by means of a REST service integrated with the eXo platform which manages all the annotations stored in the JCR database and provides a special download method that supports the HTTP "range" parameter. The REST service is also accessible from other clients, not only by the eXo platform users, making the annotations' data also available to other applications.

This platform has been tested on a dedicated server with a 6-core CPU, 16 GB RAM and 150 GB of storage running Ubuntu 16.04 LTS.

5   Conclusions

In this paper we presented a brief overview of the existing systems for Cultural Heritage management, then illustrating the SACHER project, a platform designed to better manage CH restoration processes. At this stage we are still conducting a feasibility study using the prototype described earlier; in the near future we plan to improve our system providing a more customizable interface and by expanding the annotation capabilities of 3DHOP.

Acknowledgments. This project is partially funded by the SACHER project of the Emilia Romagna region in collaboration with the Municipality of Bologna. *SACHER: Smart Architecture for Cultural Heritage in Emilia Romagna. Piattaforma Innovativa di gestione dei BBCC tangibili per l'Industria Culturale e Creativa*; Acronym: SACHER; CUP Project No: J32I16000120009; POR-FESR 2014–2020, Axis 1, Action 1.2.2; Period: 01/04/2016-31/03/2018; Scientific Project Manager: Rebecca Montanari (CIRI-ICT); Coordinator: CIRI ICT (Alma Mater Studiorum Università di Bologna); Partners: Softech-ICT (Università degli Studi di Modena e Reggio Emilia), Centuria Agenzia per l'Innovazione della Romagna; Other participants: Comune di Bologna, Imola Informatica s.p.a., Engineering Ingegneria Informatica s.p.a., Leonardo s.r.l.

References

1. Apollonio, F.I., Baldissini, S., Beltramini, G., Borgherini, M.M., Clini, P., Gaiani, M., Palestini, C., Sacchi, L., et al.: I geo-modelli per la PALLADIO Library: un archivio condiviso e in divenire. Disegnare Idee Immagini **47**, 46–59 (2013)
2. Apollonio, F.I., Corsi, C., Gaiani, M., Baldissini, S.: An integrated 3D geodatabase for palladio's work. Int. J. Architect. Comput. **8**(2), 111–133 (2010)
3. Apollonio, F.I., Gaiani, M., Benedetti, B.: 3D reality-based artefact models for the management of archaeological sites using 3D GIS: a framework starting from the case study of the Pompeii Archaeological area. J. Archaeol. Sci. **39**(5), 1271–1287 (2012)
4. Baracchini, C., Boscaino, I., Levi, D., Maffei, A.: ARISTOS: archivio informatico per la storia della tutela delle opere storico artistiche. Bollettino d'informazioni del centro Ricerche Informatiche per i Beni Culturali **12**(2), 57–81 (2002)
5. Baracchini, C., Fabiani, F., Grilli, R., Vecchi, A.: SICaR w/b, un Sistema Informativo per la progettazione, il monitoraggio e la condivisione delle attività di restauro: verso un network della conservazione. In: Atti del Convegno di Studi Scienza e Patrimonio Culturale nel Mediterraneo. Diagnostica e conservazione: esperienze e proposte per una Carta del Rischio, pp. 507–519 (2009)

6. Baracchini, C., Lanari, P., Scopigno, R., Tecchia, F., Vecchi, A.: SICAR: geographic information system for the documentation of restoration analysis and intervention. In: Proceedings of SPIE 5146, Optical Metrology for Arts and Multimedia, vol. 13, pp. 149–160 (2003). doi:10.1117/12.501505

7. Berardi, E., Marsicola, C., Sanzi Di Mino, M.R.: L'utilizzo della digitalizzazione nell'ICCD: stato dell'arte e prospettive. DigItalia 1, 97–100 (2005)

8. Capponi, G., Lanari, P., Lodola, S., Magnatti, C., Parrini, U., Vecchi, A., Vedovello, S., Veniale, F.: Il software Akira GIS Server - un'applicazione nella mappatura dei materiali costitutivi e dello stato di degrado della Torre di Pisa. Bollettino del Centro di Ricerche Informatiche per i Beni Culturali 5, 115–126 (2000)

9. Capponi, G., Vedovello, S., Vecchi, A.: Realizzazione del sistema informatico Akira GIS Server. In: Il restauro della Torre di Pisa: un cantiere di progetto per la conservazione delle superfici, pp. 46–53 (2001)

10. Cucchiara, R., Grana, C., Borghesani, D., Agosti, M., Bagdanov, A.D.: Multimedia for cultural heritage: key issues. In: Grana, C., Cucchiara, R. (eds.) MM4CH 2011. CCIS, vol. 247, pp. 206–216. Springer, Heidelberg (2012). doi:10.1007/978-3-642-27978-2_18

11. De Luca, L., Busarayat, C., Stefani, C., Renaudin, N., Florenzano, M., Véron, P.: An iconography-based modeling approach for the spatio-temporal analysis of architectural heritage. In: SMI Conference 2010, pp. 78–89. IEEE (2010)

12. Desiderio, M.L., Mancinelli, M.L., Negri, A., Plances, E., Saladini, L.: Il SIGECweb nella prospettiva del catalogo nazionale dei beni culturali. DigItalia 1, 69–82 (2013)

13. Jiménez Fernández-Palacios, B., Remondino, F., Stefani, C., Lombardo, J., De Luca, L.: Web visualization of complex reality-based 3D models with NUBES. In: Digital Heritage International Congress (DigitalHeritage), vol. 1, pp. 701–704. IEEE (2013)

14. Mancinelli, M.L.: Sistema informativo generale del catalogo: nuovi strumenti per la gestione integrata delle conoscenze sui beni archeologici. Archeologia e Calcolatori 15, 115–128 (2004)

15. Meyer, E., Grussenmeyer, P., Perrin, J.P., Durand, A., Drap, P.: A virtual research environment for archaeological data management, visualization and documentation. In: 35e Conférence du CAA Layers of Perception, Advanced Technological Means to Illuminate Our Past, pp. 1–6 (2007)

16. Ponchio, F., Dellepiane, M.: Multiresolution and fast decompression for optimal web-based rendering. Graph. Models 88, 1–11 (2016)

17. Potenziani, M., Callieri, M., Dellepiane, M., Corsini, M., Ponchio, F., Scopigno, R.: 3DHOP: 3D heritage online presenter. Comput. Graph. 52, 129–141 (2015)

18. Potenziani, M., Callieri, M., Dellepiane, M., Corsini, M., Ponchio, F., Scopigno, R.: 3DHOP: una piattaforma flessibile per la pubblicazione e visualizzazione su Web dei risultati di digitalizzazioni 3D. Archeomatica 6(4) (2015)

19. Shi, W., Kotoula, E., Akoglu, K., Yang, Y., Rushmeier, H.: CHER-Ob: a tool for shared analysis in cultural heritage. In: EUROGRAPHICS Workshop on Graphics and Cultural Heritage (2016)

20. Siotto, E., Baracchini, C., Santamaria, U., Scopigno, R.: Sperimentazione del Sistema Ministeriale SICaR w/b per la gestione e la consultazione informatizzata dei dati sulla policromia. Archeologia e Calcolatori 27, 131–151 (2016)

Applications

Language Identification as Process Prediction Using WoMan

Stefano Ferilli[1,2]([⊠]), Floriana Esposito[1,2], Domenico Redavid[3],
and Sergio Angelastro[1]

[1] Dipartimento di Informatica, Università di Bari, Bari, Italy
{stefano.ferilli,floriana.esposito,sergio.angelastro}@uniba.it
[2] Centro Interdipartimentale per la Logica e sue Applicazioni,
Università di Bari, Bari, Italy
[3] Artificial Brain S.r.l., Bari, Italy
redavid@abrain.it

Abstract. Several high-level tasks in the management of Digital
Libraries require the application of Natural Language Processing (NLP)
techniques. In turn, most NLP solutions are based on linguistic resources
that are costly to produce, and so motivate research for automated ways
to build them. In particular, Language Identification is a crucial NLP
task, that is preliminary to almost all the others, since different linguistic resources must be used for different languages. This paper investigates
process mining and management approaches as a possible solution to the
Language Identification problem. Specifically, it casts language identification as a process prediction task, and exploits the WoMan framework
to carry it out. Experimental results are encouraging and suggest to further explore this approach.

Keywords: Natural Language Processing · Language identification ·
Process mining and management

1 Introduction

In order to perform several kinds of analysis, categorization and understanding
of documents in a Digital Library, Natural Language Processing (NLP for short)
techniques are needed. Research on NLP has developed a number of strategies,
tools and resources that allow to perform many different tasks, from low-level
ones, aimed at preprocessing the text, to high-level ones, aimed at extracting
different kinds of information from it. These tasks may be connected in a sort of
pipeline in order to extract many features and components from texts, through
different levels of increasing complexity (morphological, lexical, and syntactic;
more recently, also the semantic level, which is clearly the most challenging one,
has been approached) [8]. Typical examples of steps in this pipeline are Language
Identification (aimed at automatically discovering the language in which a document is written), Stopword Removal (that removes the terms that are widespread

© Springer International Publishing AG 2017
C. Grana and L. Baraldi (Eds.): IRCDL 2017, CCIS 733, pp. 159–172, 2017.
DOI: 10.1007/978-3-319-68130-6_13

and frequent in any kind of text and hence are not informative about the specific text content), Normalization (that standardizes to a single form, stem or lemma, different inflected occurrences of the same term), PoS Tagging (that associates each term to its grammatical function), Parsing (that builds the syntactic structure of sentences), and Word Sense Disambiguation (that associates each term in the text to the underlying concept, to attack the synonymy and polysemy problems that affect natural language).

NLP tasks are typically based on linguistic resources, that must be available for them to work properly. Most such resources have been built for English, both because it has a simpler syntactical structure than other languages, and because it has established itself as the standard for scientific and administrative interaction all over the world. Much less has been done to deal with a few other important languages or with the vast majority of minor languages, dialects, jargons and slangs, that nevertheless represent a significant piece of our cultural heritage and a precious source of information. Unfortunately, experimental evidence shows us that approaches which perform well on a language are not ensured to behave in the same way on others. Building linguistic resources usually requires the intervention of human experts, and thus it is typically a time-consuming, costly and error-prone task. This motivates research to automatically learn such resources.

In this landscape, Language Identification plays a crucial role. Not only may it provide significant help to librarians, scholars or enthusiasts working with collections of multilingual documents. It is also fundamental for the whole NLP pipeline, because, depending on the language in which a text is written, different, language-specific, tools and resources must be exploited in the various steps of the pipeline. So, in order to answer Gordon's question (2005): "How well do existing language identification techniques support languages which form the bulk of the more than 7000 languages identified in the Ethnologue?", carrying on previous research in this direction [6,18], this work proposes the automatic learning of a tool for Language Identification. More specifically, the approach adopted for this purpose relies on Process Mining and Management techniques. Compared to existing approaches in the literature, it provides a more powerful representation of models, which might be leveraged in the future to improve the model's predictive performance, and allows the incremental learning and refinement of language models, which is important to improve the performance of existing language models and to add new languages at need, without having to learn from scratch using all at once huge datasets.

This paper is organized as follows. The next section recalls some background and related work on Language Identification and Process Mining. Section 3 describes the WoMan framework for process management. Then, Sect. 4 proposes the process-based approach to language identification and reports experimental results. Finally, Sect. 5 draws some conclusions and outlines future work issues.

2   Background and Related Work

As for many other NLP tasks, also Language Identification relies on the availability of suitable linguistic resources. A variety of features have been proposed in literature as relevant to determine in which language a given text is written [19]. Sequences of letters, called n-grams, are a typical example [17], but also stopwords (as the words most frequently used in a language), or the suffixes used for inflection are significant [6].

Many works are based on the presence of particular character n-grams and often exploit n-gram probability distribution [1,3,11,15]. An n-gram is an n-character substring of a text, which can also refer to any co-occurring set of characters in a string. Typically, a string is sliced into a set of overlapping n-grams. The n-gram based approach introduced in [3] for text categorization, provides a popular, high-performance methodology for language identification. Attempts to build automatically resources for the task of language recognition are often based on statistics concerning n-grams occurrence. Some techniques are based on Recurrent Neural Networks (RNNs), as in [10], which have the drawback of requiring a large amount of data to be trained. Other solutions adopt Hidden Markov Models (HMMs), where visible states are considered to be a sequence of n-grams [2,12] and the probability of an observation is assumed to depend only on the previous $n - 1$ observations [20].

Other works are based on words. E.g., [3] states that human languages invariably have some words which occur more frequently than others, which implies that there is always a set of words which dominates most of the other words of the language in terms of frequency of use. Many techniques, along the various steps of the NLP pipeline, consider only the list of terms appearing in the text (Bag-of-Words based processing), possibly associated to weights (often directly or indirectly related to their frequency). This approach has proven to be a good trade-off between efficiency and effectiveness in many applications.

As said, this work aims at checking whether a technique based on a Process Mining approach [9], where a text in natural language is seen as a process based on n-grams representation, may be effective for language identification. So, a quick recall of Process Mining basics may be helpful here. A *process* consists of actions performed by agents (humans or artifacts). A *workflow* is a formal specification of how these actions can be composed to result in valid processes. Allowed compositional schemes include sequential, parallel, conditional, or iterative execution. A process execution can be described in terms of *events* associated to the performed activities. A *case* is a particular execution of activities compliant to a given workflow. Case *traces* consist of lists of events associated to time points. A *task* is a generic piece of work, defined to be executed for many cases of the same type. An *activity* is the actual execution of a task.

Interestingly, early research on Process Mining used HMMs as the underlying learning and representation approach, before being superseded by more specific solutions. Inspired by this connection with the Language Identification literature, here we would like to make the opposite journey, starting from Process Mining-specific approaches and checking whether they can be profitably exploited on a task where HMMs have proved effective.

While Process Mining and Management techniques have been typically motivated by and exploited in business and industrial domains, and their typical tasks have been of mining and supervision of process enactment, more recently other application fields (such as Ambient Intelligence, and even Chess) have been approached with these techniques, and also the additional task of prediction has gained increasing attention [7]. In this perspective, given a formal model of the desired process behavior and an intermediate status of a process execution, the goal is predicting how the execution might proceed, or what kind of process is being enacted, among a set of candidates. Interesting solutions for the process prediction task adopt the WoMan framework for process management [5], that proved able to support the prediction task in other application domains [7]. Specifically, it is based on a representation formalism that can support the prediction task.

3   The WoMan Framework for Process-Related Prediction

The WoMan framework [4] lies at the intersection between *Declarative* Process Mining [16] and Inductive Logic Programming (ILP) [14]. It introduced some important novelties in the process mining and management landscape. Experiments proved that it is able to handle efficiently and effectively very complex processes, thanks to its powerful representation formalism and process handling operators. The technical details of how WoMan works for process prediction are out of the scope of this paper. The interested reader is referred to [7] for a more technical description of this. In the following, we briefly and intuitively recall its fundamental notions.

WoMan takes as input trace elements consisting of 6-tuples $\langle T, E, W, P, A, O \rangle$, where T is the event timestamp, E is the type of the event (one of 'begin_process', 'end_process', 'begin_activity', 'end_activity'), W is the name of the reference workflow, P is the case identifier, A is the name of the activity, and O is the progressive number of occurrence of that activity in that case.

WoMan models describe the structure of workflows using two elements:

tasks: the kinds of activities that are allowed in the process;
transitions: the allowed connections between activities.

The core of the model, carrying the information about the flow of activities during process execution, is the set of transitions. A transition $t : I \Rightarrow O$, where I and O are multisets of tasks, is enabled if all input tasks in I are active; it occurs when, after stopping (in any order) the concurrent execution of all tasks in I, the concurrent execution of all output tasks in O is started (again, in any order). Any task or transition t is associated to the multiset C_t of training cases in which it occurred (indeed, a task or transition may occur several times in the same case, if loops or duplicate tasks are present in the model). It allows us to compute the probability of occurrence of t in a model learned from n training cases as the relative frequency $|C_t|/n$. As shown in [4,5], this representation formalism is more powerful than Petri or Workflow Nets [21], that are the current standard in Process Mining. It can smoothly express complex models involving invisible or duplicate tasks, which are problematic for those formalisms.

WoMan's supervision module, **WEST** (Workflow Enactment Supervisor and Trainer), takes the case events as long as they are available, and returns information about their compliance with the currently available model for the process they refer to. The output for each event can be 'ok', 'error' (e.g., when closing activities that had never begun, or terminating the process while activities are still running), or a set of warnings denoting different kinds of deviations from the model (e.g., unexpected task or transition, preconditions not fulfilled, unexpected resource running a given activity, etc.).

The learning module, **WIND** (Workflow INDucer), allows one to learn or refine a process model according to a case. The refinement may affect the structure and/or the probabilities. Differently from all previous approaches in the literature, it is *fully incremental*: not only can it refine an existing model according to new cases whenever they become available, it can even start learning from an empty model and a single case, while others need a (large) number of cases to draw significant statistics before learning starts.

While in supervision mode, WoMan can make several kinds of predictions. Specifically, **WoGue** (Workflow Guesser), given the events of an unknown workflow, returns a ranking (by confidence) of a set of candidate process models. Confidence here is not to be interpreted in the mathematical sense. It is determined based on a heuristic combination of several parameters associated with the possible alternate process statuses that are compliant with the current partial process execution.

4   Language Identification with WoMan

Using process prediction approaches for the Language Identification problem, predictions are more complex than in industrial processes, because there is a much larger set of possible task and much more variability and subjectivity in the users' behavior, and there is no 'correct' underlying model, just some kind of 'typicality' can be expected.

4.1   Language Identification as a Process

Following mainstream literature, we adopt the n-gram based approach to Language Identification. Compared to the stopword-based approach, it is more directly applicable, because there is no need to know the set of stopwords in advance (which would require a further linguistic resource to be available). Also, we consider only lowercase letters, shifting to lowercase all uppercase ones and ignoring spaces, punctuation and other symbols.

So, in our solution, each n-gram is a task in a process perspective. Using the basic latin alphabet, that underlies most natural languages (and can be used to transliterate most other languages using different alphabets), and ignoring punctuation and other symbols, this yields overall 26 unigrams, $26^2 = 676$ bigrams and $26^3 = 17576$ trigrams. In a process mining setting, 676 or 17576 tasks are a really huge number, often outside the reach of state-of-the-art systems [5]. Transitions among tasks happen whenever a new character is read from the text, and consist in stepping from the current n-gram to the next one obtained by removing the first character of the previous n-gram and appending the new character to the result. So, for instance, the sentence '*Hello, world!*' would generate the following sequences of n-grams (where blanks, punctuation and other symbols have been replaced by a star *):

1-grams: *, h, e, l, l, o, *, w, o, r, l, d, *
2-grams: **, *h, he, el, ll, lo, o*, *w, wo, or, rl, ld, d*, **
3-grams: ***, **h, *he, hel, ell, llo, lo*, o*w, *wo, wor, orl, rld, ld*, d**, ***

Clearly, our process models will not involve any concurrency, which simplifies the mining task and allows a fair comparison to HMMs. However, these models will involve loops (including nested and short ones), optional and duplicate tasks, which are among the main sources of complexity in process mining.

In our setting, a case is a sentence. Compared to using full texts as cases, this results in short cases, each of which involves just a very small fraction of all possible tasks (i.e., n-grams), making it more difficult for WoMan to find a training case that exactly matches a new case to be processed for predictions. However, this allows to get a larger set of training cases from a restricted set of long texts. This setting requires a way to chunk sentences in a text. Instead of relying on off-the-shelf chunkers, we adopt the baseline solution that splits sentences whenever a full stop is encountered. While possibly returning wrong sentences from time to time, this avoids the need for a further resource, which is one of the fundamental requirements for our work.

4.2 Datasets Description

We collected a dataset involving 7 languages: English, Italian, Spanish, French, Portuguese, German and Squinzanese. So, it includes both latin languages and german ones. Also, very close languages are included, to make the learning and prediction task more difficult. Squinzanese, in particular, is a dialect from Southern Italy, which mainly comes from Latin but was also affected by the Spanish and French dominations, and more recently by the spread of Italian as a national language. It also has some connections to German and Arabic in a few words.

11 texts per language were collected: 10 to be used for training, and 1 for testing. In order to have texts of medium size, and based on the available literature, tales were considered. We tried to have translations of the same texts in the different languages. This should ensure a more standardized base. Especially for closer languages, this made the recognition problem more difficult (because they use similar words and, thus, similar n-grams). For this purpose, we considered well-known tales taken from the Grimm brothers collection (www.grimmstories. com), whose translation was available for all languages except for Squinzanese. In fact, dialects have a mainly oral tradition and it is not easy to find written stuff for them. However, a book of tales was available also for Squinzanese [13], and

Table 1. Dataset statistics

Language	Training set		Learning runtime (sec)						Test set	
	#sent	#char (avg)	1-gram		2-gram		3-gram		#sent	#char (avg)
			Tot	Avg	Tot	Avg	Tot	Avg		
English	679	133.486	385.216	0.57	254.248	0.37	267.432	0.39	49	119.367
French	855	110.991	1996.724	2.34	2555.46	2.99	1874.72	2.19	61	104.049
German	665	141.883	372.992	0.56	373.6	0.56	996.272	1.5	45	130.022
Italian	801	146.571	344.708	0.43	403.46	0.5	457.064	0.57	100	157.91
Portuguese	823	113.205	346.648	0.42	321.972	0.39	334.732	0.41	56	98.911
Squinzanese	696	152.927	287.348	0.41	324.78	0.47	355.852	0.51	199	138.548
Spanish	742	119.923	186.48	0.25	213.244	0.29	263.948	0.36	46	124.5

we were lucky enough that it reported also the Italian translation of the tales. So, for Italian we used the translations of the tales selected for Squinzanese instead of those by the Grimm brothers, so that the former have representatives in at least two languages.

Table 1 reports some statistics on the experimental dataset. Specifically, for each language, it reports: number of sentences (i.e., cases in a process perspective) and average number of characters per sentence (each character determines a new task for all n-gram settings), both for the training set and for the test documents. As regards the training set, the number of sentences ranges from 679 for English to 855 for French, which is interesting because they were translations of the same texts, and the average number of characters per sentence is comparable. More variability is present in the test set, where Italian and Squinzanese include a almost twice as much sentences as the other languages, but still involve a comparable number of characters.

4.3 Model Training

Concerning the learning procedure, we fixed a random sequence S of the training texts, and then learned 30 models for each language, one for each setting (n, m), where $n \in \{1, 2, 3\}$ is the size of n-grams and $m \in \{1, \ldots, 10\}$ means that the first m texts in S were used for training. Table 2 shows some statistics for models $(1, 4)$, $(2, 9)$ and $(3, 10)$, which provided the best average performance on the overall test set. Figures are comparable for all settings and languages, except Italian (somehow smaller) and Squinzanese (significantly smaller), possibly due to the different tales used for them. The number of tasks (i.e., n-grams) grows exponentially for increasing n, but its proportion compared to all possible n-grams is smaller and smaller. In any case, for $n = 2, 3$ this number is still huge, compared to the usual numbers handled by state-of-the-art process management systems in industrial environments. Nevertheless, WoMan was able to deal with this complex task. Tables 1 and 2 also report the runtime needed to learn the models (overall and/or average per sentence). Except for French and for German as regards 3-grams, average runtimes per sentence are comparable in all settings (n, m), regardless of the number of texts used, ensuring acceptable performance.

Table 2. Models statistic

Language	#cases			#tasks			#transitions			Avg runtime (sec)		
	(4, 1)	(9, 2)	(10, 3)	(4, 1)	(9, 2)	(10, 3)	(4, 1)	(9, 2)	(10, 3)	(4, 1)	(9, 2)	(10, 3)
English	370	639	679	29	404	2655	378	2619	8586	0.29	0.37	0.39
French	462	786	855	40	478	2935	436	2890	9421	0.24	0.34	2.19
German	350	623	665	34	518	3033	478	2968	9182	0.69	0.60	1.5
Italian	366	751	801	30	330	2339	319	2298	8602	0.36	0.49	0.57
Portuguese	399	757	696	43	552	2095	494	3007	8586	0.22	0.27	0.41
Squinzanese	208	589	823	29	345	3084	283	1995	9993	0.45	0.45	0.51
Spanish	372	694	742	38	505	3156	464	3095	10516	0.22	0.35	0.36

Figure 1 shows the plots of the learning behavior for the different n-gram settings, where the i-th point represents the number of changes applied to the model after processing the i-th sentence. Plots associated to the various language models are superimposed, in order to give the reader an overall idea of the learning trend. The fact that peaks become lower and sparser as long as the plot proceeds to the right confirms that the learned models actually converge. Of course, as long as n is increased, convergence comes later, as expected due to the increasing number of features to be handled.

4.4   Language Identification Performance

Concerning the testing procedure, for each set of 7 models/languages associated to the same (n, m) pair, we tested performances on the test set made up by all test texts (one for each language) as follows. On each event in the test set, WEST was called on each model to check compliance with the various languages and suitably update the process statuses, then WoGue was called using as candidate models the 7 models for the various languages. WoGue always returns a prediction, expressed as a ranking of the models/languages by decreasing confidence.

Each setting was evaluated according to four measures (see Tables 3 and 4). One is accuracy (Acc), computed as the average position of the correct prediction in the ranking, normalized to $[0, 1]$, where 1 represents the top of the ranking, and 0 its bottom. The other measures assess, on average, for what percentage of the case duration the prediction was:

correct (C): i.e., the correct process was alone at the top of the ranking;
uncertain (U): i.e., the correct process was at the top of the ranking together with others; or
wrong (W): i.e., the correct process was not at the top of the ranking.

Figure 2 shows the trend in accuracy and correctness (averaged on all languages) of the models learned for 1-, 2- and 3-grams as long as more texts are processed. While one might expect that the plots would always be monotonically increasing, we note that this somehow holds for 3-grams only, while for both 1-grams and 2-grams the plot reaches some kind of plateau after processing 4 texts. It is also very interesting to note that, after processing 2 texts or

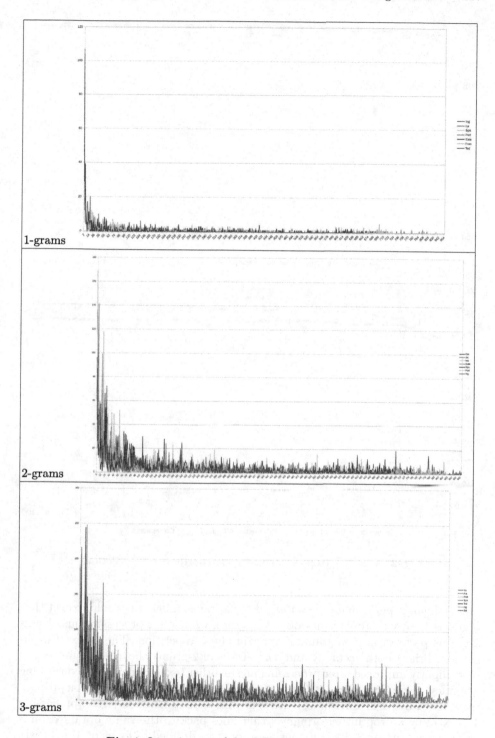

Fig. 1. Learning trend for different n-gram settings

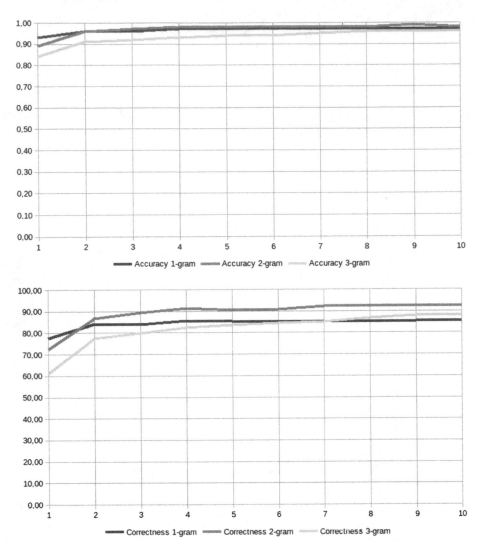

Fig. 2. Accuracy (top) and correctness (bottom) for predictions.

more, the best performance is obtained by 2-grams, albeit we would expect that 3-grams convey more information. Even more, while after processing just 1 text 1-grams perform best, 3-grams never win the competition. The 4-text threshold also brings both accuracy and correctness of 2-grams above 90%, and this is only slightly improved after processing all the other texts. Specifically concerning accuracy, some improvement (from 98% to 99%) is obtained only after processing 9 texts, but it is unreliable, since it is immediately followed (when processing 10 texts) by a drop in performance, that goes back to the value obtained for 8 texts. Given these results and considerations, we decided to focus on the 4-texts

Table 3. Predictions statistics: best for language

Language	1-gram				2-gram				3-gram			
	Acc		C		Acc		C		Acc		C	
	Text	Value	Text	Value	Text	Value	Text	Value	Text	Value	Text	Value
English	2	0.98	9	95.4	2	0.99	2	95	10	0.98	10	95.3
French	9	0.96	9	80.3	6	0.98	9	91.5	7	0.97	9	90.9
German	6	1	5	96.8	4	1	10	97.5	9	0.99	10	95.7
Italian	2	0.98	2	85.5	3	0.98	9	91.2	8	0.96	9	88.2
Portuguese	9	0.97	9	83.7	4	0.98	4	91.7	5	0.95	6	87.3
Squinzanese	1	0.96	7	83.6	9	0.98	9	88.8	9	0.93	10	75.6
Spanish	4	0.97	4	85.2	7	0.99	7	94.7	9	0.97	9	87.7

Table 4. Predictions statistics: average

n	N	avg	avg	Eng		Fre		Ger		Ita		Por		Squ		Spa	
		Acc	C	Acc	C	Acc	C	Acc	C	Acc	C	Acc	C	Acc	C	Acc	C
1	4	**0.97**	**85.58**	0.98	93.3	0.94	75.8	1	96.6	0.97	83	0.96	82.7	0.96	82.5	0.97	85.2
2	9	**0.99**	**92.33**	0.99	93.1	0.98	91.5	1	97.3	0.98	91.2	0.98	89.9	0.98	88.8	0.99	94.6
3	10	**0.96**	**87.91**	0.98	95.3	0.96	90.9	0.99	95.7	0.95	87.1	0.94	83.1	0.93	75.6	0.97	87.7

setting for 1-grams, 9-texts setting for 2-grams and 10-texts setting for 3-grams, which provided the best average performance on the overall set of languages.

Table 3 summarizes the performance on language identification, cast as a process prediction task, for a few settings selected as more relevant. U and W are not reported, since the former is always negligible (around 2.6%) and thus the latter is almost complementary to C. Looking at the detailed results, independently of the specific values, we see that in all settings German is best recognized, followed by English. This suggests that anglo-german languages are more characterized. Among latin languages, Spanish recognition is above average for 2-grams and mostly above average for 3-grams, then Italian has good performance on accuracy for 1-grams and Portuguese has some good performances on accuracy and/or correctness for 3-grams. The worst performance (Squinzanese) is still above 90% accuracy and 80% correctness for 2-grams.

Table 4 reports, for each n-gram, the number N of texts that provided the best average value for Acc and C, along with the performance on single languages. As regards Latin languages performances, they are close to average values; for each n-gram setting of French and English, their performances exceed the average values, while Squinzanese still has the worst performance.

To assign a language to a sentence, we used the last prediction in the sentence's n-grams. This quite basic decision rule allowed us to obtain 94% for (1, 4), 98% for (2, 9) and 92% for (3, 10) in predictive accuracy. Statistical significance of the results is supported by the size of our test set, that includes 556 sentences overall, compared to the overall population including 3083 sentences, so that the tolerance interval is ± 1.16 at 95% confidence, and ± 1.52 at 99% confidence.

The best performance, obtained using 2-grams, is comparable or even better than most other approaches in the current state-of-the art [11,12,19]. [11] works on 12 languages, reaching an average accuracy of about 91% overall and the following accuracy on languages we also considered: English 100%, French 99%, German 96%, Italian 80%, Portuguese 95%, Spanish 87%. [12] reports results on 4 languages only, 2 of which using different alphabets: Serbian, English, Chinese and Arabic. [19] works on 18 languages, reaching the following performance on languages we also considered: English 96% (97/101), French 83% (90/108), German 94% (94/100), Italian 98% (95/97), Latin 95% (100/105), Portuguese 92% (96/104), Spanish 95% (79/83). We are slightly worse than the Naive Bayes approach [1], which reached 100% but considering just 5 languages.

Additionally, our approach has several advantages over those solution: it can learn models using a few hundred sentences instead of thousands; and, most importantly, it is incremental both as regards training examples (i.e., it can refine and improve models as long as new training data are available, without the need to start from scratch each time) and as regards the target classes (i.e., we learn independent models for each language, and thus new languages can be added at any moment without affecting the existing models and without the need to learn them from scratch). Moreover, there is room for us to improve our performance in several directions: we can use the data gained during the whole path of a sentence to refine our decision rule; we may use WoMan's denoise feature to simplify the models by removing irrelevant components that possibly lower performance; we may use WoMan's model analysis features to identify the most characterizing or discriminating components in the models, and focus on these components hopefully improve performance.

5   Conclusions and Future Work

Several high-level tasks in the management of Digital Libraries require the application of Natural Language Processing (NLP) techniques. In turn, most NLP solutions are based on linguistic resources that are costly to produce, and so motivate research for automated ways to build them. In particular, Language Identification is a crucial NLP task, that is preliminary to almost all the others, since different linguistic resources must be used for different languages. On the other hand, for many languages that may be of interest in Digital Libraries, tools and resources for carrying out language identification are not available. This motivates the research for automatic approaches to do this.

While traditionally exploited for checking process enactment conformance, process models may be used to make predictions about a partial execution of a process. This paper proposes a way to see a text as a process, casts the Language Identification task as a process prediction problem, and investigates process mining and management approaches as a possible solution. Experimental results show very good performance. Also, some outcomes are not obvious. For instance, processing more texts does not always improve performance significantly. Also, 2-grams are the best, and 3 g are the worst, even if the latter embed more information than the former. These results suggest several directions for future research. First, we will check if and how the performance changes when adding more languages, especially with ones who are completely different from each other. Also, we will check whether performance can be improved by suitably selecting more relevant components of the models and by refining our decision rule.

Acknowledgments. This work was partially funded by the Italian PON 2007–2013 project PON02_00563_3489339 'Puglia@Service'.

References

1. Ahmed, B., Cha, S.H., Tappert, C.: Language identification from text using n-gram based cumulative frequency addition. In: Proceedings of Student/Faculty Research Day, p. 12-1. CSIS, Pace University (2004)
2. Brown, P.F., deSouza, P.V., Mercer, R.L., Pietra, V.J.D., Lai, J.C.: Class-based n-gram models of natural language. Comput. Linguist. **18**(4), 467–479 (1992)
3. Cavnar, W.B., Trenkle, J.M.: N-gram-based text categorization. In: Proceedings of 3rd Annual Symposium on Document Analysis and Information Retrieval (SDAIR 1994), pp. 161–175 (1994)
4. Ferilli, S.: WoMan: logic-based workflow learning and management. IEEE Trans. Syst. Man Cybern. Syst. **44**, 744–756 (2014)
5. Ferilli, S., Esposito, F.: A logic framework for incremental learning of process models. Fundamenta Informaticae **128**, 413–443 (2013)
6. Ferilli, S., Esposito, F., Grieco, D.: Automatic learning of linguistic resources for stopword removal and stemming from text. Procedia Comput. Sci. **38**(C), 116–123 (2014)
7. Ferilli, S.: The WoMan formalism for expressing process models. In: Perner, P. (ed.) ICDM 2016. LNCS, vol. 0728, pp. 363–378. Springer, Cham (2016). doi:10. 1007/978-3-319-41561-1_27
8. Ferilli, S.: Natural language processing. In: Ferilli, S. (ed.) Automatic Digital Document Processing. Advances in Pattern Recognition, pp. 131–155. Springer, Cham (2015). doi:10.1007/978-0-85729-198-1_6
9. van der Aalst, W., et al.: Process mining manifesto. In: Daniel, F., Barkaoui, K., Dustdar, S. (eds.) BPM 2011. LNBIP, vol. 99, pp. 169–194. Springer, Heidelberg (2012). doi:10.1007/978-3-642-28108-2_19
10. Jozefowicz, R., Vinyals, O., Schuster, M., Shazeer, N., Wu, Y.: Exploring the limits of language modeling (2016)
11. Martins, B., Silva, M.: Language identification in web pages. In: Proceedings of the 2005 ACM symposium on Applied Computing, pp. 764–768. ACM (2005)
12. Mathew, T.: Text categorization using n-grams and hidden Markov models (2006). http://www.slideshare.net/thomas_a_mathew/text-categorization-using-ngrams-and-hiddenmarkovmodel
13. Messito, A.: Cuntame nnu cuntu! PhotoCity (2014)
14. Muggleton, S.: Inductive logic programming. New Gener. Comput. **8**(4), 295–318 (1991)
15. Nagarajan, T., Murthy, H.: Language identification using parallel syllable like unit recognition. In: Proceedings of the IEEE International Conference on Acoustics, Speech, and Signal Processing (ICASSP 2004), vol. 1, p. I-401. IEEE (2004)

16. Pesic, M., van der Aalst, W.M.P.: A declarative approach for flexible business processes management. In: Eder, J., Dustdar, S. (eds.) BPM 2006. LNCS, vol. 4103, pp. 169–180. Springer, Heidelberg (2006). doi:10.1007/11837862_18
17. Pierce, J.: Symbols, Signals and Noise: The Nature and Process of Communication. Harper, New York (1961)
18. Rotella, F., Leuzzi, F., Ferilli, S.: Learning and exploiting concept networks with connektion. Appl. Intell. **42**(1), 87–111 (2015)
19. Sibun, P., Reynar, J.C.: Language identification: examining the issues (1996)
20. Vatanen, T., Väyrynen, J.J., Virpioja, S.: Language identification of short text segments with n-gram models. In: Proceedings of the Seventh International Conference on Language Resources and Evaluation (LREC 2010). European Language Resources Association (ELRA), Valletta, May 2010
21. Weijters, A., van der Aalst, W.: Rediscovering workflow models from event-based data. In: Proceedings of the 11th Dutch-Belgian Conference of Machine Learning (Benelearn 2001), pp. 93–100 (2001)

An Annotation Tool for a Digital Library System of Epidermal Data

Fabrizio Balducci$^{(\boxtimes)}$ and Guido Borghi

Dipartimento di Ingegneria "Enzo Ferrari",
Università Degli Studi di Modena e Reggio Emilia, Via Vivarelli 10,
41125 Modena, MO, Italy
{fabrizio.balducci,guido.borghi}@unimore.it

Abstract. Melanoma is one of the deadliest form of skin cancers so it becomes crucial the developing of automated systems that analyze and investigate epidermal images to early identify them also reducing unnecessary medical exams. A key element is the availability of user-friendly annotation tools that can be used by non-IT experts to produce well-annotated and high-quality medical data. In this work, we present an annotation tool to manually crate and annotate digital epidermal images, with the aim to extract meta-data (annotations, contour patterns and intersections, color information) stored and organized in an integrated digital library. This tool is obtained following rigid usability principles also based on doctors interviews and opinions. A preliminary but functional evaluation phase has been conducted with non-medical subjects by using questionnaires, in order to check the general usability and the efficacy of the proposed tool.

Keywords: Annotation · Epidermal images · Skin · Usability

1 Introduction

The interest of biomedical and computer vision communities in acquisition and analysis of epidermal images has been increased during the last decades: the possibility to automatically detect and classify early melanomas is investigated because it is one of the most common and danger skin cancer. Only considering United States, 100,000 new cases are diagnosed every year with over 9,000 deaths correlated [9,11]. In this context new automated system for fast and accurate skin image acquisition and investigation, melanoma detection and classification are well accepted in the biomedical community, also considering that the diagnostic accuracy with trained clinicians is around 75–84% [19].

Traditionally, clinical experts manually categorize and examine printed medical images so it becomes a very time consuming task; to avoid this issue, advanced user-friendly annotation tools must be developed, in order to improve the digital libraries in biomedical and related fields in size and quality of annotated data that will be processed by machine learning and pattern recognition

© Springer International Publishing AG 2017
C. Grana and L. Baraldi (Eds.): IRCDL 2017, CCIS 733, pp. 173–186, 2017.
DOI: 10.1007/978-3-319-68130-6_14

techniques. The usability of the tools, with also the assurance that their hardware devices are medical-compliant, is a fundamental element due to user's lack of deep IT-skills.

This paper is organized as follows: Sect. 2 describes literature based on epidermal and, in particular, melanoma images while Sect. 3 proposes an architecture for the digital library with the implementation details of the annotation tool; Sect. 4 reports results obtained by the experimental evaluation and, finally, conclusions and future work are illustrated in Sect. 5.

2   Related Work

A complete and rich survey about lesion border detection is in [7]. The first step for skin inspection is the acquisition of digital images: the main techniques involve *Epiluminence Microscopy* (ELM, or dermoscopy), *Transmission Electron Microscopy* (TEM) and the acquisition through standard RGB cameras [24]. In last decades, standard video devices are commonly used for skin lesion inspection systems, in particular in the telemedicine field [33]. However, these solutions present some issues, like low camera spatial resolution (melanoma or other skin details can be very small) and distortions caused by the camera lenses. Moreover, variable illumination conditions can strongly deteriorate the quality of acquisitions [2, 24].

After the digital acquisition, the second step consists in the analysis and investigation of the epidermal images acquired: several works in literature have been proposed for automated epidermal image analysis, in order to support biomedical experts; most of them are based on Computer Vision approaches, typically combining low-level visual features representation, image processing techniques and machine learning and pattern recognition algorithms [9].

In [8] manually pre-segmented images, already cropped around the region of interest, have been used in conjunction with hand-coded and unsupervised features to achieve state-of-the-art results in melanoma recognition task, with a dataset of 2,000 dermoscopy images. Specifically, a combination of sparse coding, deep learning and Support Vector Machine (SVM) learning algorithms are exploited. In [5, 26] several machine learning classifiers, like SVMs and K-nearest neighbors (kNNs), based on color, edge and texture descriptors are investigated and compared. Learning approaches [29, 30] and deep learning techniques [6, 12, 18, 25] have been exploited in literature while a combination of hand-coded features extractors, sparse-coding methods, SVMs and deep learning techniques are used focusing on melanoma recognition and segmentation tasks in dermoscopy and dermatology domain [9].

Finally, in 2016 a new challenge, called *Skin Lesion Analysis toward Melanoma Detection* [16], has been presented: the aim is to use one of the most complete dataset of melanoma images, collected by the *International Skin Imaging Collaboration* (ISIC) and obtained with the aggregation dataset of dermoscopic images from multiple institutions, to test and evaluate the automated techniques for the diagnosis of melanomas; best scores in classification and segmentation are achieved using deep learning approaches [17, 22].

Before this challenge, the exploitation of deep learning techniques, like Convolutional Neural Networks (CNNs) was partially bounded by the limited size of datasets present in literature. Generally, the amount if training data and high quality annotations are key aspects for deep learning approaches [20].

3   Our Proposal

This paper presents a new user-friendly annotation tool for epidermal images which must also be mobile oriented by running on smartphones and tablets. The annotation tool is the first step to create an heterogeneous integrated system, which architecture is depicted in Fig. 1.

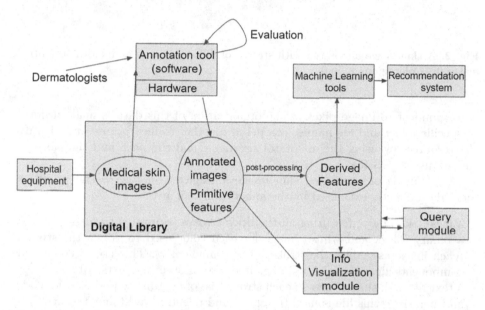

Fig. 1. The general architecture proposed for a biomedical digital library. The digital library and the annotation tool are the core of the presented method.

The system core is the Digital Library which stores and organizes the dataset acquired from hospital equipment: it currently consists of 436 medical skin images in standard JPEG format with a high spatial resolution of 4000×2664 or 3000×4000 pixels. The software has been developed to enable the annotation of images by domain experts, like dermatologists, and it is described in the following subsection: it permits to easily draw strokes with different colors (8 choices) and pen sizes (4 choices), where each color denotes a specific semantic given by dermatologists (this aspect will be addressed in future works).

The main goal of this tool is the retention of annotations in the form of a new enriched images also indexing each drawn stroke (in turn composed by points

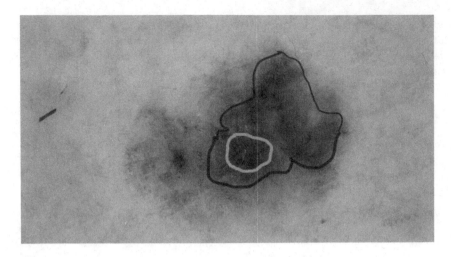

Fig. 2. A skin image annotated with strokes of different colors and width (primitive feature). (Color figure online)

correspondent to image pixels). The organization of this data is made in form of specific folder and file names, composed together to incorporate and identify the resources by using the annotator username and the path and the name of the original JPEG file.

An example of annotated skin image is depicted in Fig. 2. The primitive meta-data directly extracted by the annotation tool are:

- a new color image, featuring all the draw strokes (primitive features)
- a binary (black and white) image for each color used to drawn the strokes (each image assembles the strokes of the same color). This uses a connected components algorithm [14,15], exploited also in other contexts [10].
- a text file with the features of each stroke (list of coordinate points, color code and pen size): this file is used to rebuilt and reload a saved annotation.

After the annotation phase and the *primitive features* extraction and storing, it is necessary to perform a pre-processing phase before the extraction of *advanced features* to check two essential requirements for each annotated image:

1. remove thick hairs, because this artifacts influence the shape and contours extraction [21,34]
2. assure that for each stroke and color all the drawn contours are closed [28], to preserve the consistency of extracted features

After this pre-processing phase new images are then created:

- a binary image for each color channel (RGB) used for the thick hair removal phase
- a new color image without thick hairs

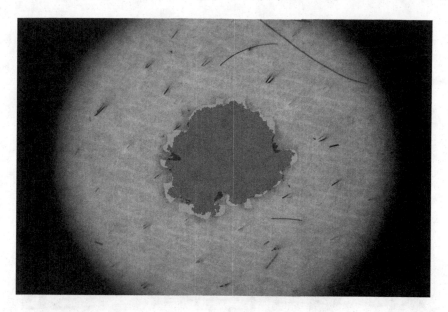

Fig. 3. An example of derived feature: the automatic area (red) made by the system and the intersection area (blue) obtained with the manual one (green) made by a dermatologist. (Color figure online)

Now it is possible to apply internal image processing functions and algorithms to extract *derived features* like contours, shapes, intersections, color features and numerical values, as shown in Fig. 3.

By using the new extracted features it will be possible to use *Machine Learning tools* to develop the *Recommendation module*. Image classification, to distinguish between benign and malignant (melanomas) lesions, could be carried out exploiting deep learning techniques; recently, this kind of approach reached best performances in many Computer Vision research tasks like image and video classification [3,4], objects detection and pose estimation.

Given an epidermal input image, a Convolutional Neural Network (CNN) could be used to produce the classification: a CNN is a neural model composed by sequences of convolutional layers that apply a set of filters (typically followed by Spatial Pooling layers) to down sample the input tensor in spatial dimensions, and by Fully Connected layers in which each neuron could be linked with all other neurons in the following layers. An activation function is exploited to introduce non-linearity inside the architecture [20]. Finally, a loss function represents the cost associated to the achievement of a final goal, like correct classification, regression and so on. The main issue of CNN is the huge amount of data needed in the training phase: with an unbalanced or small dataset they are prone to both over fitting and under fitting phenomena; to avoid this, data augmentation is often performed so an annotation tool to easily acquire and produce high-quality annotated biomedical images could be really useful and important.

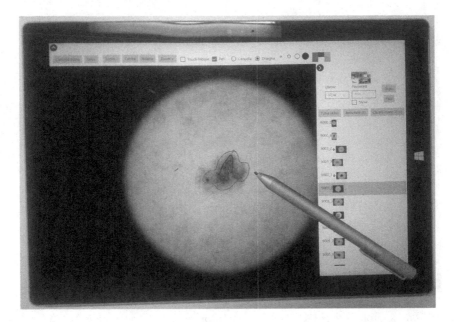

Fig. 4. The *Microsoft Surface Pro 3* is the hardware platform chosen for the annotation tool. In this way, portability and error-free annotations (thanks to the *Surface Pen*) are guaranteed.

Finally, in the architecture we considered an *Information Visualization module* for various and dynamic data visualization and a specific *Query module* to permit search facilities [1].

An example of standard for handling, storing, printing, and transmitting information in medical imaging is the DICOM (Digital Imaging and Communications in Medicine, ISO standard 12052:2006) of which the National Electrical Manufacturers Association (NEMA) holds the copyright. This standard has been widely adopted by hospitals and is making inroads in smaller applications like dentists' and doctors' offices: it includes a file format definition and a network communications protocol which uses TCP/IP to communicate between systems and enables the integration of medical imaging devices like scanners, servers, workstations, printers and network hardware from multiple manufacturers.

The different devices come with DICOM Conformance Statements which clearly state which classes they support; a DICOM data object consists of attributes (such as name, ID, datetime) with a special one containing the pixel data: in this way the medical image contains for example the patient ID within the file so that the image can never be separated from this information (similarly to the JPEG format that embeds tags to describe an image).

3.1   Developing the Annotation Tool

We decided to use as hardware platform the *Microsoft Surface Pro 3*, depicted in Fig. 4: this is a portable tablet device, powerful as a modern PC but less invasive, so it can be used in mobility into a medical environment like an hospital. Dermatologists can annotate images with the assurance that the only strokes recognized by the touch screen are those which comes from the specific *Surface Pen*, avoiding unwanted strokes coming from touch gestures or oversight movements.

To acquire the necessary data for the digital library, we developed an annotation tool following the principles of usability and *Human-Computer Interaction* [32] bearing in mind the following principles:

1. final users are domain experts that could be unfamiliar with technical tool or data organization and analysis
2. physician are usually overworked so they do not have much time to skill themselves on externals tools
3. physician and specialists like dermatologists have peculiar working protocols and pipelines, so the tool must be non-invasive with the aim to not impact on their daily activities
4. the image annotation task must be as much as possible fast and user-friendly for a dermatologist, imitating what they would do naturally
5. the medical environment has peculiar safety and security requirements so, in addition to the software tool, the hardware introduced in this areas must be considered

The task of *annotate* with a precise technological pen on a glass screen is natural and intuitive and shows the characteristic of *Affordance* [13]: in the field of psychology the term includes all actions that are physically possible on an object or environment (like what a physician wants to performs on a real medical printed photo). In a general way, when the concept is applied to design and develop activities it refers to those action possibilities that the user is aware of, also considering the available or permissible peripherals that allow such interactions. The *perceived affordance* refers not only to the user physical capabilities but also on his goals, beliefs, and past experiences [27] so that an object (real or virtual) can naturally'suggests' how to interact with it.

Another usability aspect is the *direct manipulation* allowed by the gestures on the touch screen like *to pitch* (zoom-in and zoom-out operations) and *to drag* (scrolling) which are alternatives to the button widgets provided by the user interface. Formally, Direct manipulation is an *interaction style* in which users act on displayed objects of interest using physical, incremental, reversible actions whose effects are immediately visible on the screen [31].

In his works Shneiderman identified several principles of this interaction style:

– continuous representation of the objects of interest: while performing an action user can see its effects on the state of the system

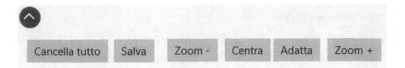

Fig. 5. The top panel of the annotation tool (part 1): here, user can save or delete the annotation and manipulate the image display.

Fig. 6. The top panel of the annotation tool (part 2): here, user can set the interaction and input modalities and manage the stroke features.

- physical actions instead of complex syntax: in contrast with command-line interfaces, actions are invoked physically via input peripherals, visual widges (button, menu,) and gestures.
- continuous feedback and reversible incremental actions: it results easy to validate each action and fix mistakes
- rapid learning: users learn by recognition instead of remember complex syntax commands

The interface is minimal but functional and presents two retractable panels at the top (separated in Figs. 5 and 6 and at the right (Fig. 7) part of the screen. The top panel contains a set of functionalities regarding image and annotation processing:

1. delete or store the annotation strokes
2. manipulate the image display (zoom in/out, center, scale adaptation)
3. select the input device (mouse/touch or pen)
4. manage the stroke features like color and width

The right panel presents two horizontal sections: the superior one permits the login and the exit from the application (exploiting the internal users database that also allows the meta-data organization previously described); the lower panel allows the image selection and loading by showing a list with a small preview of them (if an image has been annotated previously a green rhombus appears next to its name).

In the previous panel there are three tabs that have a dual functionality, in fact they show respectively the total number of images, the number of the annotated images and the number of the images that shall be annotated; moreover, when the user selects one tab, a *dynamic filter* updates the image list based on the selected preference.

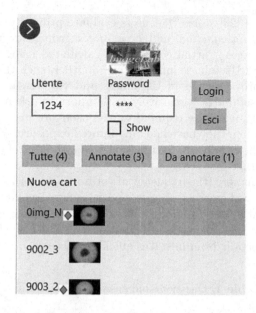

Fig. 7. The right panel of the annotation tool: it contains the login module, the list of images (with a thumbnail) and the tabs that dynamically filter them.

4   Experimental Setup

A preliminary evaluation was performed to test the annotation facilities and to understand if the user interface and its functionalities were easy to understand and perform; we used six non-medical students which, after a small brief on the capabilities and the target of this tool, were observed while carrying the annotation task on a subset of 25 images, encouraged to explore the tool.

Strongly Disagree			Indifferent			Strongly Agree
1	2	3	4	5	6	7

Fig. 8. The 7-degree *Likert* scale used for answer to a question.

After each experimentation phase, a questionnaire made by following Human Computer Interaction studies guidelines and consisting by 20 questions was given to the subjects. The evaluation for each question was given by a 7-degree ordered *Likert* scale as in Fig. 8 and was asked to rate agreement with the statements, ranging from strongly disagree to strongly agree. Questions are divided into four sections concerning *Usefulness*, *Ease of Use*, *Ease of Learning* and *Satisfaction*.

In its work, Lund [23] states that users evaluate primarily using the dimensions of *Usefulness, Satisfaction,* and *Ease of Use* which are used to discriminate between interfaces. Partial correlations calculated using scales suggested that Ease of Use and Usefulness influence one another, such that improvements in Ease of Use improve ratings of Usefulness and vice-versa; while both drive Satisfaction, the Usefulness is relatively less important when the systems are internal systems that users are required to use; users are more variable in their Usefulness ratings when they have had only limited exposure to a product while, as expected from the literature, Satisfaction was strongly related to the usage (actual or predicted).

Questions and answers (the frequency of votes in *Likert* scale) are reported in Table 1: the majority of answers expresses positive agree as for question j (Both occasional and regular users would like it) or question f (It is easy to use). Few low votes in interval [3–5] considering question t (I feel I need to have it) and question k (I can recover from mistakes quickly and easily).

Table 1. Questions and answers in likert scale

	1	2	3	4	5	6	7
(a) It gives me more control over the activities	0	0	0	0	0	3	3
(b) It makes the things I want to accomplish easier	0	0	0	0	0	3	3
(c) It saves me time when I use it	0	0	0	0	2	4	0
(d) It meets my needs	0	0	0	1	0	4	1
(e) It does everything I would expect it to d	0	0	0	0	2	1	3
(f) It is easy to use	0	0	0	0	0	2	4
(g) Using it is effortless	0	0	0	0	0	2	4
(h) I can use it without written instructions	0	0	0	0	0	3	3
(i) I don't notice any inconsistencies as I use it	0	0	0	0	2	3	1
(j) Both occasional and regular users would like it	0	0	0	0	0	1	5
(k) I can recover from mistakes quickly and easily	0	0	1	0	2	1	2
(l) I learned to use it quickly	0	0	0	0	0	2	4
(m) I easily remember how to use it	0	0	0	0	0	2	4
(n) It is easy to learn to use it	0	0	0	0	0	3	3
(o) I quickly became skillful with it	0	0	0	0	0	2	4
(p) I am satisfied with it	0	0	0	0	2	4	0
(q) I would recommend it to a friend	0	0	0	0	0	5	1
(r) It is fun to use	0	0	0	0	1	3	2
(s) It works the way I want it to work	0	0	0	0	1	3	2
(t) I feel I need to have it	0	0	1	1	2	0	2

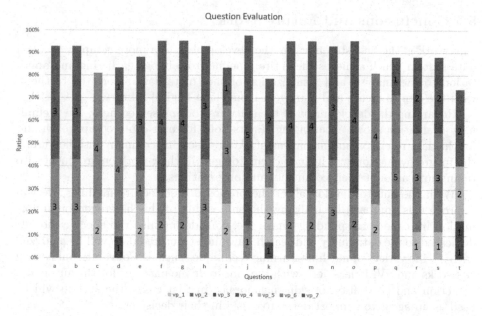

Fig. 9. The histogram about questionnaire answers. (Color figure online)

In Fig. 9 is shown a plot which summarizes and visualizes all the questionnaire results: it consists in an histogram featuring various dimensions:

1. X-axis: question code
2. Y-axis: the overall score in percentage, expresses the polarization towards a "strongly agreement" by considering a weighted vote for each given answer
3. Color: associated to a rating value of the *Likert* scale [1–7]; they go from blue palette (dislike mood) to the yellow (medium liking mood) and to the green palette (positive mood)
4. Number (into a bar): answer frequency, how many subjects answered to the question with the same rating
5. Sub-bar: its width expresses the weight that have a specific answer on the overall score (100% would be all subjects scoring the highest vote of 7).

Observing the plot it becomes evident that, by considering the overall score in percentage, for all questions subjects expresses a positive liking mood (all bar height exceed 80%). By exploiting this visualization the differences between questions become evident, for example between question *a* and question *c*: in the second one two subjects answered value '5' (yellow color evidences that the value expresses a medium liking mood) and, since the sub-bar height is related to the liking mood, expressing such a value prevents that the global bar height could exceeds one with better scores.

5 Conclusions and Future Work

This work is the first step towards the development of a more complex medical data system which achieves the entire pipeline from image gathering and annotation to the analysis and visualization of the (meta)data associated to them, with the aim to create and manage a biomedical Digital Library.

Regarding the development of the software tool presented here, the preliminary evaluation shows encouraging results both for user-centered approach and for the data retention and management. After observing common unskilled users, the future evaluation will include dermatologist in their work environment also taking into account their comments and observations.

With the aim to develop all of the proposed architecture modules, we will improve this approach by realizing the embedding of this heterogeneous information into the corresponding image file, considering also the specific module dedicated to the data query and search; raw and structured data will be analyzed with a wide variety of machine learning techniques such as Convolutional Neural Networks and SVM classifiers, with the aim to define patterns for the automatic detection and prevention of skin melanomas; in that cases, the system will be used as an agent to support dermatologists in their decisions.

The final step will be the evaluation of information visualization facilities by using the domain experts suggestions and also by the proposition of new and more effective techniques.

References

1. Ahlberg, C., Williamson, C., Shneiderman, B.: Dynamic queries for information exploration: an implementation and evaluation. In: Proceedings of the SIGCHI Conference on Human Factors in Computing Systems. CHI 1992, pp. 619–626. ACM, New York (1992). http://doi.acm.org/10.1145/142750.143054
2. Ali, A.R.A., Deserno, T.M.: A systematic review of automated melanoma detection in dermatoscopic images and its ground truth data. In: SPIE Medical Imaging, p. 83181I. International Society for Optics and Photonics (2012)
3. Baraldi, L., Grana, C., Cucchiara, R.: Hierarchical boundary-aware neural encoder for video captioning. In: Proceedings of the IEEE Conference on Computer Vision and Pattern Recognition (2017)
4. Baraldi, L., Grana, C., Cucchiara, R.: Recognizing and presenting the storytelling video structure with deep multimodal networks. IEEE Trans. Multimedia **19**(5), 955–968 (2017)
5. Barata, C., Ruela, M., Francisco, M., Mendonça, T., Marques, J.S.: Two systems for the detection of melanomas in dermoscopy images using texture and color features. IEEE Syst. J. **8**(3), 965–979 (2014)
6. Binder, M., Steiner, A., Schwarz, M., Knollmayer, S., Wolff, K., Pehamberger, H.: Application of an artificial neural network in epiluminescence microscopy pattern analysis of pigmented skin lesions: a pilot study. Br. J. Dermatol. **130**(4), 460–465 (1994)
7. Celebi, M.E., Wen, Q., Iyatomi, H., Shimizu, K., Zhou, H., Schaefer, G.: A state-of-the-art survey on lesion border detection in dermoscopy images. In: Dermoscopy Image Analysis, pp. 97–129. CRC Press (2015)

8. Codella, N., Cai, J., Abedini, M., Garnavi, R., Halpern, A., Smith, J.R.: Deep learning, sparse coding, and svm for melanoma recognition in dermoscopy images. In: Zhou, L., Wang, L., Wang, Q., Shi, Y. (eds.) MLMI 2015. LNCS, vol. 9352, pp. 118–126. Springer, Cham (2015). doi:10.1007/978-3-319-24888-2_15

9. Codella, N.C.F., Nguyen, Q., Pankanti, S., Gutman, D., Helba, B., Halpern, A., Smith, J.R.: Deep learning ensembles for melanoma recognition in dermoscopy images. CoRR abs/1610.04662 (2016). http://arxiv.org/abs/1610.04662

10. Corbelli, A., Baraldi, L., Balducci, F., Grana, C., Cucchiara, R.: Layout analysis and content classification in digitized books. In: Agosti, M., Bertini, M., Ferilli, S., Marinai, S., Orio, N. (eds.) IRCDL 2016. CCIS, vol. 701, pp. 153–165. Springer, Cham (2017). doi:10.1007/978-3-319-56300-8_14

11. Diepgen, T., Mahler, V.: The epidemiology of skin cancer. Br. J. Dermatol. **146**(s61), 1–6 (2002)

12. Ercal, F., Chawla, A., Stoecker, W.V., Lee, H.C., Moss, R.H.: Neural network diagnosis of malignant melanoma from color images. IEEE Trans. Biomed. Eng. **41**(9), 837–845 (1994)

13. Gibson, J.J., Shaw, R.: Perceiving, acting, and knowing: toward an ecological psychology. The Theory of Affordances, pp. 67–82 (1977)

14. Grana, C., Baraldi, L., Bolelli, F.: Optimized connected components labeling with pixel prediction. In: Blanc-Talon, J., Distante, C., Philips, W., Popescu, D., Scheunders, P. (eds.) ACIVS 2016. LNCS, vol. 10016, pp. 431–440. Springer, Cham (2016). doi:10.1007/978-3-319-48680-2_38

15. Grana, C., Bolelli, F., Baraldi, L., Vezzani, R.: Yacclab-yet another connected components labeling benchmark. In: 2016 23rd International Conference on Pattern Recognition (ICPR), pp. 3109–3114. IEEE (2016)

16. Gutman, D., Codella, N.C., Celebi, E., Helba, B., Marchetti, M., Mishra, N., Halpern, A.: Skin lesion analysis toward melanoma detection: A challenge at the international symposium on biomedical imaging (isbi) 2016, hosted by the international skin imaging collaboration (isic). arXiv preprint arXiv:1605.01397 (2016)

17. He, K., Zhang, X., Ren, S., Sun, J.: Deep residual learning for image recognition. arXiv preprint arXiv:1512.03385 (2015)

18. Jaleel, J.A., Salim, S., Aswin, R.: Artificial neural network based detection of skin cancer. IJAREEIE **1**, 200–205 (2012)

19. Kittler, H., Pehamberger, H., Wolff, K., Binder, M.: Diagnostic accuracy of dermoscopy. Lancet Oncol. **3**(3), 159–165 (2002)

20. Krizhevsky, A., Sutskever, I., Hinton, G.E.: Imagenet classification with deep convolutional neural networks. In: Advances in neural Information Processing Systems, pp. 1097–1105 (2012)

21. Lee, T., Ng, V., Gallagher, R., Coldman, A., McLean, D.: Dullrazor: a software approach to hair removal from images. Comput. Biol. Med. **27**(6), 533–543 (1997)

22. Long, J., Shelhamer, E., Darrell, T.: Fully convolutional networks for semantic segmentation. In: Proceedings of the IEEE Conference on Computer Vision and Pattern Recognition, pp. 3431–3440 (2015)

23. Lund, A.M.: Measuring usability with the use questionnaire. Usability Interface **8**(2), 3–6 (2001)

24. Maglogiannis, I., Doukas, C.N.: Overview of advanced computer vision systems for skin lesions characterization. IEEE Trans. Inf Technol. Biomed. **13**(5), 721–733 (2009)

25. Marín, C., Alférez, G.H., Córdova, J., González, V.: Detection of melanoma through image recognition and artificial neural networks. In: Jaffray, D.A. (ed.) World Congress on Medical Physics and Biomedical Engineering, June 7-12, 2015, Toronto, Canada. IP, vol. 51, pp. 832–835. Springer, Cham (2015). doi:10.1007/978-3-319-19387-8_204

26. Mendonça, T., Ferreira, P.M., Marques, J.S., Marcal, A.R., Rozeira, J.: Ph 2-a dermoscopic image database for research and benchmarking. In: 2013 35th Annual International Conference of the IEEE Engineering in Medicine and Biology Society (EMBC), pp. 5437–5440. IEEE (2013)

27. Norman, D.A.: Affordance, conventions, and design. Interactions 6(3), 38–43 (1999)

28. Pellacani, G., Grana, C., Seidenari, S.: Comparison between computer elaboration and clinical assessment of asymmetry and border cut-off in melanoma images. Exp. Dermatol. 11(6), 609–609 (2002)

29. Rastgoo, M., Morel, O., Marzani, F., Garcia, R.: Ensemble approach for differentiation of malignant melanoma. In: The International Conference on Quality Control by Artificial Vision 2015, p. 953415. International Society for Optics and Photonics (2015)

30. Schaefer, G., Krawczyk, B., Celebi, M.E., Iyatomi, H.: An ensemble classification approach for melanoma diagnosis. Memetic Comput. 6(4), 233–240 (2014)

31. Shneiderman, B.: 1.1 direct manipulation: a step beyond programming languages. Sparks of innovation in human-computer interaction 17, 1993 (1993)

32. Shneiderman, B.: Designing the user interface: strategies for effective human-computer interaction. Pearson Education India (2010)

33. Singh, S., Stevenson, J., McGurty, D.: An evaluation of polaroid photographic imaging for cutaneous-lesion referrals to an outpatient clinic: a pilot study. Br. J. Plast. Surg. 54(2), 140–143 (2001)

34. Zagrouba, E., Barhoumi, W.: A preliminary approach for the automated recognition of malignant melanoma. Image Anal. Stereol. 23(2), 121–135 (2011)

The Use of Hashtags in the Promotion of Art Exhibitions

Marco Furini[1], Federica Mandreoli[2], Riccardo Martoglia[2(✉)],
and Manuela Montangero[2]

[1] Dipartimento di Comunicazione ed Economia,
Università di Modena e Reggio Emilia, Reggio Emilia, Italy
marco.furini@unimore.it
[2] Dipartimento di Scienze Fisiche, Informatiche e Matematiche,
Università di Modena e Reggio Emilia, Modena, Italy
{federica.mandreoli,riccardo.martoglia,manuela.montangero}@unimore.it

Abstract. Hashtags are increasingly used to promote, foster and group conversations around specific topics. For example, the entertainment industry widely uses hashtags to increase interest around their products. In this paper, we analyze whether hashtags are effective in a niche scenario like the art exhibitions. The obtained results show very different behaviors and confused strategies: from museums that do not consider hashtags at all, to museums that create official hastags, but hardly mention them; from museums that create multiple hashtags for the same exhibition, to those that are very confused about hashtag usage. Furthermore, we discovered an interesting case, where a smart usage of hashtags stimulated the interest around art. Finally, we highlight few practical guidelines with behaviors to follow and to avoid; the guidelines might help promoting art exhibitions.

Keywords: Art exhibition · Twitter · Hashtags

1 Introduction

The simple query *current art temporary exhibitions* placed on Google on December 2016 returns more than two millions results. Obviously, this does not imply that there are more than two millions distinct art temporary exhibitions, but it gives a clear indication that there is a large number of exhibitions going on all over the world. A more accurate investigation, done by checking the Web pages of some well-known museums in the world, shows that all of them have at least one active art temporary exhibition at any time during the year. Indeed, temporary exhibitions became more frequent and important in recent decades [15] and tend to attract not only local visitors, but also tourists that take such exhibitions into consideration when organizing their trips.

There are two very important issues that a museum has to address when setting up a temporary exhibition: promotion and evaluation. The former should be done to reach as many potential visitors as possible, in order to let them

© Springer International Publishing AG 2017
C. Grana and L. Baraldi (Eds.): IRCDL 2017, CCIS 733, pp. 187–198, 2017.
DOI: 10.1007/978-3-319-68130-6_15

know all information needed to properly organize a visit during the period the exhibition is open. The latter should give organizers a clear overview of the level of success of the exhibition and of the reasons for that outcome. These two issues obviously arise in general also for permanent museum exhibitions, but are really critical for temporary ones: a certain amount of money has to be invested in an exhibition that lasts for a (relatively) short time and this investment should return in this short period.

For what concerns promotions, traditional channels can be used, such as advertisements on newspapers, playbills, fliers, radio etc. or new channels, in particular Web sites and social media. Needless to say, the potential of these new channels is huge: the possibility to reach visitors world wide, to update and disseminate information in real time and especially at low costs. It is nevertheless important to point out that new media require constant maintenance and activity, or the visitors might get the impression that the site or the accounts are neglected and this bad impression might be translated to the exhibition itself.

In this paper, we focus on the promotion aspect of temporary art exhibitions and investigate the benefits of using social media for such task. To the best of our knowledge, this is the first paper that addresses promotion rather than evaluation. In particular, we focus on Twitter and the use of hashtags that is done by organizers and visitors. Recent studies show that Twitter can be successfully employed in a wide range of situations in many different environments, such as understanding citizens feelings concerning life conditions in towns and cities [7], or identifying influencer users that can be employed to efficiently spread information and/or marketing campaigns [17].

In the specific case of temporary art exhibitions, Twitter can be regarded as an interesting tool for promotion, due to its one-to-many publicly available communication. In addition, the use of hashtags associated to the art exhibition itself makes it very easy to follow conversations concerning the exhibition. The use of hashtag is successfully done in the entertainment industry, for example for popular TV talent shows. Needless to say, the costs associated to this kind of promotion is extremely reduced compared to the ones of traditional channels. Our main goal is to understand if and how hashtags are actually used to promote and stimulate interest around temporary art exhibitions.

Our investigation shows a very fragmented and incoherent use of hashtags for temporary exhibitions, pointing out many levels of criticality. Hence, we conclude with a reasoned list of guidelines that can be followed to make an effective use of Twitter and hashtags in the context of temporary exhibitions.

2   Related Work

Twitter is one of the biggest and most popular social network platforms. Every day, on average, 500 million tweets are posted on Twitter and monthly number of active users exceeds 300 million [1]. Beyond its institutional role where it is used to display news and report, Twitter is mainly a worldwide place where users share their real feelings freely, tell where they are, what they are doing and express and exchange opinions on a wide range of topics, such as places, people and products [20]. Twitter users use hashtags to add context and metadata to tweets. Hashtags are community-driven keywords or phrases used to categorize messages and highlight topics. The extensive and accurate use of hashtags makes Twitter more expressive [19].

Various approaches have been recently proposed in the literature that analyse Twitter. Most of them can be classified in two main streams of research. As tweets are text, a large body of work has concerned sentiment analysis and opinion mining. Here the main goal is to understand opinions, sentiments and attitudes concerning different topics, as expressed in the text. One typical application scenario concerns enterprises that can discover opinioned information and detect the sentiment polarity of their customers about their products or their competitors [18]. Twitter represents a novel and very challenging domain for sentiment analysis and opinion mining [9–11]. Tweet length and textual informalities are the main issues that must be faced in this context. The majority of the proposed approaches applies machine-learning approaches to message contents and/or tags (e.g. [2,12]) while the remaining approaches are mainly lexicon-based (e.g. [13]). The other stream of research concerns social network analysis. Most of the research in this context is focused on the identification of social influencers [4,17,21] and their role in diffusing information [3]. Moreover, the fact that Twitter is most used via mobile devices makes the issue of finding relationships between the social network or the terms in the messages and geographic proximity worth of being investigated [8,22].

The diffusion of Twitter and other social network platforms can have a great impact on the Cultural Heritage sector. Some papers already investigate this phenomena, mainly concentrating on the evaluation aspect. [16] proposes a social-based solution for a fast and effective gathering of feedbacks from museum visitors. The idea is to engage online users as contributors through a mobile application that allows visitors to post their ideas, feelings, and feedbacks on Twitter and Facebook at any time in the exhibition. [5] introduces a set of Key Performance Indicators (KPIs) for quantitative estimation of Cultural Heritage Sensitivity as expressed by social network users. The approach is data driven: it analyzes terms and concepts belonging to Twitter users' messages and compares them to concepts from domain specific and general ontologies, such an analysis is then integrated with geo-referencing and temporal analysis. [6] provides a quantitative and qualitative study of the messages sent on Twitter during the MuseumWeek event. "MuseumWeek" is a communication event that was designed and planned by Twitter in 2014 together with various European museums to improve their visibility. The organization principle was simple: each day was dedicated to a theme, with specific hashtag, and users were encouraged to use the hashtag of the day as well as the generic hashtag #MuseumWeek. The outcomes show that the main goals of this promotional event were achieved. [14] studies how the relation between archives, museums and users is changed thanks to the large diffusion of social networks. The analysis is based on case studies of Danish archives and museums using Instagram for digital curating, outreach and communication. The conclusion shows that the relation between cultural heritage institution and user is not even. The media offer a room for involvement, even if it seems to be the institution not the audience that decides the arena in most cases.

3   Experimental Evaluation

Our goal is to measure the interest around topics related to art and whether it is possible to stimulate it towards art topics. From this analysis, we plan to design practice guidelines for a profitable and effective usage of hashtags in the art exhibition field.

3.1   Preliminary Investigation

As a first preliminary investigation we analyze the use of hashtags done by organizers of current (December 2016) temporary exhibitions. We look for specific hashtags explicitly created for temporary exhibitions organized by some of principal museums in Europe and U.S.A. Table 1 reports some representative results[1]. We check whether official hashtags are reported on the exhibition Web Site and on the museum Twitter account. Moreover, we check if, on the Web Site, there is a Twitter share button. Whenever an hashtag is not reported, this means that we did not find one[2]; if an hashtag is reported but the first two check boxes are not checked, this means that we found an hashtag that is actually used in tweets but it is not clear who created it (users or organizers). A particular case is the Dalì exhibition in Pisa: the museum Web site dedicates a page to the exhibition with a link to dedicated Web site. The latter shows a small Twitter button that redirects to the exhibition Twitter account containing an official hashtag (#DaliPisa).

The situation depicted by our investigation shows that the attention on hashtags creation and diffusion by organizers is quite scarce. Moreover, it is worth mentioning that: (1) the share button presents a default tweet in which the exhibition hashtag is not reported; (2) hashtags reported in the Twitter account are usually only of the most recently opened exhibitions.

3.2   Dataset Collection

We collected Twitter data (`text, UTC-creation_time, number_of_retweets, user_id, number_of_followers`) for 7 days filtered by hashtag of current exhibitions and of popular painters. Please note that while the first three entries are related to the specific tweet and the time is the local time of creation the last two ones concern the Twitter user. In particular, we considered exhibitions

---

[1] Others are omitted due to lack of space, but no significant result has been elided.

[2] We did not make a too big effort to find one, as we assume that users are not willing to do.

Table 1. Investigation of the use of hashtags in current temporary exhibitions (on December 2016).

Museum	Exhibition	Exhibition hashtag	# on Web Site? # on Twitter? Share Button?
British Museum London	South Africa The art of a nation	#SouthAfricanArt	☐ ☑ ☑
	Modern design and graphics ...		☐ ☐ ☐
Tate Gallery London	Wilfredo Lam	#wilfredoLam	☐ ☐ ☑
National Gallery London	Beyond Caravaggio	#BeyondCaravaggio	☐ ☑ ☑
Louvre Paris	Miroirs	#expoMiroirs	☐ ☐ ☐
Centre Popmpidou Paris	René Magritte	#ExpoMagritte	☐ ☑ ☑
Milan Museum Milano	Escher	#EscherMilano	☐ ☐ ☐
Uffizi Firenze	L'alluvione e gli Uffizi		☐ ☐ ☐
Palazzo dei Diamanti Ferrara	Orando Furioso	#OrlandoFurioso	☐ ☑ ☑
Palazzo Albergati Bologna	La Collezione Gelman	#MexixoFrida	☑ ☐ ☑
Albertina Museum Wien @AlbertinaMuseum	Seurat, Signac, Van Gogh	#SerautSignacVanGogh	☑ ☑ ☑
Guggenheim New York	Agnes Martin	#AgnesMartin	☐ ☐ ☐
MoMA New York	A Revolutionary impulse	#ArevolutionaryImpulse	☐ ☐ ☐

organized by well-known museums in Italy, Austria, UK and France and we used the official hashtag (e.g., #dalipisa, #mexicofrida, #seuratsignacvangogh, #beyondcaravaggio, #orlandofurioso and #expomagritte) and we considered well-known and famous painters (e.g., #cezanne, #monet, #chagall, #pollock, #goya, #picasso, #klimt, #klee, #escher, #vangogh).

3.3   Dataset Composition

The resulting dataset is composed of 10,376 tweets and its composition is shown in Table 2. First rows are related to painters' hashtags, whereas the last 6 rows concern official hashtags of current art exhibitions.

The absolute number of tweets shows a large difference between tweets concerning painters and tweets related to art exhibitions. For instance, during the observed period, more than half of the contents concerned only two painters (i.e., Van Gogh and Picasso), whereas very few were related to official hashtags of art exhibitions. To understand the reasons for this diversity, we deepen our analysis by focusing on contents published around the most tweeted painter (i.e., Van Gogh) and on those related to the most successful art exhibitions hashtags (i.e. #beyondcaravaggio and #orlandofurioso). By looking at the #vangogh tweets,

Table 2. Dataset composition: first rows are related to painters, whereas the last six rows concern official hashtags of current art exhibitions.

Hashtag	Percentage of tweets	Volume of tweets
#cezanne	3,24%	337
#chagall	2,44%	254
#escher	1,27%	132
#monet	15,84%	1646
#goya	6,18%	642
#klee	5,28%	549
#klimt	4,48%	465
#miro	2,52%	262
#picasso	25,10%	2608
#pollock	1,83%	190
#vangogh	27,85%	2894
#vermeer	3,75%	390
#beyondcaravaggio	1,18%	123
#dalipisa	0,00%	0
#expomagritte	0,08%	8
#mexicofrida	0,07%	7
#orlandofurioso	0,32%	33
#seuratsignacvangogh	0,06%	6

we observed that the interest towards the painter is stimulated by @VanGoghDetails, a single Twitter account created on June 2016 that has around 2,500 followers. The most successful art exhibitions hashtags are promoted by the National Gallery museum with the official Twitter account @NationalGallery (created on April 2010, 741,000 followers), and by Palazzo Diamanti museum with the official Twitter account @PalazzoDiamanti (created on January 2013, 5,009 followers).

3.4   Content Analysis

The three official Twitter accounts post contents very differently. Before analyzing the contents in details, it is worth noting that, on average, @VanGoghDetails posts 2.1 tweets per day, @NationalGallery posts 0.6 tweets per day concerning #beyondcaravaggio, @PalazzoDiamanti posts 2.5 tweets per day concerning #orlandofurioso.

Number of users who retweet messages. Figure 1 shows the average number of users who retweet tweets published by the official account. The tweets related to the Caravaggio Exhibition and published with the official hashtag (#beyondcaravaggio) by the official Twitter account of the National Gallery are retweeted on average by 25 different users. VanGoghDetails achieves a similar number:

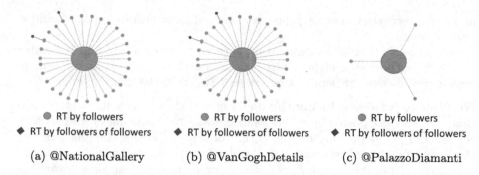

Fig. 1. Average number of followers and followers-of-followers who retweet tweets published by the official account.

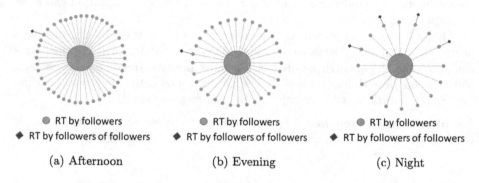

Fig. 2. Average number of followers and followers-of-followers who retweet tweets published by @VanGoghDetails grouped into three different periods of the day.

every published tweet is retweeted on average by 26 different users. However, on average, two retweeted messages are retweeted again by people who are not followers of the VanGoghDetails account. The situation is completely different for the @PalazzoDiamanti account: tweets published with the official hashtag (#orlandofurioso) are retweeted, on average, by 3 different users.

If the number of people who retweet a message is a measure of the interest around the topic, it seems clear that @VanGoghDetails and @NationalGallery diffuse the most interesting posts. However, the number of followers cannot be overlooked. Indeed, by considering that @NationalGallery has around 741,000 followers and @VanGoghDetails has around 2,500 followers, it is clear that @VanGoghDetails publishes very interesting tweets.

Figure 2 shows the average number of users who retweet tweets published by @VanGoghDetails grouped into three different periods of the day. On average, a tweet is retweeted by 44 different users if published during the afternoon, is retweeted by 31 different users if published during the evening and is retweeted by 16 different users if published during the night. In addition, the retweeted message is retweeted again by people who are not followers of the @VanGoghDetails account.

These numbers show how important is to post contents throughout the day, even if tweets posted at night receive less interest than others. It is not clear the reason why @VanGoghDetails does not post tweets in the morning hours.

Number of retweets during the day. Figure 3 shows the number of retweets that the messages posted by @VanGoghDetails, @NationalGallery and @PalazzoDiamanti get depending on the period of day. @VanGoghDetails produces the largest number of retweets, in particular for tweets posted in the afternoon and, above all, in the evening/night. This is even more evident for #beyondcaravaggio, where the retweets are centered around the afternoon. In the case of #orlandofurioso a lower number of retweets is triggered and the original tweets appear more scattered throughout the whole day, i.e. less focused on the most favorable moments of day.

Figure 4 shows the cumulative number of retweets that all the messages posted by @VanGoghDetails, @NationalGallery and @PalazzoDiamantmessages get over time. @VanGoghDetails has the most positive trend, reaching nearly 350 retweets over the monitored time span, as opposed to #beyondcaravaggio and #orlandofurioso, which reach 120 and 60, respectively.

Number of users reached by tweets. Figure 5 shows the number of people reached by the retweeted messages. Also in this case, it is possible to observe

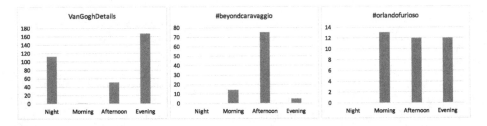

Fig. 3. Total number of retweets per period of day of original message for analysed cases.

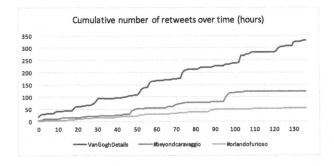

Fig. 4. Cumulative number of retweets over time (hours) for analysed cases.

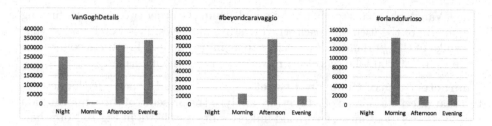

Fig. 5. Total number of followers per period of day of original message for the analysed cases.

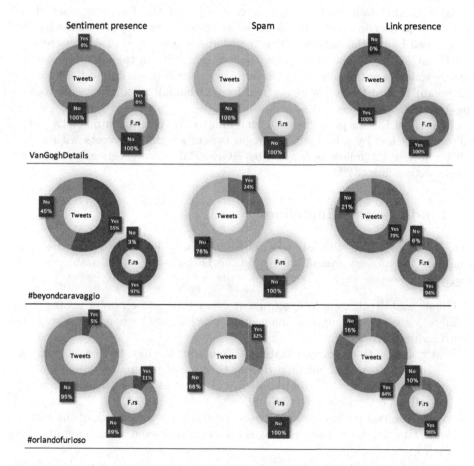

Fig. 6. Analysis of the tweet contents for VanGoghDetails (upper), #beyondcaravaggio (mid) and #orlandofurioso (lower). Large pies refer to the number of tweets, small ones to the number of followers.

that @VanGoghDetails reaches more people than the other two cases, confirming the quality of the used approach when posting messages. It is worth noting that the spike of the #orlandofurioso is due to a single popular Twitter account (i.e., more than 120,000 followers) that retweeted one of the messages.

Characteristics of the posted tweets. To understand if there are characteristics that affect the spread of a tweet, we analyze the presence of three information within a tweet: sentiment, spam and link. Results are shown in Fig. 6. Note that, sentiment is computed using the AFINN python library and messages are considered as spam when more than 4 hashtags or more than 1 link or more than 3 mentions are present in a tweet [17].

@VanGoghDetails posts neutral tweets, 97% of the followers reached by #beyondCaravaggio tweets are due to 55% of positive tweets; 11% of the followers reached by #OrlandoFurioso tweets are due to the 5% of positive tweets.

@VanGoghDetails posts tweets without spam; 100% of the followers reached by #beyondCaravaggio and by #OrlandoFurioso tweets are due to tweets without spam; 11% of the followers reached by #OrlandoFurioso tweets are due to the 5% of positive tweets.

@VanGoghDetails posts tweets with a link to Van Gogh painting; 94% of the followers reached by #beyondCaravaggio tweets are due to tweets with a link (79%); 90% of the followers reached by #OrlandoFurioso tweets are due to the tweets with a link (84%).

4   Findings and Guidelines

The dataset analysis allowed us to outline some guidelines to advertise and stimulate the interest around art exhibitions through the use of hashtag and of Twitter.

- Create and divulgate a hashtag, use it every time and on every means (e.g., fliers, websites, newspapers, magazines, playbill, etc.) when advertising the art exhibition.
- Post tweets with the official hashtag throughout the day. Indeed, it is important to post contents not only during the opening hours of the exhibition, but also when the exhibition is closed (e.g., at night and during the evening). This allows reaching people with different habits.
- Always insert a picture into the tweet, preferably a framework of the exhibition. Data show that these messages are more retweeted and, therefore, they reach more people.
- Avoid using multiple hashtags in the message to increase its spread. Multiple hashtags produce negligible positive effects, and greatly reduce the interest around the message and around the accounts who post it.
- Avoid retweeting messages that embed the official hashtag. It only confuses followers. People who want to follow the conversation around the official hashtag can do it without any problem and without the official account to retweet it.

– Be focused on the exhibition contents, thus avoid posting mere courtesy messages like "Thank @user for visiting us" or "Welcome @user to our exhibition". These messages greatly reduce the interest around the account who posts them.

5   Conclusions

In this paper we focused on the use of hashtags to promote and stimulate the interest around art exhibitions. We observed very different behaviors: those who do not consider hashtags at all in the means used to promote the exhibition (e.g., fliers, playbill, webpages, etc.); those who create official hashtags, but hardly mention it; those who create multiple hashtag for the same exhibition; those who create an official hashtag, but hardly use it; those who create an official hashtag, but are very confused about their usage. We analyzed the tweets posted with hashtags related to famous painters and with official hashtags of art exhibitions. We observed that a smart usage of hashtags might stimulate the interest around art. Indeed, we highlighted positive aspects and behaviors to avoid and we outlined few practical guidelines that might help in better use of hashtags while promoting art exhibitions.

Finally, we observe that a good use of hashtags and Twitter resolves in the creation of a large corpus of tweets that can be used to evaluate the art exhibition in terms of measuring the visitors feelings and their geographical origins, their opinions, their involvement and engagement and many other useful information that might be helpful to propose and promote future art exhibitions.

References

1. Twitter Usage Statistics - Internet live stats (2016). http://www.internetlivestats.com/twitter-statistics/
2. Aston, N., Liddle, J., Hu, W.: Twitter sentiment in data streams with perceptron. J. Comput. Commun. **2**(3), 11–16 (2016)
3. Bakshy, E., Rosenn, I., Marlow, C., Adamic, L.: The role of social networks in information diffusion. In: Proceedings of the 21st WWW, pp. 519–528 (2012)
4. Bujari, A., Furini, M., Laina, N.: On using cashtags to predict companies stock trends. In: 2017 14th Annual IEEE Consumer Communications and Networking Conference (CCNC), January 2017
5. Chianese, A., Marulli, F., Piccialli, F.: Cultural heritage and social pulse: a semantic approach for CH sensitivity discovery in social media data. In: Proceedings of the 10th ICSC, pp. 459–464 (2016)
6. Courtin, A., Juanals, B., Minel, J., de Saint Léger, M.: The museum week event: analyzing social network interactions in cultural fields. In: Proceedings of the 10th International Conference on Signal-Image Technology and Internet-Based Systems (SITIS), pp. 462–468 (2014)
7. de Albornoz, J.C., Plaza, L., Gervás, P.: SentiSense: an easily scalable concept-based affective lexicon for sentiment analysis. In: Proceedings of the Eighth International Conference on Language Resources and Evaluation, May 2012

8. Furini, M.: Users behavior in location-aware services: digital natives vs digital immigrants. In: Advances in Human-Computer Interaction (2014)
9. Furini, M., Montangero, M.: TSentiment: on gamifying Twitter sentiment analysis. In: 2016 IEEE Symposium on Computers and Communication (ISCC), pp. 91–96, June 2016
10. Furini, M., Tamanini, V.: Location privacy and public metadata in social media platforms: attitudes, behaviors and opinions. Multimed. Tools Appl. **74**(21), 9795–9825 (2015)
11. Giachanou, A., Crestani, F.: Like it or not: a survey of Twitter sentiment analysis methods. ACM Comput. Surv. **49**(2), 28:1–28:41 (2016)
12. Hamdan, H., Béchet, F., Bellot, P.: Experiments with DBpedia, WordNet and SentiWordnet as resources for sentiment analysis in micro-blogging. In: Proceedings of the 7th International Workshop on Semantic Evaluation (SemEval@NAACL-HLT), pp. 455–459 (2013)
13. Hu, X., Tang, J., Gao, H., Liu, H.: Unsupervised sentiment analysis with emotional signals. In: Proceedings of the 22nd WWW, pp. 607–618 (2013)
14. Jensen, B.: Instagram as cultural heritage: user participation, historical documentation, and curating in museums and archives through social media. In: 2013 Digital Heritage International Congress (DigitalHeritage), vol. 2, pp. 311–314 (2013)
15. Johnson, P.: Museums. In: Towse, R. (ed.) A Handbook of Cultural Economics, pp. 315–320. Edward Elgar, Cheltenham (2003)
16. Lin, Y.-L., Bai, X., Ye, Y., Real, W.: Constructing narratives using fast feedback. In: Proceedings of the 2012 iConference, pp. 486–487 (2012)
17. Montangero, M., Furini, M.: Trank: ranking Twitter users according to specific topics. In: 2015 12th Annual IEEE Consumer Communications and Networking Conference (CCNC), pp. 767–772, January 2015
18. Ravi, K., Ravi, V.: A survey on opinion mining and sentiment analysis: tasks, approaches and applications. Knowl. Based Syst. **89**, 14–46 (2015)
19. Romero, D.M., Meeder, B., Kleinberg, J.: Differences in the mechanics of information diffusion across topics: idioms, political hashtags, and complex contagion on Twitter. In: Proceedings of the 20th WWW, pp. 695–704 (2011)
20. Wang, X., Wei, F., Liu, X., Zhou, M., Zhang, M.: Topic sentiment analysis in Twitter: a graph-based hashtag sentiment classification approach. In: Proceedings of the 20th ACM CIKM, pp. 1031–1040 (2011)
21. Yang, J., Leskovec, J.: Modeling information diffusion in implicit networks. In: Proceedings of the 10th IEEE ICDM, pp. 599–608 (2010)
22. Yardi, S., Boyd, D.: Tweeting from the town square: measuring geographic local networks. In: Proceedings of the 4th International Conference on Weblogs and Social Media (ICWSM) (2010)

Author Index

Printed in the United States
By Bookmasters